Jeremy Seabrook is a
recent books include *Paup...........................Poor in Britain* and
People Without History: India's Muslim Ghettos.

Praise for *Pauperland: Poverty and the Poor in Britain*

'This is a beautifully written book that suggests that our current debates about welfare dependency and entitlements are nothing new.'
— *The Sunday Times*

'Seabrook makes an eloquent case that wealth, which now "commands many of the rites and observances formerly associated with religion", is founded on an ideology of limitless desires fuelling limitless economic growth. [...] His prophetic question will not go away: "Since growth and expansion in perpetuity are impossible, can the transition to a more modest way of living be accomplished peaceably, or will it occur only as a consequence of some great catastrophe?"' — Jonathan Benthall, *Times Literary Supplement*

'Seabrook's history of the poor and attitudes towards them is a powerful political and moral polemic.' — *The Times*

'Seabrook takes readers on a journey through what he calls the "fallibility of economic reason," in which humanity becomes a commodity to be brought and sold to the highest bidder...recommended for those interested in the making of public policies, specifically concerning poverty and poor.' — *Choice*

'Jeremy Seabrook chronicles the history of the poor with a fine anger and compassion and a deep understanding of his subject. This is a fine book as well as a relevant one.' — Ian Jack, former editor of *Granta*, 1995-2007 and author of *Before the Oil Ran Out: Britain 1977-86*

'Nothing changes, the poor are always with us — and so are the punitive attitudes of those who confine others to that condition. From Speenhamland to the work house to Iain Duncan Smith, Jeremy Seabrook's enlightening tour through this sorry history reveals the unceasing need of the comfortable to remoralise the paupers, not themselves.' — Polly Toynbee, columnist for *The Guardian* and author of *Hard Work: Life in Low-Pay Britain*

The Song of the Shirt

The Song of the Shirt

The High Price of Cheap Garments

from Blackburn to Bangladesh

JEREMY SEABROOK

.

HURST & COMPANY, LONDON

Published in the United Kingdom in 2015 by
C. Hurst & Co. (Publishers) Ltd.,
41 Great Russell Street, London, WC1B 3PL
© Jeremy Seabrook, 2015
All rights reserved.

First published in India in 2014 by Navayana Publishing Pvt Ltd,
New Delhi

Printed in India

Distributed in the United States and Latin America by
Oxford University Press, 198 Madison Avenue, New York, NY
10016, United States of America.

A Cataloguing-in-Publication data record for this book is available
from the British Library.

ISBN: 978-1-84904-522-3

www.hurstpublishers.com

This book is printed on paper from registered sustainable
and managed sources.

Oh, Men, with Sisters dear!
Oh, Men, with Mothers and Wives!
It is not linen you're wearing out,
But human creatures' lives!
Stitch — stitch — stitch,
In poverty, hunger and dirt,
Sewing at once, with a double thread,
A Shroud as well as a Shirt.

—from "The Song of the Shirt" by Thomas Hood (1843)

Contents

The Indian Subcontinent and Bengal

India

Indian Ocean

Bangladesh

West Bengal

Bay of Bengal

Not to scale

Bangladesh, 1971

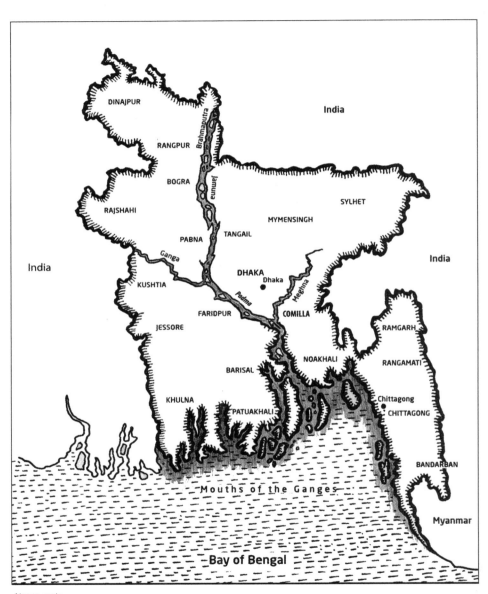

Not to scale

Industrial England: Centres of Production

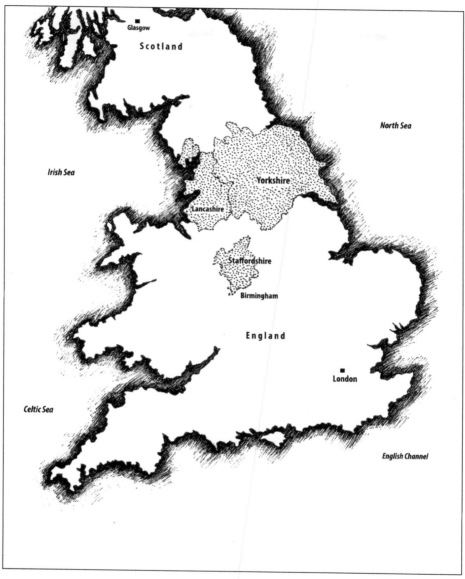

Not to scale

Preface

This book reflects on the mutability of progress. The evolution of industrial society is generally thought of as a deterministic, linear process, but experience in the clothing and fabric industry suggests certain areas of the world are liable to periods of industrialization, but equally, to de-industrialization. Bengal and Lancashire offer a mirror image of how this works: the loss of the weaving industry in Bengal in the late eighteenth century coincided with the mechanized production of cotton goods in Manchester and its satellite towns. While Dhaka became a ghost city, Manchester was the centre of intense economic dynamism.

The British textile industry enjoyed a long period of supremacy, but began to decline during the First World War, and the disappearance from Lancashire of cotton goods was almost complete by the closing years of the twentieth century; by which time, Bangladesh had become one of the world's major producers of garments, exporting its goods, in a ghostly replay of traffic in the other direction, of the machine-made clothing that had displaced so many of the spinners and weavers of Bengal almost two centuries earlier. As Dhaka has grown into one of the world's most congested cities, with its 2,500 garment factories, Manchester has lost population: despite a vibrant service and cultural sector, the original reason for its existence still haunts the city: the loss of manufacture of necessary material goods leaves an ache and a sense of depletion which cannot be easily remedied.

I have used a variety of resources in compiling this book: archival sources; work by contemporary writers; interviews with academics, historians, and especially workers, in order to gain as rounded a view as possible. The material has been assembled over a long period—since I was introduced to Dhaka's garment sector by the British NGO, War on Want, in the early 1990s— and I have had to rely upon my own notes and diary entries, which makes the origin of particular quotes quite difficult, and occasionally impossible, to trace. Since the book is a reflection on how the shifting sites of industry influence labour and lives, I have preferred not to interrupt the narrative with too many references: for instance, chapter 32 of this book, 'A Haunted Culture', draws upon the work of Major J.H. Tull Walsh (1902) and other functionaries of the British, whose curiosity about Bengal turned them into accomplished ethnographers. A broad list of works cited and consulted is given at the end of the book.

If the book appears to Western readers South Asia-centric, there is good reason for this: Bengal in the eighteenth and nineteenth centuries, and Bangladesh in the twentieth and twenty-first, were scarcely the initiators of the epic processes described in the book: it focuses on how they responded to, and made sense of, great economic and social movements that originated elsewhere. It is the story of weavers, spinners and factory workers; among whom the oppressed of Lancashire were also, at least for a time, victims.

I am indebted to many individuals for insight into these processes, particularly to the many young women workers in the garment sector of Dhaka, who generously shared the stories of their life and work. I am grateful to union organizer Amit Sarkar (not his real name, for fear of reprisals against him as a result of his disclosures). I would like to thank Professor Muntassir Mamoon, Professor Shafique uz Zaman, Professor Sirajul Islam of the Bangladesh Asiatic Society; and especially my dear friend, Mr Abdur Rob, for his understanding of, and love for, Barisal. I am thankful to Syed Shamsul Haq, Hameeda Hossain, Kamal Uddin and Khushi Kabir, Iqbal Hossain and Imran Ahmed Siddiqui; the Clean Clothes Campaign and Labour Behind the

Label, and all those for whom the makers of the clothes wear are a matter for continuing concern.

I cannot over-emphasize my debt to S. Anand of Navayana, and Rimli Borooah and Arif Ayaz Parrey, for their superbly creative editing work. Versions of some parts of the book have appeared elsewhere, particularly in *Race and Class*, journal of the Institute of Race Relations in London, and I would like to express my affectionate regard for A. Sivanandan, Jenny Bourne, Hazel Walters, Liz Fekete and all the staff, for their support. At least one piece has appeared in *New Internationalist*, and I would like to acknowledge the work of the collective for bringing to the attention of the world the vital issues underpinning of globalization and development.

Jeremy Seabrook
December 2014

Part I
Fire

1 | Dhaka, a temporary settlement

I would have begun with the fires in the garment factories that have claimed the lives of many garment workers, but the death of more than 1,100 people in the building collapse on the edge of Dhaka in April 2013 was a story of such appalling contempt for human life that it must rank among the most callous in the brutal history of industrialism. Even after the structure had been declared unsafe, workers were coerced into entering the factories under threat of loss of wages. In the tangle of metal and concrete that followed, bolts of cloth had to be used as improvised chutes for bringing people to safety; workers—more skinny and sinuous than police or medical personnel—made their way into pockets where people were trapped, and had to amputate limbs with a saw. The bodies laid out in front of the ruins stretched hundreds of metres in the dust and debris.

Anyone looking at Dhaka and its hundreds of garment factories, its tens of thousands of cycle rickshaws, its construction workers provisionally living in the shells of apartments they will never own, its maidservants, faces patterned by grilles on the verandahs which keep them captive, can only wonder at the bleakness of alternatives that has driven people to find a precarious sanctuary in this place. For Dhaka—this constricted camp for the evicted of development—scarcely merits the name of 'city'. Is it the poverty of ancient fishponds and rice fields, fallen orchards and abandoned homesteads that has sent people here, or the promise of wages which are eaten up in advance by the price of rent and food that rises as fast as the greedy floodwaters that have chased them from home?

It is difficult to conceive that the humiliations which young women and men endure in the scanty choices for their labour in this labour camp masquerading as city can be more bearable than the indignities of villages they called home until only the day before yesterday: the woman transplanting rice seedlings, miming the gestures of her drowned sister in the waters of the paddy field; the woman beating sheaves of rice against the threshing stone; the man carrying his implements over his shoulder at the end of a long day hoeing and weeding on land he will never own; the family contemplating the eroded fields that will be deposited elsewhere as someone else's fertile silt; the woman for whom the charity of the mosque is the only thing that stands between her children and destitution.

Hope is inscribed in the ugly landscapes of the city, in the white light of its factories that shed their radiance on the slums below, in the market with its pyramids of scarlet and green vegetables, in the rented shelter shared with strangers—hope that has been chased from places where land is lost to the Padma, the moneylender or the shifting topography of the country, where fields can no longer provide sustenance and the ties of kinship have become fetters.

It is not only daily working conditions, an income that limps behind prices, the demands of the home place for remittances that make life in the city appear intolerable. There are sleepless nights under burning tin roofs, the absence of water, the darkness of electricity outages, the airless tenements; to all this is added the harassment from overseers and foremen, compulsory overtime when orders have to be finished, sexual advances by those who exercise power over them, and even worse, periodic catastrophes—explosions, fires and the collapse of buildings that leave scores or hundreds of bodies wrapped in white cerements, where their loved ones can barely recognize them through their disfigurement.

The position of Bangladesh in the division of labour of

globalism today is not to clothe the nakedness of the world, but to provide it with limitless cheap garments. The workers are disposable, rags of humanity, as it were, used up like any other raw material in the cause of production for export. Dhaka is criss-crossed with vehicles stamped in red with the words 'On Emergency Export Duty', as though it were the highest priority of Bangladesh to send out of the country as quickly as possible all it can produce.

Fire remains the single greatest hazard to workers in the garment industry. The most recent—and deadly—fire in Bangladesh occurred in Dhaka on 24 November 2012, in the industrial suburb of Ashulia. Over one hundred people died in the inferno at the Tazreen factory. In the past ten years, at least five hundred garment workers, mostly young women, have been killed in factory fires. In most cases, doors were locked to prevent pilfering of goods or unauthorized absence from work, especially during night shifts when supervision is less stringent. This event, which threw the light of its flames upon many transnational importers of Bangladesh's ready-made garments, including Walmart, was described by the owners, by the government and the Bangladesh Garment Manufacturers and Exporters Association (BGMEA) as 'sabotage'. The supply broker had moved orders to Tazreen from the official supplier, without permission from Walmart. Corruption, as well as chains of middlemen, brokers and intermediaries, creates a maze of subcontractors, which permits unauthorized factories to fulfil orders. These are often unsafe, ramshackle and negligent.

As in the Tazreen conflagration, most of the twenty-seven who died by fire in December 2010 at the sadly named That's-It sportswear factory, also in Ashulia, perished, not from suffocation, but from injuries sustained when they jumped from the tenth floor of the building where the factory was located.

Fire and the fear of fire have haunted the garment workers of Bangladesh ever since the garment sector became a major employer of labour thirty years ago. Twenty-three died in a fire at Macro Knitwear in Dhaka in 2000, twelve at Globe Knitting, also in 2000. In January 2005, twenty-eight were incinerated at the Shan Knitwear factory in Narayanganj. In February 2005, three disasters struck Bangladesh factories. Fire destroyed the four-storey KTS Textile Industries building in Chittagong, with the loss of at least fifty-four lives. On the same day, fifty-seven workers at the Imam Textile Group in Chittagong were injured in a stampede following the explosion of a transformer. A few days later, nineteen people were reported dead when a nine-storey building collapsed in Dhaka. Forty-five workers, including ten children, were killed at the Chowdhury Garment factory in Shibpur, east of Dhaka, in November 2006. In February 2010, twenty-one workers were killed and more than fifty injured in a fire at the Garib & Garib Newaj factory in Gazipur. A large stock of synthetic acrylic sweaters burned, producing thick toxic smoke. Exit doors were said to have been locked by management "to prevent theft".

All such disasters have much in common: faulty fire equipment, no fire escapes, factories stacked in increasingly high-rise buildings, staircases and doorways encumbered by bales of flammable material or finished goods awaiting dispatch—synthetic fabrics which burn readily and release toxic smoke.

In March 2011, eight workers died in a fire that broke out in a shed on the roof of a four-storey garment-dyeing factory, where chemicals were stored. According to witnesses, a huge plume of black smoke was seen in the early hours of the morning of 10 March, and the eight victims "were trapped inside their room". It is quite common for workers to live on rooftops of factories, or in the same spaces where they perform their daily labour, so that their experience of the capital city is one of confinement, if not incarceration. It is not unusual to meet people who have never left the immediate neighbourhood where they live and work. Three of the five rooms in the shed were occupied by workers, the other two by chemicals. The whole building was served by a single entrance through which 250 workers passed daily. There was no emergency exit. The family of each dead employee was offered 10,000 taka (about $130) "for burial expenses". *The Daily Star* reported that between 2010 and 2011, 155 people died in separate chemical-related incidents in Dhaka alone, including some in the—once again—sadly named 'Goodnight Mosquito Coil and Spray' warehouse.

Fires are not a recent bringer of death to the cities of Bengal. As early as 1837, it was prohibited to build huts with thatched roofs in Calcutta, since in the preceding years, the Black Town—as the area occupied by 'natives' was designated—had been periodically ravaged by fires that spread through the slums that stood in the shadow of the mansions of the rich Bengali banias, dewans and landlords; and it was feared that such fires might also spread to the European quarter.

During one of my first visits to Dhaka, February 1995, at M/S Proster Garments, a joint venture between Hong Kong and Bangladesh, panic over an outbreak of fire caused five deaths, as twelve hundred workers tried to flee the building. There had been a minor fire three days earlier, but at that time, the factory was unoccupied, since it was the time of *iftar*, the breaking of the daily fast in the month of Ramadan.

A rumour quickly spread that the building was on fire. Four young women in their early twenties were trampled to death, while another was killed when she leaped from the roof of the five-storey building. Many others, injured in the crush, were taken to hospital.

When we spoke to people at the site of the accident, we were told not to believe the official casualty figures: at least one hundred had died. This was an exaggeration, but it is well known that industrial accidents are often concealed or played down by the authorities in order to minimize their impact. It is not unknown for hospitals to dispose of the dead, with the connivance of the police, so that only the grieving relatives know that their loved ones have perished, and no public scandal occurs. I was reminded of the example given by J.L. Hammond and Barbara Hammond (1925) of mining conditions in South Wales in the early nineteenth century: "The Commissioner [of the Children's Employment Commission] could write as follows of deaths in the mines, 'When a man dies, the viewer looks at the body and sends for the coroner, and unless a case of suspicion is made out, he does not come, but sends an order to the constable to bury, and frequently, the coroner does not attend until there are five or six cases to clear.'"

The site of the Dhaka fire in 1995 was a four-storey building. We couldn't go inside, since there was a heavy police presence. Management representatives explained it was simply an unfortunate accident. If the workers had not panicked, the deaths and injuries could have been avoided. In other words, the victims were blamed for their own deaths.

Blaming the victims or 'outsiders' or 'agitators' has become a common response to such disasters. If disaffected workers are not the culprits, the 'hidden hand' of rival countries—usually India—can be detected. The domestic lack of regard for the cheapest garment workers in the world, and the repudiation of responsibility for them by employers and government, both have a long history in Bengal.

On a piece of ground opposite the factory—not, as far as one could tell, an official cemetery—lay the sad red earth mounds of five newly dug graves of the young women. This also evoked the practice in early nineteenth-century Britain, of burying in the factory compound the bodies of pauper apprentices who had died. The community was tense and uneasy. The factory was to remain closed for three days as a mark of respect to the dead. The workers laid off did not expect to be paid for the period of mourning. The factory was making baseball caps. Deaths, caused by the manufacture of such trivial, often throwaway, items, suggest disproportionate sacrifices.

There is a heavy and tragic irony in these burnt offerings to industry, since water has always been the most usual element that brings death to Bangladesh: tidal surges, cyclones and floods have traditionally taken a heavy toll of human life. Perhaps fire is a fitting agent of destruction in the city today; it is, after all, an expression of the modern sector and industrial development. Fire has a cruel resonance—people displaced by water find they have a rendezvous, in their place of safety, with the element which is regarded as the opposite of that they have fled from.

For the first time in history, the people of Bengal are now flowing against the rivers—rivers which have determined their lives, their movements and their sensibility for centuries—making their way to the new sources of livelihood in Dhaka and Chittagong. Just what a reversal of culture this involves is suggested by this passage: "Rivers are the life-blood of Bangladesh. The people of Bengal have always wanted to be near to rivers. Lovingly, they have given such names as *Modhumati* (the honey-sweet one), *Ichhamati* (the desiring one), *Dudhkumar* (the milk river), *Karnafuli* (where a princess lost her earrings)." But what brings life can also bring ruin. "Many settlements and achievements have been submerged into the waters of these rivers. It is for this reason that people have named the rivers *Kirtinasha* (the destroyer)" (Mamoon, 2010).

Radhakamal Mukerjee (1938) describes the unique landscapes and riverscapes of Bengal—a place of perilous beauty and dangerous mutability—which have had such a powerful influence upon the culture of the people. "On account of the natural defence presented by a network of rivers and watercourses, Bengal was virtually independent of the sway of Hindustan after the Turkish conquest of Delhi, and later carried on a long-drawn-out struggle against the mighty organization of the Moghul empire." Mukerjee relates how recent the present geography of Bengal is, since no fewer than six new rivers appeared in the final decades of the eighteenth century, which reshaped the economic history of Bengal—a result of the catastrophic floods of 1769–70 and of 1786–88, as well as the earthquake of 1762. "Both geography and history were remade." Mukerjee's evocation of the delta also conveys the hardship and endurance of those who survived there.

The waters here widen out into endless vistas, and the lands are in a process of perpetual building and unbuilding by a wide and interlaced network of canals and streams, while an endless procession of cocoanut-clad villages and itinerant hamlets, containing a swarming population, fringes the marshes or river-banks, which are higher than the surrounding country, and are always accessible by water. Fishes are abundant here throughout the year, and the paddy-lands extend right up to the doors of the peasants' huts. Man here is essentially a child of the river. His crops and farming practice are closely adjusted to the timely inundations of floodwater; indeed if the rivers do not rise in flood and submerge the country, he will be a fish out of water. He has discovered a variety of paddy which shoots higher and higher as the flood-water rises and submerges the entire landscape. When sandbanks are uncovered, he sows seeds by supporting himself on a raft of bamboo, or grows some quick-growing vegetables, still maintaining his connection with the parent village by means of boats, and leaving the settlement when the wayward river drowns his fields and leaf-made huts. In the interior he ploughs his fields with buffaloes on standing water and reaps his harvest, often in breast-deep water, and goes for shopping on earthen tubs or plantain rafts along the innumerable creeks that intersect the country. His traffic and transport are determined by tides and winds, and he himself lives a more or less amphibious life. The peasants' cottages here are found in isolation from one another on sites which have been artificially raised above flood-level, or built on mounds of earth, separate islets, amidst bhils or marshes, which are partially dry and covered with rice in the cold weather, but which during the rains form an almost unbroken fresh-water sea bordered by the river-banks rising only a few feet above the flooded country.

Loss of land is a continuous injury to the poor of Bangladesh: two-thirds of the people have little or none. Even if the loss occurred generations ago, it is still felt with the keenness of a recent bereavement. Land is not only livelihood, but life itself; and landlessness creates a sense of collective disinheritance, a predicament that follows people into trackless city slums, precarious structures on government land or sites where ownership is disputed, and they are subject to extortion, illegal taxes and sudden eviction.

In the village landscapes, keeping one's head above water is more than metaphor; it suggests the origin of the endurance and tenacity of the people, even when they have entered the city, with its own landscapes, its sea of humanity, floods of people and of course, the ebb and flow of its economic tides. If Bengali is rich in metaphor, this is perhaps because the landscapes which have shaped it themselves suggest the images captured in the music of the language.

It was estimated in the late eighteenth century that tens of thousands of people depended for their livelihood on boats; while many more lived on boat-making, fishing, harvesting water-grown vegetables and reeds for thatch. It is impossible to overestimate the upheaval involved in today's crowds, struggling against the flow of water to reach the fortresses, islands of prosperity, represented by the cities—pre-eminently Dhaka.

In the two decades since I first went to Bangladesh, Dhaka has been transformed. In the early 1990s it was already growing at breakneck speed, as migrants poured into the city, from where rumours of work had spread as swiftly as the fires that were to claim so many of them in the course of their labour. Much of the city had a ramshackle, improvised air, with people settling in rough self-built shelters of *chetai* (woven bamboo), wood and industrial debris floating around the ponds and waterways that criss-crossed the city. The city was in the throes of a great transformation, from a place of tightly embracing rivers to a washed-out concrete jungle. It evoked an eerie feeling of how it must have been in Manchester or Leeds in the 1820s and 1830s. In 1825, when the German architect Karl Schinkel visited Manchester, he reported, "The enormous factory buildings are seven to eight stories high ... where three years ago these were only meadows." In the 1990s, people, bewildered by the hardening tide of concrete which obliterated ancient waterways and mango orchards, were saying the same of Dhaka.

In the early 1990s, most garment factories of the city

compared favourably with their counterparts in Jakarta, Bombay and Bangkok. The majority of the structures were still new, far from the squalid sweatshops of popular imagination. They had been, it is true, thrown up in no time in this mushroom-city of labour, five or six storeys high, each floor occupied by a different factory. As a result, there was usually plenty of light and even air, although these amenities are qualified in Dhaka, since the city is heavily polluted with vehicle fumes and particulate matter. They were, however, even then, extremely cramped, all available space taken by machines and their operatives, finished goods accumulating in the aisles between them. In recent years, the industry has expanded, colonizing new areas around Dhaka: Savar, Gazipur, Naryanganj, Ashulia, with towers of twelve, fourteen, sixteen storeys; the only infrastructure is roads to convey the finished products away from the desolate sites of their manufacture. I visited one factory in 2010, whose owner, devoutly religious, employed only men, since he didn't believe women should work outside the home. This was rare; commerce overrides piety almost everywhere, and women are reckoned to be—perhaps mistakenly—more docile and pliable. As a result, the conditions in factories today vary widely. In some, workers are treated humanely and with consideration, but it is hard for employers to resist the compulsions of competition, and the word cut-throat is sometimes more than mere metaphor.

The first factory I saw in Dhaka in 1993 belonged to Mifkif Apparel, where workers were making denim shirts and shorts, mainly for export to the US. Many products clearly evoked those who were going to wear them: some intended for Russian or Canadian winters, others obviously leisurewear for poorer people in the West. Some suggested summer evenings in clubs in Europe, while others were durable working wear for manual labourers. This factory was on the second floor of a new concrete building. A grille barred access to the workshop which, when we arrived, was padlocked, but the key was at least present on the premises. In none of these factories did I meet the owner, and none of the workers was able to name him.

Two hundred people were working on a floor space of 4,000 square metres. The windows had grilles through which air could circulate, but curtains of coarse blue cloth were necessary to shield the workers from the heat of the May sun. There were sixty-eight machines in the room, mostly sewing machines, but some for making buttonholes. There was a plastic floor covering, on which helpers were working, mainly children or recent school dropouts. People were so pressed that one helper sat under the cutting table to do her work. Others sat beneath the machines, cutting threads on the finished articles. There were about twenty different operations: making collars, cuffs, buttonholes, sleeves, body shape.

Ahmed Garments was a quite different environment. It was a cramped ground-floor building within a small compound, where other industrial units were also operating. Next door, most employees of a unit making cardboard containers for tubes of Clean-o-Dent toothpaste were children. In Ahmed Garments there was only one small, barred window open at the far end of the factory, and the atmosphere was stifling. One hundred and twenty-five workers were packed in close columns, sitting at machines from Japan making products for the US. The material was from Pakistan, mainly flannel, in red-and-black or green-and-blue checks for padded winter jackets; the quilting was from Korea—a bewildering global geography in every object. A number of children were working here, the youngest about eleven. They wielded huge pairs of scissors, trimming the rough edges of garments after they had been stitched. Some boys were pressing the finished items. The atmosphere was hot and dusty; cotton waste from the material and threads had caught in the protective metal webs of the fans, so these resembled circular cocoons.

Silver Garments factory was also in the central district near

Topkhana Road. Just before eight in the morning, I watched young women arrive at the factory. They had emerged from huts of woven bamboo, of tin and hammered industrial metals, radiant and smiling in a blaze of primary colours, with, only here and there, an occasional burka. To present themselves so that they could maintain their self-respect, they rose at 4.30 in the morning, to take a bath, wash their clothes and oil their hair. If we present a cheerful face to a sometimes cruel world, said one young woman of about twenty, it is because it is *haram* in our religion to be pessimistic—an insight, both significant and appalling, into the sorrow in the ubiquitous smile of Bengal.

Silver Garments employed 500 workers. Although in close lines, sitting before their machines like students at desks performing a daily ritual of perpetual examinations, they at least had air and light. The factory was decorated with gold and crimson streamers, as though in celebration of some industrial festival that does not yet appear on any known almanac. They were working on a consignment of shirts for Walmart in the US. The target was to complete 500 pieces a day, the hourly production rate chalked on a blackboard in front of the workers, which reinforced the impression that they were engaged on a prolonged course of intensive study.

Silver Garments paid wages regularly, and offered twelve days paid holiday annually. The production manager, formerly a worker himself, had been at pains to persuade the owner to take some responsibility for the lives and conditions of his workers. He said this was an exception in Dhaka. Many employers regard their workers as dispensable, since 'labour in Bangladesh flows like water'; both are in excess of what is required. While little can be done to stanch water in Bangladesh, at least some of its flood of labour can be diverted elsewhere. Almost a million workers go abroad each year, and the flow of their remittances to Bangladesh—12 per cent of the country's GDP—helps keep the economy afloat.

The children of mainly landless families, the garment workers have come from river-depleted land close to the Bay of Bengal, the workless inertia of small towns, the broken rural economy of the Indian border areas. Some came as children with their parents, their land devoured by the Meghna, by sickness, by debt, by powerful land-grabbers.

However hard they work, however many hours they labour, they are unable to fulfil the measureless obligations to kin and neighbours in the villages and the countryside. They had come to the city in order to assist families wearied by floods and cyclones, by expenses for sickness, dowry or lost land, and they find that their only gift to those they love is their own absence—one less mouth to feed. It is a poor offering and scant consolation for the discomforts they must endure in these alien places for purposes they never sought and which were never clearly explained to them. In any case, the garment factories—brightly illuminated aerial palaces of glass—represent no permanent settlement for the people whose labour they consume. Their penitential labour is reminiscent of Bengali weavers, who, in the late eighteenth century, were so indebted to the East India Company and the money 'advances' on which they depended, that no matter how hard they worked, they could never discharge their debt.

They are people transplanted, like the rice seedlings which many used to separate by hand, bending in pools of water beneath the burning sun and drenching rain. To the city these recent migrants bring the sincerity and artlessness of rural life—qualities ripe for transformation into exploitable labour: an unhealing injury to the country sensibility, since it is irreversible. Their horizons in the city are not broadened: if anything, the wide skies and ferocious cyclones that eat up land and flood crops tell them more about the world than the factory twilight in which they live. They are people who have no idea of the identity of their ghost-employer: most have never seen the managing director, and cannot name the owner. They know only their role in the productive hierarchy—their status as an operative and the level of skill they have attained. They have no knowledge of the garments that pass through their dexterous hands. They do not know how garments become apparel, gathering profit as they fly across the world, attracting value from buying house to exporter, from importer to wholesaler and to retailer on the global high street or in the worldwide mall.

Their income is, like the land which many have lost, eaten up in advance. House rent now typically accounts for between a third and a half of their monthly wages, and their diet is one of meagre survival: dal, rice and vegetable. They never have meat, eggs, milk or fruit. Home is a concrete shell shared with five or six others or a tin shed, heated by the sun and uncooled by malfunctioning nocturnal fans.

Between 80 and 90 per cent of workers in garment factories are young women. Many of the young women workers share rented rooms in slum communities on private land; some landowners own fifty or sixty huts. Others occupy government land, from which self-declared proprietors, sometimes supported by MPs, bureaucrats or criminals, claim 'rent', a euphemism for protection money, which means protection from them and their hirelings.

There had been no rise in the minimum wage for garment workers for four years between 2006 and 2010, in spite of the continuous increase in living costs. The announcement of a rise in the minimum wage from November 2010—from 1,662 taka to 3,000 taka ($20 to $38) per month—although apparently generous, was far behind the workers' costs. After industrial unrest and riots in September 2013, the minimum wage was raised to 5,000 taka ($68) but by February 2014, almost 40 per cent of factories had not implemented the increase. Workers' representatives had claimed a minimum of 8,000 taka (just over $100), but this was rejected by the Bangladesh Garment Manufacturers Export Association (BGMEA) and the government.

In any case, many factories impose unofficial fines and deductions from the official wage, as well as withhold bonuses and money for overtime. Sometimes long delays occur in payment for labour performed, and some garment establishments are three or even six months in arrears. The government hinted at subsidized rice for garment workers for some years. In 2009, the BGMEA had set up a scheme to subsidize four kilos a week per worker, an initiative that was to last one year. How far this was implemented is unclear. In June 2012, the National Garment Workers Federation reported an agreement had been reached with the government to allow garment workers to buy food staples at subsidized prices—up to twenty kilos a month—from government-approved providers. The government promised subsidized rice for workers in the ready-made garment sector; but nothing happened. Garment workers quote a Bengali poem, 'Chailam ek ghoti jol, Dilo adkhana bel'—I asked only for a drop of water and you gave me dry fruit. That's how they feel.

A World Bank report in May 2010 stated that Bangladesh is now the third largest garment exporter in the world after China and Turkey. The sector earns seventy percent of the country's foreign exchange. According to a 2011 McKinsey Consultancy Survey of twenty-eight European and US purchasing officers for apparel companies, as China loses market share, Bangladesh could be the next 'hot spot' for ready-made garment exports. Within ten years these could draw another 3.5 million people into the industry, despite infrastructural constraints on power, roads, harbours. Workers are paid US$ 1.66 an hour in China, fifty-six cents in Pakistan, fifty-one cents in India, forty-four cents in Indonesia, thirty-six cents in Vietnam and thirty-one cents in Bangladesh. This is an overestimate: even after the rise in minimum wage, for anyone working a sixty-hour week, the rate is around eighteen cents an hour.

Amit Sarkar, a labour organizer, explained to me in March 2011 the scale of rewards in the sector:

> There are seven grades of operatives. At the bottom are the unskilled 'helpers', who earn the minimum wage. The next three grades suggest slightly raised levels of skill, and are paid accordingly. These low-paid workers constitute more than two-thirds of the labour force, and 80 per cent of them are women. The grades are assigned arbitrarily, and do not necessarily reflect the ability of the operative. Supervisory grades begin at level three, while lower management starts at level two. In the top management grade, 75 per cent are male.

In June 2004, *The Daily Star* reported that fifty or more suicides by garment workers had taken place in Konabari industrial village near Gazipur, where mostly young women killed themselves in the first five months of that year, a time of lay-offs and reduced orders for the factories. One young woman who attempted suicide was saved by neighbours and, it was reported, she now lives "on the pity of others". One factory manager said he did not know if any of their workers had committed suicide. "If anyone dies or commits suicide at her home, it is not our concern," said Mujibur Rahman, manager of Swan Sweaters. *The Daily Star* correspondent saw the body of a young man, a helper at Standard Garments, whose colleagues said he had probably committed suicide after having been sacked the previous day. The deputy general manager of the factory at first denied any deaths in his factory, but later said, "I need clearance from my management and top authorities to speak about any deaths." Many such deaths go unreported or are attributed to fictitious causes: 'personal problems' or 'an unhappy love affair'.

In the factories I visited when I first came to Dhaka in the early 1990s, two or three hundred workers sat in long rows, bent over Juki or Brother sewing machines. Helpers stitched and cut threads on the floor in the aisles between the machines. The work was monotonous and intensive: the fingers of the women guided the fabric between the needles which darted at a speed that deceived the eye. Although the workers were young, the ruinous effect of work upon their health was already evident—failing eyesight, damage to the spine, respiratory diseases from the dust and lint in the air.

This was the mid-1990s when the US Congress was threatening to pass a bill that would ban the import of garments from factories in which child labour was used. As a result, about two-thirds of the children working in the industry in Bangladesh were dismissed. There was no record of the fate of these unemployed waifs, nor of the families who may have depended upon their scant income. The US Congress exhibited no concern for the crowds of children employed in even more hazardous occupations than garments; and this drew criticism that their primary interest lay in protecting their own garment industry rather than the vulnerable youth of Bangladesh. As it turned out, there were children in all the factories I visited at that time.

A group of girls had recently arrived in Dhaka; Moshada was twelve, Nayantara thirteen, Rafiya thirteen, Mussamad Amina Khatoon fourteen and Ruma fourteen. They had come from the same village near Dinajpur, in one of the poorest parts of the country—part of the constantly changing pool of workers in the industry, the young women who replenish the supply of labour in the city. They were chaperoned by Mostara, twenty-five, the second wife of Moshada's grandfather, technically her step-grandmother.

I met them at the house of Jehanara Begum, an older

woman whose life has been devoted to the prevention of abuse and overwork of young women in industry. She said, "Although the factories are no longer supposed to employ children, you tell me whether twelve- and thirteen-year-olds are considered children or not. They have to send money back to their families. What choice do they have?" Jehanara raised a significant question. She asked what is childhood—not at all a rhetorical question in a country where young people take responsibility for their siblings, for minding cattle, for guarding crops as soon as they are able. Just like their counterparts in rural Britain of the early nineteenth century, their economic function is often necessary for family survival. The Western idea of childhood as a kind of holiday from life is, says Jehanara, alien and impossible here; and although adamantly against exploitative labour, she nevertheless doubts whether doing away with any useful function for children is in their own best interests.

The fact is child labour appears here in a quite different light from that in which it is presented in the West. The high-minded abolitionists have not been able to tell us how the families of working children are to survive (including the children themselves) without their contribution to an income just about sufficient to nourish and maintain them. If the children here are victims, they are victims of globally systemic wrongs, which the government of Bangladesh is powerless to address. It is one thing for Western moralists and reformers to swoop down upon 'ruthless employers', but when they cannot contextualize the processes that have driven the children into these places, their outrage strikes ineffectually against hard reality. Who is going to guarantee a living wage to adults that will permit them to bring up their children in security, particularly in a world where the 'competitive advantage' of ill-paid labour is the only recourse of a country like Bangladesh? By whose ordinance will these great injustices be healed?

There is, however, a difference between serving a necessary

economic purpose and excessive hours of labour. These young women had been working only for a few months, and Ruma had started only four weeks earlier. Work began at 7.30 a.m. and went on until 6 p.m., but when there was an urgent export order, they were sometimes detained in the factory as late as 10 p.m. It was not unknown to work through the night. Everything depended upon delivery times; and this tyranny—which came from the wholesalers and consumers in the countries where the products of their labour were sold—governed their life. At the beginning of their day's labour, they often did not know at what time it would end. Moshada was experienced, and worked sometimes as a machinist, and sometimes checking the quality of the finished articles. The factory where they worked made shirts, jackets, 'half-pant', 'full-pant' and 'genji' (a vest). Moshada knew the goods were exported, but did not know their destination. She was earning 1,600 taka a month, the others between 1,200 and 1,600 ($15–20).

The girls had gone to school in the village, but this did not equip them with the skills to read and write. Mostara was living with her husband and daughter. He had been a rickshaw driver, but was no longer working after an injury in a road accident. Mostara herself owned two rickshaws, which she was renting out to drivers at forty-five taka a day, so she had a basic daily income besides her factory wage.

There were five people in Moshada's family. Her father was a rickshaw driver, her mother also worked in a garment factory. Moshada gave all her wages to her father. When she needed new clothes, she asked her father for money and he gave it to her—a practice echoing that of early industrial Britain, where young people continued to hand their wages over to their parents until they were married. Moshada said she liked the factory, because she was earning and making a contribution to the family. This gave her a status she would not have in the village, working at home or in the fields. Factory life, she felt, was part of the modern world. "When I first saw the factory I was frightened. I was shocked, overwhelmed by the noise, the crowds, the speed of everything. In the village life is slow, in the city everyone is in a hurry."

Nayantara's family—her parents, two brothers and sister—have remained in the village. She came to Dhaka three months earlier, and found many friends and relatives from home who all lived close together. When she first saw the city, she was amazed by its size, the dust and the traffic. But she came to prefer Dhaka to the village, not because life was better here, but because there was money to be earned.

Rafiya was working as helper in a factory, still learning to operate the sewing machine. "If you are talented, you can become an operator after four or five months, but if you are slow, it can take a year or more." Rafiya's father was dead. Her two sisters, both married, and her two brothers remained in the village. Rafiya was sending 500–600 taka ($9–10) a month to them. She was living with three other girls in a room in Dhaka, for which they were paying 700 taka a month. By the time they shared their money for food, they were left with little to spare. Rafiya had never before held money in her hand. She said they were buying small items of luxury such as powder, lipstick, nail polish, toothpaste, and occasionally fruit and chocolate. "We do not buy soft drinks, because each one costs ten to fifteen taka, which is a waste of money." Rafiya took a tiffin to work—roti, banana, rice, vegetables, dal, which she ate during the half-hour lunch break. Apart from that, work was continuous. "It is very hot in the factory. Although there are fans, they do not cool the air. Sometimes the overseers get angry. They scold and curse us if we make a mistake."

Mussamad Amina Khatoon was living with an aunt and uncle in Dhaka. Her father had died, and her mother remained in the village with her two brothers and sister. She would rather be in the village, where there was peace and quiet, and where her family lived. She said she had no friends in Dhaka, no one to talk to or to play with. She saw Dhaka as a temporary place, and did not doubt that she would return home.

Ruma had two brothers and a sister. Her mother and father quarrelled because their land was too small and could not provide enough for the family's survival. Ruma's mother came to Dhaka as a maidservant. Ruma followed later, with her father, who was now working on a construction site. Ruma left school at ten, and had just started work in the factory. She gave all she earned to her parents, and they sometimes gave her money to spend on fruit and chocolate. She sometimes watched TV in a neighbour's house.

When I asked them about their ambitions and dreams, Mostara said sharply, "What dreams? Their only dream is to go to their house, cook, eat and sleep. That is the dream of young women in Dhaka—they dream that their working day will at last end."

In the place where we were sitting, a grey concrete bench, the eyes and the silvery smiles of the children—these young women trapped between childhood and womanhood, between rural and urban, between history and modernity—gleamed in the darkness. There was something haunting in their presence, a fugitive sense that these were indeed the descendants of earlier spinners and weavers in Bengal, survivors of those whose skills had been struck from their fingers, whose livelihoods had been curtailed and lives abridged by famine, hunger and the imperial will that had destroyed the precious craft of making muslin so sheer that a whole mythology grew around it: that it was so fine thirty yards could pass through a wedding ring or be shut away in a matchbox; material referred to as 'dew' or 'woven wind' or 'running water'. Is it the ghosts of their forebears that animate the youth and energy of these dingily beautiful young women, sending them out of a rural purdah to which imperialism had dispatched them when it laid waste an industry far superior to anything known in Britain, which was then to send its machine-made cotton goods to Bengal, a land which now, in its turn, dispatches the fruits of its degraded labour back to Britain and the rest of the Western world?

We know from what desolate, drowned or diminished land these young people have come; but who knows what landscapes their forefathers and mothers knew during the long and painful process of 're-ruralization' of a Bengal that had achieved a high degree of industrial proficiency—so high, it posed a threat to Britain on the brink of its own industrial revolution, and had its resourcefulness erased by the traders-become-rulers of the East India Company.

The young women also recall apologists for child labour in Britain during the early industrial era who insisted children should be initiated into factory labour at a young age. Andrew Ure, the Scottish doctor and scholar, wrote in 1835:

> To devise and administer a successful code of factory discipline, suited to the necessities of factory diligence, was the Herculean enterprise, the noble achievement of [Sir Richard] Arkwright. Even at the present day, when the system is perfectly organized, its labour lightened to the utmost, it is found nearly impossible to convert persons past the age of puberty, whether drawn from rural or from handicraft occupations, into useful factory hands. After struggling for a while to conquer their listless or restive habits, they either renounce the employment spontaneously, or are dismissed by the overlookers on account of inattention.

These wise and prescient sentiments have been well absorbed by the employers of Dhaka.

In December 2010, the twenty-seven deaths at Ashulia did not complete the toll of victims in that unhappy month. Earlier in the same week, four people died after police fired on demonstrators at a South Korean-owned factory in an Export Processing Zone in Chittagong, who were protesting at the company's failure to pay the newly agreed minimum wage of 5,000 taka a month ($60). Ten thousand workers took to the streets. When they arrived at their places of work, they found eleven factories had shut down in response to 'unrest' over wages.

Scores have also been killed over the past decade as a result of actions by the state against workers demonstrating against low pay, delayed wage payments, underpayment or other irregularities: in May–June 2006, October 2006 and June 2009, workers were shot in clashes with the police, and there was even police firing at workers inside the FS Sweater factory in Sripur in 2006, where dozens were injured.

There have also been persistent outbreaks of rioting by garment workers in Bangladesh over the past decade, sometimes in response to disasters in factories that have snuffed out fellow workers' lives. These have usually been spontaneous and uncoordinated, and have involved fire: burning vehicles and buildings, blocking the highway, wrecking factories and vandalizing the materials of their labour. In April 2010, what the papers euphemistically call 'unrest' sent six thousand workers from twenty-two factories in Mirpur to blockade the Dhaka–Chittagong highway at Kanchpur and to halt traffic on the road to Sylhet.

Rage among garment workers is intense and palpable. Their rage and despair at their lot in life, at the indifference of the authorities, finds expression in crowds that take to the streets with sticks and staves, torching vehicles, vandalizing buildings, venting their fury in a wild, unfocused frenzy of grief. Such displays of violence are a measure of the powerlessness of the workers, the forbidden solidarities and prohibited collective endeavour of these victims of a development about which they have never been consulted. Whoever thought of asking young countrywomen in Barisal or Dinajpur if they wanted to stitch clothes for the people of Frankfurt or San Francisco, Tokyo or Manchester? The factories simply sprang up, in response to the sophisticated sensors of the market.

Amit Sarkar, the labour organizer, told me in March 2011:

> The garment industry here is still growing. Certain garment sectors in China have closed down, and have relocated to Bangladesh because the wages are even lower. The only constraint here on the industry growing even faster is the lack of power, meaning electricity; but we might also say, a lack of workers' power is our biggest constraint.

For the garment workers a vital issue is: how would they use the vast potential of their own collective power to ensure that they are protected from economic violence—an unfashionable phrase, since 'the economy' and its miraculous workings are supposed now to be the source of all conceivable good. This means a representative trade union, preferably industry-wide and united, recognized by workers, employers and government, elected freely and voluntarily by factory operatives. One of the puzzling aspects of the continuous demonstrations by workers in Bangladesh has been the relative ineffectiveness of trade unions.

It is not that these do not exist in Bangladesh. There are at least fifty working in and around Dhaka. But many are either corrupt or company-controlled. Some are financed by Western non-governmental organizations or are supported by Western trade unions and consumer groups. They fail to command widespread support. Is this because the industrial model, which produced a rooted and committed trade union movement in Britain in the nineteenth century, does not exist in Bangladesh? The thousands of factories are simply assembly units. Most of the materials come from elsewhere, and remain in the country just long enough to be stitched into garments for export. The industry is not a consequence of any deeper transformation; and the workers well understand its provisional sojourn in Bangladesh: it would not take much for it to fly away to more lucrative sites, if they should interrupt the delicate balance of a global rag trade, in which it is their destiny to perform a single, if vital, task.

So although workers may be 'volatile', they are pressed by family urgencies that make whole villages dependent upon remittances from Dhaka or Chittagong; they are afraid of any kind of organization that might deprive them of labour; they know that the implicit bargain struck between factory owners and exporters has caught them up in a promise that is broken every day.

It is not surprising that the rulers of Bangladesh do not appreciate the circumstances under which so many young women and men labour—a fact not unconnected with the position of a significant proportion of lawmakers who have some financial interest in the industry. About 10 per cent of parliamentarians are factory owners, but as many as half have some financial interest in the garment industry. The owners live in secluded compounds in great luxury, protected from the public by high walls, frontiers that resemble those of another country, guards in watchtowers—a semi-military image of a citadel or fortress, beneath which workers pass each day on their march to work, kicking up dust with their chappals on the margins of the road. Factory owners will spend as much on a night out as those they employ will earn in a year.

While the industry involves only the shaping and stitching of the material that comes from outside the country, the factories themselves are more durably sewn into the structures of privilege. Owners and foreign buyers blame each other for the pressure on the workers, but their interlocking relationship ensures that both make enormous profit at the workers' expense. The garment lords of Dhaka lament that Western brands are constantly demanding increases in productivity, even though their own yield from the labour of the people has bypassed any possible description of justice—they are obscenely, extravagantly rich. I once travelled in the business class of Biman Bangladesh Airlines, and it was like being present at a cocktail party of the ruling elite. They all knew each other, and shared stories and exchanged gossip about visiting their kinsfolk in London, Rome, Washington, California, the places where their children were studying and the specialists which their relatives had consulted. Clearly, the educational and health-care provisions of Dhaka were not good enough for them. It is a restricted, claustrophobic world, which has at its disposal resources equal to anything the global rich can boast of.

The factory owners find it incomprehensible that disturbances should break out, and can only imagine that these are a consequence of conspiracy; as though malice and not misery prompt people to react against injustice. And so the patterns are repeated: workers cheated, denied fair remuneration for their work, overly supervised and spied on, threatened by musclemen if they resist, and all the time fragmented and scattered, so that collective resistance is undermined: the rich grow richer as individuals, but the impoverished are made poorer collectively.

Since about 80 per cent of the foreign exchange of Bangladesh is now dependent upon a single industry, it is understandable that the leaders of the country should wish to protect it; but as they do so, they often exhibit considerable insensitivity towards those upon whose work their own well-being depends, using whatever means at hand to keep the workers under their control. In March 2009, the government alerted intelligence agencies about the possible infiltration of militants or NGOs committing subversive acts to create 'anarchy' in the apparel industry. On 31 October 2010 the 'industrial police' was created, whose labour concentrates on rooting out disaffection, and advising employers on the desirability of employing certain firebrands and hotheads whose concern is with the subordinate objectives of safety and the punctual payment of wages. The industrial police would have been more usefully employed looking into abuses by developers, builders, factory owners and managers, but this is not part of their selective remit.

The issue of disturbance of the flow of wealth in Bangladesh provokes stern pronouncements. In April 2010, the home minister told the press: "No one will be spared if found to be involved in creating unrest in the garment sector." The government declared, "We have information that outsiders often fuel trouble in the sector," while the prime minister herself said, "Government will not tolerate anarchism in the garment sector, as this is the main source of foreign exchange in the country." The fear that disaffection might be instigated from outside, that it is the work of a 'hidden hand', is a customary aspect of the official paranoia that the competitors of Bangladesh are constantly striving to destabilize the country. For most, this means India—an India which, to some, is scheming to regain possession of a province which it lost, briefly, to Pakistan before it became an independent entity in the Liberation War of 1971, an emancipation in which India was also a key player.

Perhaps the single most potent factor in the factory owners' attitude is that they regard workers as a different order of human being from themselves. When challenged on the gross inequalities between them and their employees, they will lament the 'great differences that exist in our society'; but this is part of a long-established 'natural' order, and the beneficiaries of such divisions rarely show any great haste to call them into question. Rioting by garment workers in the first decade of the twenty-first century has resulted in the vandalization of factories, setting fire to cars and shops, while police have regularly fired on, and killed, protesters. These have their equivalents in past events of industrial Britain: destruction of power looms in 1812 and 1816 by 'Luddites', the march of the Blanketeers in 1817 and the cutting down by the military of people at a peaceful demonstration of workers in St Peter's Fields in Manchester in 1819. The great difference between these events has been in their effect on the popular consciousness of the time: the deaths of so many workers from industrial accidents, factory fires and police shootings in Dhaka over the past twenty years have had no impact comparable to the single event that became known as the 'Peterloo Massacre' in 1819. In Bangladesh, the well-being of the elites depends upon fulfilling contracts and realizing the foreign exchange from the delivery of garments, and the products indispensable to this: imported whisky, fast cars, luxury goods and above all, armaments that will protect them against external enemies and internal insurgents. This means the fate of some garment workers is of less consequence than any disturbance to the smooth conduct of trade—the more so since ancient ideas of caste and the distinction between *ashraf* and *ajlaf* Muslims still haunt the quasi-feudal democracy of Bangladesh.

Just as a new generation of garment workers is generally unaware that they are the distant descendants of the (almost exclusively female) spinners and the men who practised the ancient art of weaving in Bengal, political leaders who warn of 'conspiracies' among workers to subvert this most prosperous part of the economy are equally ignorant of their own role in this shadow replay of colonial history. The conditions under which weavers worked in the last decades of the eighteenth century, however archaic they appear now, foreshadow the mass employment of the twenty-first century; and the strategies, both of the workers for escaping onerous impositions, and of the employers, in imposing ever greater burdens of labour upon them, show a distinct convergence, which is easily overlooked by eyes distracted by the trappings of modernity.

When the East India Company consolidated its power over the weavers of Bengal, it imposed ever more stringent rules on the conditions of their employment. Regulations imposed by the Company aimed at two things: to compel the weavers to fulfil contracts, and to eliminate rival mercantile groups from interfering with their business.

> Much of their produce was downgraded in quality by Company officials, categorized as defective in order to cheat them of the full price. This practice was so prevalent that the 'advances' paid to them were never fully remunerated, and the weavers remained permanently in debt, and frequently worked at a loss (Mitra, 1978).

Among the many conditions placed upon the weavers was the demand that they work solely for the Company.

The weavers naturally sought to evade the system of fines, advances for production, the rejection of work as of too poor quality, growing bondage to a single employer. There was little possibility of weavers being able to organize a collective response (Hossain, 1988). Some continued to work surreptitiously for other employers, while others abandoned weaving or migrated from their villages and *arangs* (manufactories and depositories for goods). When weavers tried to avoid the commitments in these ways, they were harassed, arrested, fined, beaten and sometimes imprisoned.

Between 1775 and 1787 'reports from the Commercial Residents' (officially appointed by the Company) indicated that during this period 'combinations of weavers' were formed to resist and defy the orders of the arang (factory). From Dhaka, in 1776, there were complaints of the existence of such a 'combination'. It was reported that the weavers of two villages under Sonargaon arang refused to work for the Company. During the course of the investigation, it was learnt that they had been intimidated by the weavers of Sonargaon. "Six persons abused … and threatened us if we worked for the Company that they would use every endeavour to ruin us and prejudice our characters. We, therefore, pray for redress and protection, or we must desist working for the Company." It was ordered that an application be made to the Provincial Council to "cause proper punishment to be inflicted upon the weavers of Sonargaon, who may be proved to be concerned in the unwarrantable combination of which you advise us… The Commercial Residents ascribed such organized protest to the instigation of outside forces" (Hossain, 1988).

According to D.B. Mitra, "At Malda, the weavers showed a determined resolution not to take the Company's advances because of the penalty clause." (This stipulated that the agreed quantity of pieces of cloth must be delivered on pain of fines.)

They feared that circumstances such as sickness, inability to get proper threads in proper time, interruption due to disputes with the *zamindars*, might prevent them from fulfilling their contracts. The weavers of the city of Dacca unitedly protested against the imposition of a penalty of 35 per cent. It became so serious in nature that in order to break the combination, Mr Taylor, the Commercial Resident, had to send six ringleaders of the combination to the *Faujdari Adawlut* (criminal court) for trial and punishment (Mitra, 1978).

There are parallels in the ready-made garment industry of contemporary Bangladesh, since there are few alternatives to employment, especially for young women, who are constrained to work for wages that barely cover subsistence. Those who protest against the terms on which work is offered are liable to detention: Moshrefa Mishu, president of the Garment Workers Unity Forum, was arrested in December 2010, held in prison, mistreated and subsequently hospitalized; she was charged with being one of the 'ringleaders' of the torching and vandalism of vehicles and property following the outbreak of violence when workers protested that the new minimum wage offered in November 2010 was too small an improvement on that which preceded it to provide an adequate living.

According to labour organizer Amit Sarkar, the government has posted industrial police in the factory areas. At the first sign of trouble, the management just has to call them and they go to the factory. The private owners in any case have their own goondas with lathis and other weapons. "Some employers pay others to discipline their own colleagues; they will even give bonuses to some workers to make sure they inform them of any disaffection or efforts to organize. Our workers are young people from the village. They are not united."

The system of supervision, the use of informers and spies, fines and punishments for mistakes—all this is a ghostly reconstitution of the old imperial hierarchies of *gumashtas* (agents), *jassendars* (assessors of the quality of the material) and *dalals* (brokers). *Taggudgars* (collectors of cloth) at every arang; and peons (low-ranking officers) used to monitor the weavers and make sure they were not working clandestinely on their own account for other merchants or traders. In the eighteenth century, guards were posted at the doors of the weavers' houses to enforce compliance with the Company's contracts, to ensure they did not deal with French, Dutch or independent merchants; today's agents and eavesdroppers are employed inside the factory.

The small organized activities of workers were, of course, remote from anything understandable in terms of trade unions, and were probably a result of efforts by shared interest groups in the complex division of labour in the commissioning, financing and collecting of the weavers' labour. In spite of this, the Company strengthened legal measures against efforts by the weavers to act collectively. The status of the weaver was consistently degraded, in order to ensure the safety of the Company's 'investment', the quantity of goods ordered by London in any given year.

The censure of trade unions and their pernicious influence on the economy of the country, currently heard in Bangladesh, not only echoes the coercive regulations of the East India Company, but also reawakens memories of the horror of 'combinations' of workers in Britain, especially in the wake of the French Revolution, and the passing by Parliament of the Combination Acts of 1799. These forbade any organization of labourers; and although repealed some twenty years later, a fear of workers' capacity for collective action haunted industrial Britain, and has continued to do so. Andrew Ure (1835) thundered:

> The very name of union makes capital restive, and puts ingenuity on the alert to defeat its objects. When the stream of labour is suffered to glide on quietly within its banks, all goes well; when forcibly dammed up, it becomes unprofitably stagnant for a time and then brings on a disastrous inundation. Were it not for unions, the vicissitudes of employment, and the

substitution of automatic for handwork, would seldom be so abrupt as to distress the operative.

Late in 2009, several thousand people surrounded the Nippon Garment factory on Mymensingh Road. After the police shooting in which three people died, the police lodged scores of cases against the protesters, *including those they had killed in the firing*.

This vindictive pursuit of the dead too has equivalents in the long and baleful history of textiles in Bengal. The East India Company was remorseless in its attempt to recover lost production or debts from its deceased weavers. Hameeda Hossain (1988) cites documents that passed between the Commercial Residents and their representatives in the local areas, relating to cases to be followed up of weavers thought to be dead, absconding or incapable of repaying debts since 1787.

> In Chandpur, Sobha Behal, a deceased weaver no. 118 under *Dihi 1* (a group of villages) left only a hut which was sold for Rs 2. When Yugul died in 1799, his possessions were sold for the *shraddha* ceremony (funeral) and the Factory could not extract anything. Sitasmakar, weaver no. 503 under *Dihi 1*, absconding from Narainpur, was caught and his debt was realized in part … To escape prosecution, weavers fled with their families … When Tuku Pradhaniya of *Dihi 2* died, the Factory expected his son to accept his liabilities.

Today's factory owners have huge authority, since they are represented in government and in all policy-making forums; they are as powerful as the East India Company was. The weavers were self-employed; the garment workers are part of today's global sweatshop—both groups at the mercy of powerful interests whose reach and influence they cannot match.

The division of labour under the Company, whether under the agency system or the contract system, created a network which rendered the workers invisible to the final beneficiaries, much as happens in the garment industry in Bangladesh today. And it is the actual makers of the goods, the weavers and workers, who are always squeezed in order to ensure the 'success' of the enterprise. It is they who bear the whole edifice of creation, distribution and consumption of their labour, support the proliferation of plunderers and profiteers, who know how to skim off a portion of the value of merchandise as it makes its way across vast distances—then as now—to its final destination.

Despite the corruption and subversion of many contemporary efforts by workers to organize, some are animated by a passionate innocence and integrity. One hot afternoon in May 2010, I joined a small independent trade union demonstrating on the streets of the capital in favour of a rise in the minimum wage from its then 1,662 taka a month to 5,000—a demand which, by the time it was fulfilled in 2011, had become largely ineffective, since the cost of house rents and basic foodstuffs had in advance eroded the long-promised raise.

Before the modest procession set out, about forty people gathered in a cramped, sweltering room on the ground floor of a concrete building in the commercial centre of Dhaka. The walls were papered with patterns of green leaves, onto which were pasted photographs of aircraft in flight: significant symbols, uniting nostalgia for an abandoned rural past with hope for a super-industrial future. The room contained two grey metal desks, plastic chairs and a gunmetal cabinet. The floor was concrete, worn and shiny where the feet of countless people with grievances had shuffled and stood, recounting their sorrows. A power outage had just halted the fan, which had ceased to rotate, its blades the wings of a captive metal insect.

This modest space is the headquarters of a trade union whose officials face constant harassment and arrest. It has been donated by a travel agent sympathetic to the workers' cause. There is no computer, not even a typewriter, a lack of facilities which suggests the union is neither fraudulent nor corrupt. It relies on contributions from its 25,000 members. These are not only the lowest paid industrial workers in Bangladesh, but also the most poorly paid garment workers in the world.

Workers from outlying districts of Narayanganj, Ashulia and Tongi have paid their own fare and sacrificed a day's pay to be here. The procession that forms in the alley leading to the building is sparse but dignified. It is also mostly male: although they have no intention of provoking violence, they have advised the women workers not to come. They tell of lives exhausted even before they begin their twelve-hour day of work: unreliable supplies of water, long queues for the latrine, sweaty nights under tin roofs that retain the heat of the day, as their youth and energy are sewn fast into garments that may be worn once or twice and then discarded, eyesight impaired and back bent by years at a Juki machine on a plastic-topped table under the unwinking watchfulness of pale strip lighting.

The young people are thin and mostly small in stature; their bodies speak of undernourishment and overwork. They are clad in threadbare shirts, trousers low on their skinny hips, frayed by dragging in the rain and dust, canvas trainers from which the soles have become detached. Nothing could be less threatening. The demonstration makes little impact on the crowded thoroughfares in the humid late afternoon of Dhaka. It is soon swallowed up in the tangle of cycle rickshaws, vendors, construction workers, beggars, unemployed young men and maidservants going from house to house, the child labour at tea stalls and young apprentices welding in metal workshops, eyes unprotected from the pyrotechnics of blue and orange sparks. The slogans of the demonstration are carried away on the fumy air and drowned by the traffic; and after walking half a kilometre along Naya Paltan, they disperse, unmolested even by the police, always on the lookout, not so much for infringements of law and order, as for an opportunity to make a few extra taka in informal fines on the poorest.

This ragged column of people was not threatening. Far from

resembling the epic imagery of mass rallies, heroic flags and clenched fists, it was much more like the petitions with which the dispossessed weavers of the late eighteenth century besieged the Commercial Residents of the East India Company, begging for relief from the impossible conditions under which they were expected to deliver the Company's investment—yet another echo of those times.

The weavers of Santipore sent petitions to the Calcutta Council pointing out their grievances. The following authoritative account is to be found in the Proceedings of 2 April 1773:

> The two annexed papers which the President formed from an examination into the complaints made to him by the weavers of Santipore and which he has every reason to believe to be authentic, will show the present miserable situation of the weavers, since it appears that the prices given to them for the cloths provided on account of the Company's investment, amounted to no more and in some instances less than the cost of the materials and their labour was extracted from them without any payment. They are at the same time forbidden under pain of corporal chastisement and forfeitures to work for private merchants or to make any other assortments but those ordered for the Company's investment (Mitra, 1978).

Hameeda Hossain (1988) refers to the 'passive resistance' of weavers. "They were totally dependent on the Company and the latter's shifting economic interests had reduced them to a condition of chronic underemployment. When they could no longer meet the conditions imposed on them they either left their place of work or changed their occupation." In the end, the Company's concern with the collection of land revenue overtook its trading interests. By this time—the first third of the nineteenth century—the import of British-made goods had, in any case, rendered the work of the superior grades of weavers irrelevant; the loss of the industry involved the disemployment

of tens, if not hundreds, of thousands
women spinners were totally without oc
of yarn from Britain increased. These histo
structural and took place over long periods of tir
public scrutiny. How different these were from c
catastrophes and accidents, captured instantaneous
insomniac eyes of the global media.

of skilled weavers; while
upation as the import
ical disasters were
ne and far from
ontemporary
by the

...aza at Savar just outside
...orst industrial accidents
...was accidental only in
...iral' are, since they are
...o thousand factories of
Dhaka have been thrown up in great haste to cash in on the
garment rush of the past twenty years.

The site of the ruined building was described by many as a
'war zone'; and it is indeed a battleground, site of the ubiquitous
Third World War: the global war of attrition of rich against poor,
a conflict between limitless greed and the exhaustible energy of
flesh and blood. The costs of this are borne by ill-paid workers
with their ruined eyesight, spinal injuries, absorption of dust and
lint by the lungs, and, as in the case of more than eleven hundred
victims at Savar, with life itself. The wealth of Bangladesh is
heavily dependent upon the labour of despised and humiliated
workers, who form part of a vast machine for enriching others:
lawmakers, bureaucrats, factory owners, exporters, middlemen,
importers, retailers and international brands in the West.

Stories that emerged from the wreckage confirm official
indifference to those who worked in the factories. There was no
complete list of all employees. Even the number was unknown,
let alone the names. Some days after the tragedy, it was reported
that thirty-two unclaimed bodies had been buried in the Jurain
graveyard—a blood-chilling announcement that reinforces the
sense of the anonymity and abstraction that is 'labour'. Who
knows whether the dead were unclaimed because those they

loved were living in a remote part of the country, and did not
know where they were working: people change factories all the
time because of unpaid wages, mistreatment, beatings or fines
for 'misconduct' (which generally means making a mistake in
stitching), harassment or sexual advances by predatory male
overseers. There is a constant human tide in and out of these
unregulated workplaces; labour is dispensable and infinitely
replaceable; and only when an event like this illuminates the
monumental insentience of the system does it dawn on those who
employ them that they are more than the sum of their weekly
labour, that they have families who struggle to survive and who
depend upon the meagre sums they send home.

Who died and who perished was a matter of the caprice of
fate. Some, little more than children, had worked only for a day
or two, and had yet to receive a pay packet. Others had been
called to Dhaka by sisters or brothers, telling of opportunities in
the city's two thousand factories. A few people had failed to arrive
for work that day, summoned by sickness or family duty to more
urgent necessities. Others had distrusted official assurances that
it was safe to enter the building. One girl had sent her sister in her
place. Another young woman, reported dead, arrived home and
the family believed she was a ghost. Miracles occurred: it was
not the time to die for the woman sheltering under a staircase,
and another survived protected by the body of a colleague.

And after seventeen days, there was the wonder of the
survival of Reshma, brought out physically unscathed. The
world media reported this as an almost supernatural deliverance;
although her story, told with the skeletal brevity with which the
lives of poor people are usually evoked, is yet another tale of
hardship and sorrow. Her father died when she was three, and
she and her four older brothers and sisters were brought up by
their mother in Dinajpur. She came to Dhaka to join her sister,
and married a co-worker she met in the factory. The husband
treated her cruelly, taking control of her salary and beating her;

a few months earlier she had left him. After her rescue she was appointed to a position in the Westin Hotel at a salary of 30,000 taka a month.

In the publicity that followed Reshma's survival, politicians were not slow in making their way to her bedside. The prime minister and leader of the Opposition both arrived at the Combined Military Hospital to pay tribute to her endurance, perhaps also to earn back their lost reputation for humanitarian sentiments, and, who knows, to share with her their own secrets of survival in the relentless political conflict they have waged against each other for almost a generation.

Rana Plaza was owned by Mohammed Sohel Rana, a significant figure in the governing Awami League, who had held office in its Youth Wing, although he was disowned by the party. Official permission had been obtained for a six-storey structure, but two more floors were subsequently added, which placed further stress on the fabric of the building. No permit had been granted for its use as a manufacturing unit. It had, in any case, been constructed with substandard materials, and was also situated, like much recent building in Dhaka, on a former watercourse, which further destabilized the units. Overcrowding and the constant vibration of machinery were also found, in a provisional government report, to have contributed to the instability of the structure.

The building had been declared unsafe after cracks appeared in the masonry; and the employees of a branch of BRAC bank had been told not to report for work. The management of the factories had not only reassured the workers that it was perfectly secure, but some had also threatened them with a stoppage of wages if they failed to show up for work. Many operatives had hesitated that day before going to work; only the fear of losing their jobs appeared more compelling than the risk to their lives. After the collapse, the owner fled, and was apprehended as he tried to escape to India. Others—engineers, inspectors, officials—were arrested. The story was transformed from a social and economic disaster into a criminal case, and the prime minister declared that the guilty would be hunted down and brought to justice. In this way, a confrontation with the wider structural corruption in Bangladesh was avoided, and the issue reduced to one of wrongdoing in the erection of an individual structure.

Western companies rushed to express their concern for the welfare and safety of the workers, even though they knew nothing about the subcontractors who furnished them with their agreeably cheap merchandise. New impetus was given to campaigns conducted by organizations dedicated to fairness and 'clean clothes'. Although Primark cannot be held responsible for the faulty structure of Rana Plaza, it issued a statement: "The company is shocked and saddened", and it offered "condolences to all those involved. Primark has engaged for several years with NGOs and other retailers to review the Bangladeshi industry's approach to factory standards. Primark will push for this review to include building integrity." The company had, only a couple of days before the disaster, announced an increase in 'operating profits' of 56 per cent for the preceding six months to £238 million. Its parent company is Associated British Foods, owner of Silver Spoon Sugar and Twinings Tea (*Guardian*, 23 April 2013).

Primark felt impelled to add that it "notes the fact that its supplier shared the building with those of other retailers". Its supplier, Simple Approach, had occupied the second floor. "We are fully aware of our responsibility. We urge other retailers to come forward and offer assistance." Even the company's apparent generosity could not stand alone: it could not refrain from urging its competitors to similar compensatory acts, no doubt in the desire not to make gratuitous inroads into its own profits while its challengers kept theirs intact. The remorseful contrition expressed by Mango, Matalan, Benetton and other foreign importers was borne away on the humid death-laden breeze. The response of many workers in Dhaka to this form of industrial terrorism was also sad and troubling: the catastrophe sparked off an immediate display of violence, a manifestation of the helplessness of the workers. The image of police firing teargas and rubber bullets on the injured and humiliated of Dhaka has a haunting resonance; it is a savage emblem of a broken and corrupt system, which turns its wrath against the people forced by absence of choice into its compulsions.

After the remorse came the justification. A member of the BGMEA declared that the catastrophe had been 'an act of God'. Is it an accident that the deity, nowhere to be seen when the manufacturers are making their fabulous fortunes, puts in an appearance only when workers are killed or maimed?

The scenes of desolation of the heartbroken and bereaved rouse obscure echoes in the people of Britain. The pictures of distressed family members, and their watchful vigil at the scene of the disaster, were reminiscent of experiences familiar only the day before yesterday in the country that gave birth to the industrial revolution.

There were, of course, frequent accidents in the early mills and textile plants of Lancashire and Yorkshire: women and children, whose hair or clothing was caught up in unguarded machinery, so that their whole bodies were sucked into the system of pulleys and chains, whirled around and often severely injured. There were many fatalities. But these were widely dispersed, and could be represented as individual tragedies. Nothing occurred on the scale of the enormity in Dhaka. In Britain, industrial calamities visited upon more dangerous occupations, especially coal mining, which was to Britain in the late nineteenth and early twentieth centuries what garments are to contemporary Bangladesh, since this was the single largest employer of labour.

In 1913, pre-dating the events in Savar by exactly a century, the greatest industrial catastrophe ever known in Britain took place at the Senghenydd pit in South Wales. On that occasion, 439 miners were killed by an underground gas explosion. The rockfall from this prevented rescuers from reaching the victims: it took over a month to recover all the bodies.

The parallels with present-day serial disasters in Bangladesh are striking. The events at Savar had been preceded by many industrial misadventures—building collapses, fires and explosions—after which promises were made that greater attention would be paid to worker security. In Britain, a decade before the Senghenydd calamity, seventy-eight miners had been buried alive in the same pit. Following this earlier accident, recommendations had been made for the improvement of safety arrangements, but these had been neglected. In fact, conditions had worsened in the meantime, since increased production had led to an even greater concentration of workers in cramped and confined spaces.

The echoes are remarkable, even though a century has passed between these *non-accidental* tragedies. Pictures taken in 1913 prefigure scenes played out in Dhaka in 2013. There are the same frantic relatives, frozen in attitudes of disbelief and terror: women in shawls and long dresses looking for their sons; mothers who are nursing children, and who realize they will never see their husbands again. The impotent anxiety, the surrender to the inevitability of what has happened, the creased brow and hand clutching the throat, the faint residue of hope—long relationships, with all their pain, conflict and love, abridged, arbitrarily, in a matter of seconds.

In what other way than in terms of warfare can we interpret the struggle to make yet more profit out of the labour of those who have nothing but the nimbleness of their pliable hands to bargain with against even greater global concentrations of capital? The significance of Dhaka in 2013 is that the locus of this prolonged war has shifted, from the bleak pit-villages of Britain, places of stone and slate, to the capital of Bangladesh, a city as inimical to human well-being as almost any other on the planet. The sex of the workers, too, has changed. All the dead of Senghenydd were men, while the majority in Dhaka were women, especially young women, on whose slender remittances whole families in the countryside—indeed, whole villages—depend. But it is the same conflict: the intensification of labour, driving down of costs by competitive Western companies, disregard for the life and limb of those who know no other means of livelihood. A photograph survives of a street in Senghenydd, a row of mean one-storey cottages: every house lost at least one member of the family. It is known that the explosion left 217 widows, 480 children without a father and fifty-two other dependents without a livelihood. This was the first major disaster to have occurred since the 1897 Workmen's Compensation Act, which provided the widows with less than £300. It is also on record that compensation and relief fund grants excluded from its beneficiaries some women who had been co-habiting with dead miners and their illegitimate children.

Despite highly conspicuous arrests in Dhaka, the history of the pursuit of owners of faulty or dangerous factories reflects that the effort has been less than effective. The solidarity of the rich might offer instructive lessons to those who have nothing to conserve but their own lives. Individuals are protected by political allies; court cases wind their way through the judicial system in slow motion; evidence is lost, the accused abscond or move abroad to places where they have prudently invested in real estate and other durables which will shield them from the wrath of their countrymen and women.

After Senghenydd, the owners and managers of the pit were prosecuted; but charges against the owners were dropped, and the manager of the mine was fined £24—the equivalent of a few thousand Bangladeshi taka. A headline in the local paper declared that the life of a miner was valued at 'a penny farthing'. The Miners' Federation of Great Britain appealed against the decision, and in consequence, the owners were fined £10—about 1,500 taka. The mine remained open until 1928. A memorial was erected to those who lost their lives only in 1981—sixty-eight years after the event, and on the eve of the government of Margaret Thatcher's final battle with the miners. An official enquiry found that there had been no neglect on the part of anyone, although it was suggested that the number of inspectors of mines was insufficient.

Official remorse was perfunctory, but a relief fund soon touched £100,000, including receipts from a public viewing of the wedding presents of Prince Arthur of Connaught (grandson of Queen Victoria), and the Duchess of Fife. Charity stood in place of justice.

Such public callousness would be unthinkable today in Britain. The world has changed, but remains, in many ways, obdurately the same. In its support to the families of the dead and wounded of Dhaka, Primark offered what it called a "compensation package". This would "include the provision of long-term aid for children who have lost parents and financial aid for those injured and payouts to the families of the deceased". This conciliatory gesture deserves closer scrutiny, for any humanitarian impulse is blunted by the chill euphemisms of language. The idea of a compensation package suggests something satisfactorily despatched—a bale of clothing perhaps, or some other merchandise. 'Children who have lost parents' appears to throw on the orphans an element of carelessness; while the idea of a 'payout' is mechanistic, grudging, condescending. The people, moreover, are not 'deceased', since this implies natural causes: they were killed.

This is all in significant contrast to the immediate self-sacrifice and heroism of the rescuers—neighbours, students and workers from the neighbourhood, who could instantly identify the trapped workers with their own loved ones. They did not wait for organized help—perhaps because they had learned this was likely to be slow and ill coordinated—but tore away at the rubble with their bare hands. Rescuers talk of how they had to amputate limbs to free people trapped under heavy beams and reinforced concrete that could not be lifted; some of these improvised operations were carried out without anaesthetic, and by workers without medical experience. No one knows how many lives were saved in this way.

After the event, swarms of journalists, film crews,

photographers and commentators descended upon the scene, all supplied with the most sophisticated technology; but lifting equipment and the necessary tools for rescue were not immediately available. If a fraction of the money spent on reporting the disaster had been spent on safety, there would have been no news story to cover; in this way, few of us are entirely free of complicity in the drama. Some of the pictures, too, were unbearably graphic: a couple, half covered in rubble and pallid with dust, were caught in an embrace as they died.

The images of South Wales in 1913 and Dhaka in 2013 converge: the lines of white shrouds, the vigilant mothers and husbands and sisters who stood day and night in the same spot, clenched against the news they knew must come; the wrecked pithead and the concrete floors of the factory compressed like some monstrous sandwich, people standing with photographs of the missing, as if their picture could conjure them back from the dead.

The most vital issue for the workers was as it was in South Wales: a representative trade union. The government quickly announced a rise in wages (unspecified), and said it would henceforth be possible for unions to form "without the prior permission of the owners". Nothing about any comprehensive union to which all workers might belong. Nor did the government say anything about whether it was time to do away with company-sponsored unions, bogus welfare organizations, ineffectual and self-seeking officials; to dismiss the spies and informers. There was no mention of foreign NGOs, 'labour rights organizations' or consumer groups, which, if they have a role at all, should be to support the functioning of free trade unions in Bangladesh.

It cannot be left to Western activists, even less to the importers themselves, to determine what is good for those they and their suppliers and subcontractors employ. If workers are accorded dignity and respect, which have, so far, been withheld, all the rest will fall into place.

The women of Britain's past in the dress of Edwardian Wales, with their mute sepia-coloured grief, are kindred to the weeping mothers, whose full-colour sorrows in contemporary Dhaka are transmitted instantly by the global media; and they join together over time in a single explosive question: if this is progress, who is advantaged by it? To claim that this represents 'development' is to prioritize the lives of the rich West over those of the poor of the earth, which is simply a reconstruction of older imperial priorities. After all, 'business' is now the only area of human activity in which 'empires' are still routinely allowed to be built.

Part of the subtext of reports in the Western media was a sorrowing acceptance that since 'we' have been through such tragedies, this is part of the necessary tribulation to be endured by the people of Bangladesh, before they can emerge into the sunny uplands of (relative) prosperity and ease. Comparisons had also been made between the Tazreen fire of 2012 and the Triangle Shirtwaist fire in New York, 101 years earlier, which occurred in similar circumstances. That factory was also in a high-rise building, and overfilled elevators could not cope with the number fleeing the blaze that broke out in March 1911. Many workers were trapped on the roof; 146 people died. Similarities between disasters in present-day Bangladesh and in the US of the twentieth century and Britain of the nineteenth century illuminate the path inscribed in the iconography of 'development'; and however shocking the events, there emerges from them a sense that these human sacrifices are tragic mishaps on the road to the kind of wealth and prosperity now enjoyed in Western countries. In other words, the expressions of sorrow, the hand-wringing and the regrets serve to confirm a widely held determinist view of what is involved in the process of growing rich. Lamentable as such occurrences are, the subtext reads: these are part of the rites of passage to a world of plenty and contentment.

That all is changed, while everything remains the same, suggests the work of those who strove for social justice, emancipation, freedom from oppression and a secure livelihood which assures sufficiency has gone in vain; these will have to be won all over again, and liberty be wrested, not from the paraphernalia of imperial occupation, but from the apparently impregnable global fortresses of capital, which faithfully replicate the vanished pomp of territorial empires.

The appeal of cheap garments in contemporary Western markets is often advanced as a conclusive argument for the industry in Bangladesh (and elsewhere): the consumers have spoken, and their voices are louder in the global market than that of people who have produced the garments. The presence of 'cheap clothing' in Western stores has been dearly bought; only the price paid by the consumer—whether the preference of Bengal silks of ladies of fashion in the 1790s or the scramble for clothing in Primark, Walmart or Carrefour—bears no relation to the pain of those who produced the items for which there is such heavy 'demand'. In fact, the very term 'demand' takes precedence in the seemingly neutral equation of supply and demand: demand is imperious and dominant; supply, submissively responsive.

Part II

Barisal

In 2009, I went to Barisal City, an old provincial town in the south of Bangladesh, overwhelmed now by refugees from ruined rural livelihoods, in order to understand why so many people are drawn to Dhaka—that sombre labyrinth of hope, the site of a better life which, whatever material improvements it yields, nonetheless actually *feels* worse than the life people have left.

Barisal is still half rural, a chaotic collection of stagnant ponds, overgrown with dense weeds, arum and *kachuri panna* (water hyacinths), houses of tin and wood, ramshackle booths next to a municipal office block, small hovels close to the crumbling architecture of the Raj, zamindars' ruined houses and self-built slums. All over the city, stacks of tree trunks remain, savage harvest of the devastating cyclone Sidr, of October 2007, which felled ancient rain trees, betel, palms and mango orchards. There is no industry in Barisal, whose people eke out a living in the narrowing spaces between a degraded country life and an urban existence that has yet to establish itself.

Dipik Lal Mridha, of the city corporation, says there has been "some development" in Barisal, but it is at a low level. He says, "We have lost our feelings for the poor. Community feeling is diminished. The rich used to help the poor, but if they do so now it is only for show. Although people earn more money, prices of food have risen so much that the standard of living has fallen."

There are many agencies in the development sector, but little coordination between them. Mridha says the slums are not expanding in space, but their population is increasing, because people come and stay with relatives or former village neighbours.

Political parties control slums on government property. They levy rent and *chadda*, illegal tax, which goes to political *mastaans*, or enforcers. Crime is generally low, but addiction—to ganja, heroin and especially to Phensedyl, a cough mixture smuggled from India—is a problem. Struggles over land are the cause of most violence. All government departments concerned with land are corrupt: false registrations and bogus sales are common; land is frequently claimed or sold by two or more people. Administrative and legal chaos, insecurity and fear of eviction serve as powerful incentives for people to leave.

Although Barisal has an aura of impermanence, and many of its young are able to move on, this city is one of the provinces of globalism—where the whisperings of modern life have become louder, the imagery of wealth and power more visible, and the iconography of global luxury is more than a mirage, since it shimmers on the ubiquitous TV screens, mocking frugal lives diminished by the shadow of glamour it throws upon them. It must have been like this in the early nineteenth century, when the poor gathered at the doors of the great and the rich in London, to watch the spectacle of arrivals and departures at great balls and parties; although then, the poor had to trek to sites where the wealthy held their conspicuous festivals and celebrations. Now, it comes to them. The garment factories of Dhaka are the conduit to better life, the passage into the modern world, images of which reach young women in Barisal and other smaller towns, and urge them to leave home as the child brides of an industry erected on the graves of weavers who perished two centuries ago.

In a marshy field on the outskirts of Barisal, a group of nomadic families have set up their brief camp: hoops of bamboo cased in black polythene. These are perpetual migrants. They live an archaic culture of catching snakes, selling their meat, skins and venom for traditional medicines. They know secret remedies for shameful illnesses, how to pound the roots of jungle weeds with ginger and sulphur to cure syphilis and how to make warts disappear with a mixture of the *jamun* plum juice and the saliva of frogs. Their relationship with snakes is unique, since the creatures respond to their voice without the use of a flute or any other instrument. They know which herbs to gather and weave into amulets that can withstand the evil eye and the spells of ill-wishers. Those who wander have a knowledge withheld from sedentary peoples, out of whose credulity they make a living. Kashi Ali had ten children, of whom four died. Allah gave them this life, so why should they settle? If the children go hungry and have not enough to eat, they live or die by the grace of God. Shameto Begum's husband has gone into the city to sell charms and to practice *singha*, a traditional medicine using buffalo horn. They grind the horn, and cure the sick by cutting their veins and blowing the powder into the bloodstream: the blood that flows is black, and as it emerges, the evil that has poisoned it is made manifest.

Barisal awakens to a dawn chorus of crows. They perch, gleaming, malevolent, on stinking metal containers of waste or sagging loops of electricity lines, a stave of discordant music.

Barisal is a halting place on the road to Chittagong or Dhaka for people who have lost land, their most precious possession. Land is a source of constant violence—seized by the powerful, deeds of ownership falsified by corrupt officials, subdivided into uneconomic parcels by inheritance. But the most ferocious dispute of all is the constant struggle between land and sea. Barisal is a melting, melancholy place, battered by storms from the Bay, its waterways and canals overflowing, so gorged with water that the sea spits out land it cannot swallow, and in another mood, eats up what had been, until recently, fields of grain. People take refuge on crumbling embankments, frail shelters shaken by the wind, their only means of travel ancient country boats swept downriver by relentless currents.

Water floods the plain, sweeps the city in tidal surges, drips, an irregular heartbeat, on the tree canopy. Water turns Barisal into a fluid, mythic space: it is the edge of the world, its seventeen rivers are streams of forgetfulness, which people must cross in order to wash away the memories that attached them to life. And indeed, people here must forget all they knew about rural existence, as they are born again into the urban penumbra of Barisal, a life after the death of the countryside which made them and then expelled them. A frieze of dispossessed people makes its way through the waterlogged landscape towards this improvised city, once a place of learning and gracious zamindari structures.

Economic compulsions force an older folk culture into retreat, since the enactment of the seasonal rhythms of agriculture—songs that accompanied threshing and harvesting, the chants and poetry of weeding and transplanting rice—has become irrelevant. This is now a dying music in the flooded groves and abandoned orchards, the drowned, cyclone-stricken land, paddy fields sold for the sake of a dowry, medical treatment or education, or lost through debts incurred due to the cost of fertilizers, inputs or distress prices—since farmers have no means of preserving their crops against rats, pests or heat, and what ought to be the celebration of harvest works against them, since they must all sell at the same time.

In Barisal migrants besiege the terminal, for steamers on the turbulent river, and the bus stand, where battered Bedfords with dented chassis and modern Hinos with panoramic windows bear people away, to sell their labour, their youth and vitality, the produce of their land, the skill of their fingers—transactions in which they are always the losers.

It is not only the fragile land that is eroded by restless rivers and tides; ways of life, cultures and traditions are also washed away. Even the people are thin, two-dimensional: emblems of poverty and the subject of reports, abstracts and inquiries which have been stored away in monsoon-stained files half eaten by white ants, or now, absorbed into seldom accessed cyber data, lost in the info-glut of modernity. Microcredit initiatives, aid programmes and development projects have come and gone, but the poor remain: bony rickshaw drivers, emaciated elderly maidservants, children breaking bricks in desolate yards, faces powdered with red dust, while in the drenched villages they lure birds and fish into bamboo traps, a work increasingly necessary in the city of hunger, which cannot provide sustenance for its people.

In the early morning, to the metallic music of opening shutters and grilles, Khaled sets out his tea stall. It is a wooden shack by the roadside. The collapsible shutters, closed with a rusty padlock, are raised to form a roof over two plain wooden benches. Water boils in a big black kettle on a kerosene stove. Khaled pours tea, a long ochre ribbon, into plain cups with broken handles. A container provides drinking water at one taka a glass. Khaled's stock is meagre: on the wooden shelves rest coloured cylinders of biscuits, while snacks—flaky amber-coloured pastries and slabs of bright yellow cake—hang from nails, out of reach of the rats. Cigarettes are displayed on a tray covered with silver paper, three taka each, together with cheaper local bidis. Although there are scores of similar businesses in the neighbourhood, Khaled makes a profit of 150 taka a day ($2), enough to secure dal-bhat, dal and rice, for his wife and three children, and to pay rent for the single room, with its big wooden bed, dusty and non-functioning TV set, the ABC books which, he hopes, will miraculously bring up his children to understand English. Khaled cannot read or write. He was working by the age of nine, first in the fields of rich neighbours, in adolescence as a cycle-rickshaw driver, later in the brickfields of Dhaka, on the fish ghat and the steamer station—also, briefly, in a garment factory where, he says, he felt he could not breathe.

In the hotel—the most comfortable in this shabby town at $6 a night—hot water is delivered in a plastic bucket by young men, with their sad smiles and inherited stories of grief and loss. The rooms are high and chill, beds surmounted by a wooden frame, from which drapes may once have hung or mosquito nets been suspended. Through glassless windows a shrill sound of wedding music, the call of a muezzin to the *isha* prayer, children playing cricket in the faint glare of a wilting street light.

I had visited a slum in Barisal, Amanathganj, ten years earlier. At that time it was a ramshackle collection of poor hutments of woven bamboo, *golpatta* (nypa leaves) and polythene. At the end of the monsoon season everything was sodden, half submerged, pervaded by a smell of wet earth and damp wood, and a chaotic eruption of mildewed life over all surfaces— pale spindly mushrooms growing out of bamboo poles, fungus invading the sandbags set out to contain the water.

Ten years later, Amanathganj is changed. The houses are more substantial, mostly made of wood and brick, with tin roofs. It seems a measure of stability, even of modest well-being, has been achieved. This is partly illusion: the improvements have given people no greater security, since they own neither the land nor the houses. The poor recount their sparse biography, a brief story of bare tenements and hollow stomachs. Nilufa Begum, her mouth stained with betel nut, tells a story of land lost to erosion before she was born, a husband forced by ill health to work only intermittently, a life of famished insecurity. Two of Nilufa's four children died. Neither of the survivors goes to school: the fifteen-year-old is a peon in the office of a courier service company, earning 600 taka a month ($7.5). The younger does nothing. Nilufa shares her hut with her husband's parents. Her mother-in-law contributes to the family income by begging. Nilufa's husband has worked today, so they will eat twice, a small festival to celebrate another day's survival. Home is a single room, ten feet by twelve feet, and the monthly rent 800 taka ($10).

Mukul's family was evicted from the shelter on government

land in Barisal, where they found refuge after their small paddy land had succumbed to the greedy mouths of the Ganga. There are five children, of whom only one is at school. Mukul's husband is a rickshaw puller who pays rent of forty taka a day to the owner. Mukul makes and sells *pitha* cakes—local bread eaten with tea. Their daily income is 150–200 taka a day (about $2.5). They pay 700 taka a month ($8.5) for rent on a small hut. Mukul says it would require about 10,000 taka a month ($125) to feed her family properly—a symbolic figure, but one that conveys its meaning. Proper nourishment is far beyond their means. Her actual expenditure is about 3,000 taka ($38). Some days she borrows money to buy food, debts that must be repaid with interest. Sometimes they eat only once a day.

Mukul, like most women, can price all food items accurately. In 2009, rice is about thirty taka a kilo. The cheapest dal, watered down daily until it is thin and without nutrition, is sixty-five taka a kilo. In this, the dry season, onions are thirty, potatoes fifteen, aubergines twenty. Cooking oil costs sixty-five to seventy taka a litre. Small fish can be bought for seventy taka, but most people eat meat only at festival time. *Deshi* (local) bananas are two taka apiece, but apples, oranges and milk are luxuries. Fuel—wood or kerosene—costs around 300 taka a month. On average, the poor of Barisal are spending about 60 per cent of their income on food. The rest is taken by rent, electricity, school fees and transport. There are, says Mukul, two kinds of hunger—hunger that leaves the stomach half-empty, and the hunger that is malnutrition, when people become weak from a lack of iron and vitamins, and are vulnerable to disease that comes, a thief in the night, to rob people of those they love.

Mohammed Shahalom also received from his father an inheritance of loss, since he was born in the city long after their small piece of land in Gauronadi was sold. His father worked in Barisal as a cycle-rickshaw mechanic. Shahalom is fifty-five. He wears a lungi and a faded denim shirt, his lined face framed by a grey beard. He has been a rickshaw driver, but with age he has the strength to work only part-time, so his income is reduced to eighty taka a day ($1). He feels shame and sadness that his capacities are diminished. Of his six children, two daughters are married. One son, married in Dhaka, offers him no help. The two unmarried boys also work in Dhaka as daily labourers, and send money home. The family of five spends about 3,000 taka a month on food. They were living on government property, but in the evictions that followed the takeover by the military-backed government in January 2007, their home was broken. Shahalom has rebuilt a poorer version of the house: caught in a circle of ageing and illegal occupancy, he sees his earning power weaken with each passing year, and every fresh eviction further impoverishes the family. He pays no rent, since he is 'illegal'. In an inextricable tangle of existential and socially determined influences, time and the actions of governments conspire to make people poorer.

Abdul Sattar left Mehendiganj when his land was drowned more than twenty years ago. Abdul Sattar is fifty, and runs a business buying and selling fish. His two sons, twenty-five and eighteen, help him, and their combined income is 6,000 taka a month ($75). The older boy is married, so there are now seven family members. They were also evicted in January 2007. Abdul Sattar was unable to educate his children, because he was sick for many years, and the children had to contribute to the family income. "Landlessness is a curse that follows you, because land can never be recovered. You will be poor forever." If the people of Barisal look back, it is because they can conceive of no other wealth than the retrieval of land, and have not yet learned to place their hope in modernization, a process to which no precise date is affixed.

Mohammed Sheikh Baseduddin has organized the sixty families who squat on 2.3 acres of government land. In 1948, labourers at the steamer station took the land on lease from the district commissioner, but although it was continuously occupied for sixty years, no permanent right to settle was granted. Eviction is a periodic experience, of a piece with the cyclones and storms that drive people from their homes. This happened once more in the wave of removals after 1/11, as they now call the fateful date when the army-backed government took power. Sheikh Baseduddin's forebears were brought to work here by the British. His mother is from Bhola, where her parents were marginal peasants. He works on the fish ghat, earning 6,000 taka a month. His three boys and two girls left school at eleven, but a fifteen-year-old daughter is still studying. His dream is for her to gain professional status. Faith in education has a long history in Barisal. Brojo Mohan College, founded in 1889, and Sher-e-Bangla Medical College earned for Barisal a reputation as 'the Oxford of the East'.

If long-established families live with uncertainty, what is the chance of stability for more recent comers? Dulupa Begum is a slender young woman of eighteen, from Patuakhali district; her husband is from Bhola. Her husband's family lost their land to the river, while her father worked as a daily labourer on the land of others, intermittent, ill-paid work, which frequently left them hungry. Dulupa and her parents came here three years ago. She married a rickshaw puller and they have one girl child. Of his 150–200 taka a day ($2–3) she says she is happy when God gives food; but sometimes she must borrow money to live, taking a loan from the rickshaw owner. They have a debt of 10,000 taka ($125).

Amanathganj is low-lying and has been frequently half-submerged. The efforts of the residents have raised the land so it is now protected against flooding. But improvements in the environment are offset by the threat of eviction. The subjective feeling of people is that, even if income rises slightly, this is cancelled by insecurity. In any case, the prices of daily necessities go up constantly, so their money cannot keep up with the cost of

food. People say they are eating less. Of what use is a tin house if
you are hungry and live in fear of eviction?

Shoma, a smart young man of nineteen with a wide smile,
studied until he was twelve, but has never worked. Shoma is the
second of five brothers, and is maintained by his father, a rickshaw
puller. He wants to gain 'technical knowledge', but does not
know where to find it, or even what it means. Shoma, attractive
and indolent, is like many young men in the slums. They are
collectively a threat to the peace of Bangladesh, since their dream
of entering the modern world is always thwarted. Frustrated and
bored, they are ready for recruitment into politically affiliated
gangs, or groups of religious extremists. These are the orphans
of modernization, ubiquitous and uncounted. Their idleness
and contempt for the ignoble livelihoods on offer menace the
country that bore them. They clutch a mobile phone, symbol of
connectivity and communication, but are linked to no one but
each other.

The mobile phone has become a necessity. It is often cited
by the rich as evidence of the fecklessness of slum dwellers whose
priorities ought to lie elsewhere. But who will deny themselves
the meagre consolations of the modern world? The austerity
the rich wish upon the poor is a philosophy fit only for those
who have everything. The young men prowl the city, the tea
stalls and public spaces, possessed by other hungers than those
of the empty belly; they are seeking a use for the energy which
overspills their lean frames with as much ferocity as the rivers
burst their fragile banks.

They will not accept the humiliation of driving cycle
rickshaws, of which there are 18,000 licensed in Barisal, although
nobody knows how many actually ply the streets, with their
painted medallions of idealized country homesteads, emblems
of progress—a cityscape with flyovers and skyscrapers—or
scenes from Bengali films. The cycle rickshaw is, in fact, a
symbol of economic violence, the only recourse of those who

come to the city without skills. Each one signifies loss of dignity and servitude. When the young men who now refuse such work marry and have children, many will learn that pride is no longer an affordable luxury, and will indeed rent one of the detested vehicles. They, too, will then pedal away their youth, wasted in the heat and rain—men old at forty, whose heartbeat is visible, captive in its thin ribcage. The only fate worse than driving the cycle rickshaw is to be unable to do so, since begging is the next step in the descent to destitution.

One day we hear of the death in Barisal of a freedom fighter of the Liberation War of 1971. We go to pay our respects as he lies in the compound of his home. White plastic chairs are set out in the garden where a few pale roses bloom in the tepid February sunshine. Mourners come and go with their condolences. Asadazzaman Khastu died at the age of seventy. He had been tortured by the Pakistani army in Jessore jail in 1971. He lay in a plain coffin, a white sheet over his face. His eldest son solemnly receives all who come to pay homage. We stand around the dais on which the bier rests. The son removes the flaps of the shroud: a full face fringed by a beard, the serene remoteness of death a contrast with the closeness of the war, the injuries of which still scar Bangladeshi society. On his chest is the flag of Bangladesh and the flag of the Mukti Bahini (freedom fighters). He is dressed in his best clothes, a suit which he wears with the slight discomfort of those destined for elsewhere: the unaccustomed apparel of the migrant, the special wear of the departed, raiment for another world, yet so irresistibly reminiscent of more material migrations. His country owes its existence to this man and the comrades who have come to say goodbye. No longer young, they look upon him and make the judgement of posterity on struggles to which they gave everything.

In Jantala, lanes meander along the leisurely tracks of buffalo carts or irregular borders of former paddy land. Here lives Sudhir Sen, who, unlike many Hindu intellectuals, did not migrate to India after Partition or under Pakistani rule. His father was a traditional healer and herbalist in Gauronadi, about fifty kilometres from Barisal. An uncle, a teacher in Barisal, brought the family to town for the children's secondary education—there was none in the villages.

I matriculated in 1944, and was involved with the Quit India movement. I was arrested and jailed frequently as a dangerous man. They sometimes kept us in the condemned cell to frighten us. We were allowed no reading material. I was an only son, and although my father died while I was in prison I was not allowed to see him. The only thing worse than the British occupation of Bengal was their leaving it. Many good people made the effort, but could not stop the communal slaughter. We tried to unite people with a Peace Committee. When Gandhi visited Noakhali we asked him to come here. The British authorities had done their best to divide Muslims and Hindus; they achieved a partition of the mind, for which we are still paying.

East Bengal became part of Pakistan because that was the wish of most Muslims. But we knew that it could not last. East Pakistan lost many talents—in business, education, culture, administration. Hindus were more advanced than Muslims, and most fled to West Bengal. It took us years to fill the gap left by their departure. The Pakistanis treated Bengalis like subjects. They were worse than the British. During the language movement I was a journalist, writing reports and features against them. After 1950, when the *danga* [rioting] was going on, I worked with the Peace Mission. Arrested by the Pakistani authorities I was in and out of jail for fourteen years.

During the Liberation War, I left for India as a refugee and spent six months in a camp near Calcutta. I came back, but everything was lost, the house looted. My relatives tried to keep me in India, but I love the soil of East Bengal. In spite of Hasina's victory in the last election, the anti-liberation forces are still strong. They are highly organized, they have their underground. The British left India long ago, but the influence of their mischief remains.

Sazzad Hussein Jalal finished his working life as Additional Deputy Collector in government administration. He has devoted time and money after his retirement to a small school in his home, based on values of the humanist Bengali tradition and culture. It is named after his mother, who died when he was seven. He was raised by his older married sisters. His spacious though somewhat austere house lies in a quiet street behind one of the main town thoroughfares. Sazzad Hussein Jalal has been motivated by service and self-sacrifice. His house, like his life, is of a plain grace and beauty: a zigzag metal grille bars the window against birds rather than intruders. A chill night breeze moves the thin curtains. There is an old almirah, an armchair, a table covered with reference books. The walls are ochre coloured. White strip lighting throws a pale glare upon doors with huge metal bolts. When he evokes the history of Barisal, he makes it sound as though it had all happened in his lifetime: the pre-Christian Gupta empire, the ancient kingdom of Chandradvipa, the Sultanate, Sufi missionaries, the Mughals and the British. He says, "The Mughals ruled for 800 years, but they did not transfer resources from India to elsewhere. That was left to the British, who used every strategy their imperial experience taught them in order to exploit; and that was inherited by the leaders of free Pakistan and later, of free Bangladesh."

Sazzad Hussein Jalal is an intensely spiritual man who subscribes to no revealed religion. "How impoverished we are by the wealth of the world!"

In the morning, we visit the school, the small library with its smell of monsoon-damp history books. The children are at their desks in the rooms on the ground floor of the house. The pupils, of primary school age, are children of the intellectual secular middle class. They are a minority, but the children, who present us with a bunch of gladioli, are alert and intelligent. Their eyes shine with pleasure. Their artlessness and simplicity are deeply moving. The mother of one child says she wants him to be taught by people who are good as well as clever. She wants him to understand the world, not to exploit it, and to love his country selflessly, not at the expense of anyone else. This keeping faith with a now archaic idealism was like a visit to a distant past, a lost Bengal, a land that no longer exists, colonized now by another ideology: the supranationalism of money which has no allegiance to any known topography.

We went to a festival of street theatre on a chill February night at the Shaheed Minar in Barisal. Every town and city has a memorial of the same design, set up to commemorate the day of protest in 1952, when the Pakistani authorities declared Urdu the official language of the country. During a protest by university students at Dhaka University, five students were shot dead by the Pakistani military. The day itself, Ekushey February (21 February), is one of the great celebrations in Bangladesh, when people come at midnight to lay wreaths and flowers at the memorial.

The play was yet another dramatization of the struggle for the independence of Bangladesh: the plunder of the wealth of Bengal by the British, Partition, the new colonialism of a Pakistan which regarded its eastern province as a source of tribute, labour and raw materials. The energy of the young performers was deeply affecting. Why, I asked, are there so few stories of the sufferings of present-day Bangladesh? The young actors said with one voice that because the victory of 1971 is still under threat, nothing gained after so much suffering can be taken for granted.

There was added poignancy in the electoral victory in 2008 of Sheikh Hasina, daughter of Sheikh Mujib, the murdered first leader of free Bangladesh. During the previous seven years, the liberation forces were eclipsed by the corrupt and violent government led by their enemies, in a coalition including the Jamaat-e-Islami: a party which occupied the unique position of holding power in a country whose very existence it had resisted and had fought against, heart and soul.

The Liberation War was the defining event in the creation of Bangladesh. If it has lost none of its potency, this is because the consequences of the dissolution of East Pakistan have still not fully worked themselves out. Powerful interests inside the country, in alliance with powerful actors outside, wish to restore to Islam what was lost to Pakistan. The relative impunity with which the terrorist group Jamaat-ul-Mujahideen Bangladesh operated under the Bangladesh Nationalist Party (BNP)/Jamaat-e-Islami coalition during 2001–06, bombing secular and Bengali cultural organizations, murdering opposition politicians, journalists and writers, was one of the reasons why the country turned so decisively towards the secular Awami League in the election of December 2008. The Awami League was returned in January 2014, in an election in which the Opposition refused to participate, and as a result, its hold on power is fragile, and widely regarded as not legitimate. The forces of obscurantism do not go away. They are biding their time, awaiting the next opportunity for disruption, for reopening the old dispute over the nature of Bangladesh: whether it is primarily Bengali or Muslim, and whether the ancient culture of Bengal is compatible with the austerities of the dominant strain of contemporary Islam.

Was it for this they died, the hundreds of thousands who gave their lives for the freedom of Bangladesh, I wondered, when we went to Kaunia, one of the poorest settlements in Barisal. In this sad ghetto of ill-being, a large number of people suffer some disability or sickness. In a muddy clearing of soaring palms, many of the huts damaged by the cyclone Sidr have not been repaired. On the road, Mohammed Aslam, thirty-five, with his five-year-old daughter Fatima, is on a three-wheeler cycle which he propels by hand. At fifteen, he had polio, and a withered leg is folded beneath him. His wife, mentally ill, died recently, and he now looks after the child alone. He bought the tricycle for 4,000 taka ($50), and lives by begging. His income is unpredictable: he monitors the variable generosity of the public mood, and sometimes he feels begging is a humiliation. His daughter—a beautiful, smiling child—touches the hearts of people his disability cannot reach. They eat sparingly. Hunger is their constant companion.

Nur Islam also had polio as a young man—part of a reminder to the poor that they bear the scars of now preventable illness, which seems to mock what many had formerly regarded as a divine visitation or punishment. Nur Islam, who walks with crutches, does not know his age. He lives by begging, and 'earns' 100 taka a day ($1.2), enough to feed his mother, wife and child. He does not beg in the neighbourhood out of pride, but roams citywide. He says the four members of his family require 1.5 kilos of rice each day. This claims almost half his income, before taking into account the 400 taka monthly rent on his hut. His child goes to a 'non-registered', that is, private, primary school. His hope that she will get an education to keep her from destitution may be misplaced, since such schools are usually businesses before they are places of instruction.

Shipon, seventeen, works irregularly in a biscuit factory, and earns between 1,000 and 1,200 taka a month ($12–15). He was born in Barisal. He had no schooling and cannot read or write. He has one sister and six brothers. His father, who came, landless from Pirospur, is dead and Shipon is the principal support of his family. Two brothers are working, one as a ferry-wala on the river crossing, the other as a seller of roasted channa. The rent of their hut is 500 taka. There is rarely sufficient food. He would like a better job, but his eyes travel upwards, suggesting this is part of the divine order.

The door of a hut damaged by the cyclone stands open. Inside, it appears unoccupied: windowless, devoid of furniture— there is only what looks like a pile of rags in the corner. But the ragged clothing stirs—it covers the body of an old woman coming out of sleep. Embarrassed, I withdraw from the threshold of the little house. Despite my request to leave her in peace, someone goes in search of her husband. An old man soon joins the group of mendicant people who have gathered—leaning on a stick, elderly, haggard, grey stubble on his cheeks and white beard. He wears a vest which is a lattice of holes, a shabby lungi, plastic chappals. A *taviz* is tied to his thin upper arm. He is Abdul Majid Kazi. For a moment, he cannot remember the name of his wife, Chunburu Begum. He came with his parents from Greater Faridpur during the British time, when the river took his family's land. They applied for an alternative on *chor* land (chors are new islands and spits of land thrown up when the floodwaters recede). This is government property, and those who have lost land can lay claim to it; but the complicated bureaucratic process effectively prevents poor people from successful acquisition. Land-grabbers took what ought to have been theirs, and government officials ceded the land to those who could pay the highest price.

Abdul Majid Kazi says he is eighty-five. A former rickshaw driver, he can now do nothing. His wife, the woman sleeping in the hut, fell from a rickshaw five years ago. Her leg was broken, but since they could not afford the hospital treatment, it set awkwardly, and she can no longer walk. Their only son has moved away, and they beg for food. Their income is unpredictable, but always slender. They cannot remember a time when they were not hungry. They eat rice and poor quality dal, and occasionally vegetables. Neighbours give biscuits and other small food items, and although they also have nothing, provide them with clothing and blankets. He says his wife was unwilling to go on the road today, since she felt unwell.

In front of the hut is a rough wooden cart, with wooden wheels and a string handle by which it is pulled. Abdul Majid Kazi picks up his wife and carries her outside. She seems almost weightless. As he passes the threshold, her hair becomes unknotted and catches the jagged tin, leaving behind a few strands of grey. He places her in the cart. She blinks in the sunlight. She wears a bright green sari, from which spindly legs emerge, thin as twigs, the colour of molten chocolate; her joints are knobs of bone, obscene protuberances of want. She looks startled; profoundly deaf, she cannot reply to questions. Her husband pulls the cart over the stones of the rough ground, and as it jolts, she grimaces with pain.

"How can the poor fight for justice," asks Zilbhanu, a woman of about forty-five, "when we have no knowledge and no resources?" She has five children, two boys and three girls. The older boy, twenty-five, was working in a printing press. He lost his hand in the press machine, and has not worked since. He is now in prison, victim of a conspiracy over the land where their house stands. A developer has laid claim to it and wants to evict Zilbhanu and the family. He tried to take forcible possession of the property. There was a fight, and the boy was arrested and jailed for resisting. Zilbhanu's husband, Amir Ali Khan, is a rickshaw puller, earning 100 taka a day. There are seven in the family, including a married daughter, her husband and baby, while the younger son is studying in a madrasa.

They live on chapatis and vegetables. Some days there is no food. Seven people require a bare minimum of 1.5 kilos of rice a day. Zilbhanu picks up wood from the road for cooking fuel. The family came from Madrapasa twenty-five years ago. Her father was landless; the site where they live belonged to her father-in-law. Her husband built the present house, but when her father-in-law died, a wealthy man appeared and said he was the rightful owner. There are no documents to prove otherwise. Traditionally, occupancy is the only proof of ownership—a custom disturbed by the modern world which requires written evidence of their right to remain where they are. Zilbhanu is resigned to eviction.

This story of land stolen by others recurs almost as frequently as the tale of land eaten by the river. Anwar from Bakerganj had a small homestead, but no paddy land in his village. He was cheated of his small plot by powerful individuals, who altered official records. It is easy for people with money to bribe bureaucrats to change records in their favour. Now Anwar drives a rickshaw, earning 3,000–3,500 taka a month. He pays 400 taka a month in rent for the hut where he lives. He has three daughters. He had no schooling, and neither did they. He will allow them to go to Dhaka to work in a garment factory—a permission which maintains his dignity as father, but born of a necessity he does not wish to acknowledge.

Official figures on Barisal are puzzling and contradictory. Nothing adds up. According to the municipality, 43 per cent of people live 'below subsistence'; 27 per cent are 'lower middle class'. There is, apparently, no category between these two. Again, 18 per cent are 'upper middle class' and 4 per cent 'rich'; 70 per cent work in the 'informal sector', but this does not include cycle-rickshaw drivers. There are 34,000 households in the city, but each 'household' is multiple. It is assumed that the population will double by 2025, but estimates of existing numbers vary. Is it 200,000, 400,000 or more?

Who are the comfortable middle class in this city of starvelings? We went to Terodrone, a village a few kilometres out of the city, where Iqbal farms six acres of family land. It is a different world. In the winter sunshine, the landscape is peaceful. The water sparkles in the fish pond, and a translucent reddish growth of new leaves colours mango, jackfruit and litchi trees. Hens scratch the earth in front of the house, which is built on a platform raised against the floods. The interior is fragrant and cool, without excess or display. Fields of irrigated paddy are regular rows of acid-green plumes. In a corner is the *mazar*, the last resting place of Iqbal's parents, two slabs of stone surrounded by rusting iron railings. His father died in 1984, his mother in 1997. To lie on ancestral land is also to rest in the future: it shows confidence in possession, unlike the jealous vigilance of smaller landholders, equally afraid of the appetite of the greedy ocean and the covetousness of the land-grabber.

Iqbal and his family lead a life of restraint and modest

consumption. He was a member of the Workers' Party of Bangladesh. He says, "When there is extreme injustice in the world, membership of extremist groups makes sense." If Iqbal is privileged, this brings with it heavy responsibilities. His parents were both teachers and he is the youngest of twelve children, among whom there are academics, doctors, an NGO worker, while one brother is abroad. None of them wanted to work on the land, so he is the custodian of the shared family wealth. This is both a privilege and a duty. He does not give a regular part of the produce of the land to his siblings, but provides for them whenever they are in need. He holds the land because he had less education than they, and his right to do so is a recognition of that. The demands of an extended family upon the joint wealth he holds in trust are open and unpredictable: sudden sickness, an operation, children's education, unemployment, the cost of medicines. Iqbal offers insight into what it means to be well off in Bangladesh. It is not a private condition, but a shared responsibility.

It was late in the day when we went back to Barisal. Long shadows fell over tawny fields in dusty orange sunlight. Evening sunshine struck sparks on rice fields and fish ponds, illuminated the lean figures of people returning from work, a procession of famished servitude, the instruments of labour over their shoulder. There is always melancholy in the light of evening, and even the children playing cricket, the cows tranquilly cropping stubble appeared strangely static, trapped between day and night—an illusory moment of stasis in a country caught up in convulsive change.

We paused at Madhabpasha, which became the capital of the kingdom of Chandradvipa in the sixteenth century to avoid attacks of the Portuguese and the Mughals. A broad flight of shallow stone steps leads to the great tank, or reservoir, which belonged to the palace. It is surrounded by trees, which appear as a drowned forest in the placid water; the setting sun a great golden flower on the shimmering stalk of its reflection in the lake.

We visited the Masjid Baitul Aman at Gutia, twenty kilometres from Barisal. This vast mosque is of very recent construction, financed by a former mayoral candidate for Barisal, and aspiring BNP representative of one of its parliamentary seats. It was inspired by the mosque at Medina, and is of overwhelming opulence: dome and minaret inlaid with marble and semi-precious stones. The caretaker admitted us to the interior shortly before it was opened for the *maghrib* prayer; it is a floating space of glass, floral-patterned tiles and marble that could accommodate tens of thousands of worshippers. The symmetrical gardens are full of flowers, descendants of the Raj nostalgia for an English summer—marigolds, asters and dahlias. It strikes with the force of a mirage, a building from elsewhere, an exotic craft landed at random in the countryside of Barisal. The car park is crowded with coaches and cars. Families, women in burkas, men holding children firmly by the hand, stand patiently at the monumental gate like petitioners before paradise, waiting for the evening prayer.

Barisal City looked even more shabby after the open countryside, the ramshackle shops of wood and tin, home-bound children, women with headloads of wood, the busy markets and ubiquitous advertisements for Fair & Lovely soap. The town was stricken by news that another launch had sunk in the Kirton Khola river, with more than forty deaths and an unknown number missing. A sand-laden cargo ship had rammed the Fahmida Happy Express, which sank within ten minutes. The operators and the Inland Water Transport Authority could not say how many passengers were on board, since not all had been issued tickets. Of all transport systems, river travel is usually considered to be the safest. The frequency with which such predictable 'tragedies' occur is caused by overloaded craft, unseaworthy vessels that corruptly obtain fitness certificates, faults in construction of the boats, lack of qualified crew, absence of safety equipment. These are people of so small account that even their numbers, let alone their identities, remain 'unknown', except to the relatives who maintain their anguished vigil at the terminals in Barisal or Mehendiganj, waiting for news that does not come.

There is bound to be an element of fatalism in the sensibility of peoples living on such an unstable littoral. Those always close to calamity tend to be more socially conservative than the occupants of more solid ground. In the elections of 2008, the handful of seats garnered by the (at that time) discredited alliance of the BNP and the Jamaat were either in districts close to the border with India, or near the Bay. Barisal City remains, narrowly, in the hands of the BNP. Here, as in so many other places, Bangladeshi dreams of liberation have withered. Freedom was frozen in its moment of achievement, not only because of famine and devastating floods that followed the war of independence—to some, evidence of divine disapproval—but also by generations of kleptocratic politicians, feudal landowners and venal bureaucrats.

Barisal is where the fragrant *balam* rice was produced, which gave its name to 'golden Bengal', the ripeness of the grain shimmering in the mellow harvest season; it is vanished now, wiped out by high-yielding varieties that dispossessed many small farmers who could not keep up with the appetite of miracle seeds for fertilizer, and who were themselves devoured by the food they cultivated. Rivers, teeming with fish that provided cheap protein for the poor, have been poisoned by the run-off of pesticides; in some places the waters have become as barren as the polluted or salt-spoiled land. This is where an eclectic culture of Sufism, Hinduism and Bengali folk culture joined in common celebration of the beauty and brevity of life; where scarlet hibiscus and spiky boughs of bougainvillea were offered to ancient deities, whose serene presence remained undisturbed by the coming of Allah, apparently more merciful then than now. Here, too, the handloom weavers worked their marvels of sheer fabric, material far superior to anything produced in Britain. In the green canals and shady waterways, freedom fighters came and went at will during the Liberation War of 1971, and Pakistani soldiers perished as they tried to pursue them through treacherous labyrinths of emerald water.

Many people displaced from the coastal areas have sought shelter on the periphery of Barisal City. Kashipur is still a semi-rural settlement only recently annexed by the growing urban area. Its palms and ponds, full of coarse green weeds that choke the waters, are increasingly colonized by tin houses built by landlords and rented to the recently arrived or people dislodged from elsewhere.

Renu is a widow, originally from Bakerganj, where the houses of both her father and husband's family were washed away by a branch of the Tertulia, one of the octopus rivers whose tentacles devour whole communities. She is a dignified woman, clad in a green floral shawl for the cool winter morning. She was married in Bakerganj, and has two boys, "who can both write their own name, although they never went to school". The older boy works with a group of fishermen, who catch fish in commercial ponds, the owners of which give a proportion of the haul to the fishermen—a sixth or a quarter of the total. Sometimes, the owner sells the whole harvest to the fishermen, but few have enough capital to buy, or the facility to dispose of so much.

Renu's younger boy is in a grocery shop in Barisal City. Renu works as a domestic in the neighbourhood, and is paid 200–300 taka a month in each house for cleaning, washing vessels and preparing food. Both boys are married, and they share a house, rented for 400 taka a month. There are eight members in the family, including her grandchildren. Sometimes they eat only once a day, but when she cooks enough, some is saved for the following morning. Because of her son's work, they occasionally taste fish.

"Earlier," says Renu, "we had one acre of paddy land, but it was eaten by the river."

> But the homestead remained. Then that was lost. Now we have no land at all. We have no house. Our fortunes have declined. I was eighteen, and already married when the river consumed our house. It was terrible to watch land vanish. In one month, an area of more than a kilometre was destroyed. We rescued the tin from our house, but because we had nowhere to rebuild, even the tin was sold. I now have grandchildren. I would like them to be educated, but who will provide for them? I have four sisters and two brothers. My brothers went to Dhaka. One is serving as a peon in an office. I used to go to Dhaka to visit them, but after some time I stopped. If you have no money, no one will love you. If I have money, my brothers will love me.

Beauty Begum is one of five sisters from Bhola. Her mother still lives in her home village with one daughter still unmarried. Their father lived in Mehendiganj, but when the river took their land, they moved to Bhola. They had a small amount of paddy land and a homestead, but he fell sick and had to sell the land. He could provide a dowry to the two older sisters, but when he died, the mother had nothing to give.

Beauty has the spare elegance of swiftly vanished youth. Her husband works in an office in Barisal earning 3,000 taka a month. They have two daughters. Beauty can sew, so she rents a sewing machine for 400 taka a month and takes orders from her neighbours. She also works as a domestic in two houses, earning 600 taka a month. They pay 400 taka in house rent. "When we get dal-bhat," she says, "we are thankful to Allah. But often our hunger is unsatisfied. Sometimes we eat only dal and rice, some days there are no vegetables. Fish and meat are only for festivals." She pays thirty taka for a kilo of rice, and the family of four requires 1.5 kilos a day. Potatoes are fifteen to twenty taka a kilo, aubergines twenty, onions thirty; a litre of the cheapest cooking oil costs eighty taka. Wood for cooking costs 300 a month, and electricity fifty. The pond near their hut is suitable for washing, but drinking water has to be carried from a tube well outside the community. Beauty thinks of her mother and sister in Bhola, but can do nothing to help. "We had to leave. At home there is no income, no work. Here, with my help, we can survive." Beauty is not happy, but she is reluctant to express discontent, because they must accept what God sends. She was, she says, beautiful and healthy once; but she lost her health in the city. She speaks of her former self as though she were an old woman. Beauty is twenty-five.

Abdul Samaat thinks he is about fifty. He came as a child from Mehendiganj as a result of river erosion. The terrors of that time still live in his memory. "From July to September," he says, "the current of the Meghna is very strong. Each year, you wonder whose land and life it will carry off. The river is an even greater thief than man." His was a family of rich peasants. His forefathers had "abundant land", but it was stolen twice by the river. He clearly remembers the second time, when the earth dissolved in the water; after that his family became landless. His father came to Barisal, where he died of grief. From a substantial farmer, he had been reduced to working as a day labourer on other people's land. Abdul Samaat has six brothers. Some have acquired enough land to construct a homestead, but none has paddy land. He works as a labourer in Barisal, living in a hut on the land of his employers and paying no rent. He works in paddy fields and vegetable gardens in the rural hinterland of the city. He has three girls and five boys. One girl is studying in the eleventh class, and although she is clever, it is difficult to keep her at school; the youngest boy also goes to school, thanks to help from the neighbours and occasionally, from relatives. Three girls are married. One married son works as a carpenter in house construction. Another boy is a helper on building sites. Abdul Samaat earns 5,000 taka a month. The loss of the family land gnaws his memory remorselessly. His children will never regain the status of independent farmers. That is gone forever. Some days, he says, they have not enough to eat, which is a particular indignity for people who have always been producers of food. His children are good, but they have their own families and cannot help. He ties his lungi around his waist, and walks, shoeless, on to the beaten earth outside.

Nurul Islam Haldar bears the name of small zamindars (landowners) in the time of the British, although he now has no land. He comes from Charfasson, about 130 kilometres from Barisal. He is thirty-six, and his family lost their land—more than fifty acres—to the Meghna. His father came to Barisal. Nurul Islam left school at eleven. He was married in 1997 to a woman whose father is a small farmer in Charfasson. Nurul Islam is a rickshaw puller, and his wife also earns 200–300 taka a month, sewing, rolling bidi or making quilt at home. His earnings average 150 taka a day. He has one boy—who is at school—and two girls. "We eat what God allows. We eat meat only at *korbani* [Eid-al-Adha], and fish two or three times a month." Many poor people describe God as the provider of food, as though no intervening social structures existed.

This is a city of unwilling partings and torn kinship; of ghost farmers, displaced by high-yielding agriculture that nevertheless starves them into migration; hybrid people, caught between ruined or river-eaten land and a settlement not yet town. The remembrance of lost land pervades Barisal; it drives the relentless pedalling of cycle-rickshaw drivers, the humiliation of shabby hotel boys sleeping on stone floors and of small girls with a headload of wood scavenged from the sawmills, the endurance of women breaking bricks on construction sites, their eyes red with the lurid cosmetic of brick dust. Here, in this city, new social classes are formed—people whose lives, disarticulated from the rhythms of rural life, are not subject to the disciplines of industry; people employed only by their own ingenuity, devoid of all resources but their own resourcefulness.

We follow the path taken by thousands of young migrants, from the bus stand at the edge of the city, along the dusty highway towards Madaripur, past homesteads built on earthen mounds high above fields where ripening wheat or irrigated paddy of the dry season suggest abundant harvests in these landscapes of want. The buses are packed with people carrying away the produce of the area: jute sacks of fruit, vegetables, handicrafts, green coconuts, bamboo, betel, sugarcane, or metal cages of chickens and ducks. Some of the buses overflow with migrant labour, ragged men with rough hands and feet hardened by paddy fields in which they have stood, ankle-deep in water like the rice they transplanted. They occupy every inch of the roof of a bus, faces bronzed by the setting sun, a tableau of rural servitude.

Young women are now the most precious export of Barisal, travelling to the capital with their cardboard suitcases and sweet submissiveness, taken by unknown aunties who appear from no one knows where, promising lives of prosperity and ease. They are quickly instructed in stitching. They bend meekly over Japanese Juki or Brother machines, votaries of the religion of industry. Their necks present an image of tender vulnerability in their yielding and, apparently, freely chosen servitude. There are many girls, too, with their two or three years of schooling, the scratched signature with tongue between their teeth, thirteen- and fourteen-year-olds, child brides of industry, waiting to be claimed by raw new factories on sites that were, until yesterday, agricultural land.

Buses and trucks share the roads with ancient carts, cycles and pedestrians, women with headloads of fodder and fuel. An overturned truck lies, its cab crushed, wheels still spinning in the air. Casualties are neatly laid out on the green verge, and appear to be sleeping, exhausted by labour violently abridged. Near Faridpur, some mastaans have imposed a toll on passing vehicles. There is chaos when drivers refuse to pay. We make a detour to avoid the congestion, through village haats, scattering the market women at the side of the road with their pyramids of scarlet tomatoes, mauve onions, papery opals of garlic, foaming cauliflower. There is a long wait at the crossing of the Padma river, at Dauladtia, ancient staging-post on the river from British times, now almost totally dedicated to prostitution, a place for transgressive encounters by anonymous travellers. Since I last made the crossing, the river has shifted its course, and new chors have appeared in the water, so that what was almost an hour's journey has now been reduced to twenty minutes. The sand has settled around the edges of the river in waves, in mimicry of the water that has deposited it. The chors create slivers of molten silver that seem to have frozen as they fell. A thin crop of rice has been planted in patches on the islands, bright green rectangles snatched from the fleeting fertility of parcels of land that may be submerged by the next storm. At Aricha, where we land, the dust disturbed by the buses and trucks leaving the ferry sets up a choking fog, another reminder of land in powdery disintegration.

It is not long before the influence of Dhaka—that concentrated, crowded capital, fourteen million people crammed into a thousand square kilometres—begins to throw its anticipatory pall over the countryside. From Manikganj, long fingers of brickfield chimneys taper into the sky, getting closer until the whole landscape is filled with smoking cylinders. Between them, thin scraps of paddy field are still being cultivated; but everything is covered by dust from the bricks, which accumulate in red stacks at the side of each brickfield. Men and women carry the grey unbaked material to underground furnaces, which scald the earth, on which the workers step with great care: if they place their foot over the fires, their chappals will melt and they will be severely burned. The wind blows smoke and dust, a dim particulate mist that reduces visibility to a few metres. The trees at the side of the road are coated with red dust, so they look like metal sculptures of trees, not living things at all.

Each brick is now worth five taka; or rather, that is its market price. But the market reflects only a fragment of the true cost, which is uncounted: the lost fertility of the soil, the forfeit of future yields of paddy, the exchange of land for a single harvest of money. The market calculus represents a small fragment of the burden that this apparently easy transformation, driven by the real estate boom of Dhaka, imposes upon the Bangladesh of tomorrow and the day after.

It is the hope of livelihood that drives people to the capital. Some have achieved little more than if they had remained at home: I think of the despairing face of the boy in the hotel, whose work is to scrub away stains on the carpets, a penitential never-ending labour; the young shop worker who has received seductive instruction from the capital, that his village wife is simple and conservative—he has found new sexual excitements that have destroyed the attraction of a home-place, to which he no longer looks forward to returning; Nurjehan, an elderly woman begging in Segundabicha, injured in a fall from a bus, who now lives and sleeps in Kamlapur railway station; the grandmother living with the baby her daughter died giving birth to, offered a place to sleep on a verandah by the charity of a pious rich man in Banani.

We follow into the city the road travelled by migrants. It leads to Mirpur 14, a stony ill-made road in this meandering suburb. Mirpur 14 suggests a utilitarian numbering, a place of suitable anonymity for the nameless poor. We come to a small factory owned by a family originally from Jalakoti in Barisal, and employing people mostly from the same district. The word 'factory' is an exaggeration: it consists of the lower floor of what appears to be a substantial private house, enclosed by a high stone wall. Upstairs, a narrow passage left by boxes awaiting collection and dispatch leads into a semi-public drawing room, where tea, snacks and fruits are set out on a table. Employees from the floor below move in and out quite freely. The distinction between family and employees is not immediately clear.

A smiling boy of about eleven staggers beneath a pile of children's clothing. His name is Asgar, and he is from Noakhali on the Bay of Bengal. His father, who had lost his land, came to Dhaka, where he sells vegetables. Asgar, one of three brothers, has been working here for a year. He earns 1,600 taka a month ($20) for a twelve-hour day. He is with an older boy, Shohal, sixteen, from Pirospur in Barisal. He also came with his landless father, mother, three brothers and one sister. He earns 1,800 taka a month. He prefers Dhaka to the village, because there is work here, and he feels the excitement of being in a city that he has, however, not yet seen. He had a little schooling, but left at eight. He cannot write. His older brother sells vegetables, and his father is a flower seller, but neither job is regular and their monthly earnings are unreliable. They pay house rent of 1,800 taka for a one-room tin shed, which claims all Shohal's earnings. His younger brother is privileged—he goes to school. Shohal is sad, because he would like to study, but his salary is the only secure income. Their house has an electricity connection, but water must be brought from outside. Shohal has a dream: to become manager of a big garment factory or owner of a small one like this. His family manages to save 1,000 taka a month; just how many years it would take for those slender savings to be enough to invest in even the smallest factory unit, he has no idea.

Nipa is twenty-five. She is from the Barguna division of Barisal, and arrived in Dhaka with her parents four years ago, where they pay house rent of 2,000 taka a month. She was at school until she was eleven. Their land—the homestead—was washed away by the river. Nipa has two sisters and one brother. The older sister is married, but Nipa must wait for her parents to choose a husband for her. Her father is a construction helper who earns 2,000 taka a month ($25). She is earning 3,000 taka. It is sometimes awkward for a child to have greater earning power than the parents: this seems to many people against the order of things, particularly if the child is female. Nipa starts at eight in the morning. Her working day is twelve hours, with breaks for lunch and tea, six days a week. She packs garments for shipment. Nipa prefers life in the village. There, she says, life is peaceful and unhurried, the surrounding countryside is full of relatives and friends. Dhaka is crowded, people are indifferent, no one cares for others. There are some advantages in Dhaka: Nipa is allowed to come to work alone; and although she has more freedom than she might enjoy in the village, she has little time to exercise it. Life is, in some ways, even more constrained in the city. Nipa is very shy, and places a hand in front of her mouth when she speaks. She says her ambition is to be 'self-reliant', to earn more money and to get married.

Rabi, owner of the unit, a pleasant young man of twenty-four, joins us. His father started a small security service organization, providing guards for shops and middle-class flats in Mirpur. When he died, Rabi took over the business. He sold it and entered the garment sector. Rabi employs forty-five workers, the majority from his native Barisal. Garments are not made here; articles are 'finished', that is to say, threads are cut by hand, buttons sewn and fasteners checked. Each one is ironed, folded, packed in polythene bags, before being stacked in cartons ready for shipment. Rabi invested 600,000 taka in the unit. At the moment, business is good.

Maksuda's is the face of the uncomplaining stoicism of older women. She works as caretaker, cleaning, sweeping and washing for the family. She came to Dhaka as a young bride from Muladi in Barisal. Her husband died suddenly twelve years ago. She does not know the cause of his death. They had some small acreage of paddy land in the village, and Maksuda remembers harvesting the rice. It was swept away by the river. She has never returned since coming to Dhaka, as no trace of the village remains. She remembers the pain of that year, when the river carried off everything, even, it seems, the family's memory of all it had known. To Dhaka, she says, they brought nothing but emptiness and longing; and Dhaka took her husband.

Maksuda has two girls, fourteen and twelve. Both are studying. Maksuda earns 2,500 taka a month. Her brother, a driver, who is relatively well-to-do, helps her with the girls' education. Maksuda has many relatives in Dhaka who are kind to her; with the destruction of the village, the extended family migrated. Two brothers give her regular help, and her hope that her daughters may receive a decent education is not unrealistic. She expects nothing for herself, and thinks it only natural that she should sacrifice herself for her daughters.

Lima is a slight self-effacing girl of fifteen. She wears an orange-coloured sari decorated with black circles. The youngest of six sisters, she was five when her father died. All her sisters are married. Her mother remains in their village near the Bay of Bengal. Lima was brought by her sister to Dhaka two years ago. She lives here with the owner's family, working partly as a domestic and partly in the factory. She earns 2,000 taka a month, but sends 1,500 to her mother, who sets aside 500 for Lima. Lima longs for home—her mother and sisters are all in Barisal, and she misses them. She starts her twelve-hour day at eight in the morning. She has one day's leave each week, but stays indoors. She does not go out, and has seen nothing of Dhaka. Her ambition is, she says, to be 'self-sufficient'; and with her savings hopes one day to purchase land in the village. The cost of this is about 8,000 taka ($100) per decimal (one-tenth of an acre). Dhaka is for her a sad and lonely place, although the family she works for are kind. She can read although she left school at eleven.

What Lima does not know is that the amount of land required to be self-reliant in her home area is about sixty decimals. At the present rate of saving, it would take sixteen months to buy one decimal. Ten decimals would require thirteen years, even if there were no inflation in the price of land. In any case, the land near her village is liable to salination, which ruins paddy, and catches the full force of cyclones. Her hopes are poignant; her endurance of exile heroic; the likelihood of the fulfilment of her dreams remote. Still, she goes about her daily work meekly obedient; her trust is absolute, both in the future and the grace of a God who will not fail her.

The workshop is a plain room of about twelve square metres. In it are crowded the forty-five employees. More than half are under fourteen, the majority girls. A boy is sewing buttons with a machine. Girls trim loose threads and check that all buttons are present and firm, and fasteners functioning. Others are ironing. They stand at old-fashioned domestic ironing boards, from which the steam rises, so their flushed faces appear as though through mist. At a table, the clothes are carefully folded, and then passed to a long trestle to be sealed in transparent polythene. They are stacked in cardboard cartons by young women who handle each piece as delicately as they would a tray of eggs. The garments will go from here to shipping containers for export. All items will go abroad, to Gap and Primark in Britain, to Walmart and K-Mart in North America.

The youngest children are perhaps ten or eleven, but one or two boys appear even younger. Their work creates a strange impression: it is not only a living tableau of the 'scandal' of child labour, but the garments they are folding and packing evoke the children in Britain or America who will wear them. They are very gender specific—for little girls, short, layered skirts with a floral pattern and a low top; for boys, combat fatigues in khaki and olive and small-size denim jeans and jackets. This clothing is clearly for the lower end of European and North American markets. The children of the poor in Bangladesh are making clothes for the children of the poor in the West. It says much about the relationship between the comparatively privileged position of poor children of the inner city and peripheral estates of Britain and the US, and their impoverished Bangladeshi peers.

What of those who have succeeded in the city? First of all, they usually began with some advantage: land or capital in the family. Mintu is manager of a garment supply business, a subsidiary of a Manchester company which imports clothing. This is a supreme irony: the city once cursed by Bengalis for having taken away their jobs is now the location of a number of houses importing Bangladeshi clothing into Britain.

Mintu has a luxurious suite of offices in Mohakhali, where military officers—many of whom grew rich during the two years of army-backed government after January 2007—have their houses and businesses. Mintu also provides uniforms for the London Underground, twice-yearly consignments of 40,000, and smaller orders in between. The company in Manchester has increased its outsourcing, so that designers and pattern makers are also now based in Bangladesh. The deepened outsourcing places responsibility on Mintu for quality control, and he must monitor market changes and the slightest shifts in fashion. This also requires vigilance over the merchandise from the dozen factories he works with; and if there is any failing in quality of goods or delivery schedules, he must immediately change suppliers. Since he buys in dollars and sells in pounds, the fluctuating dollar–pound rate creates constant pressure to cut costs. Labour, he says, is as cheap as it can be in Bangladesh; but the garment exporters' organization, BGMEA, is unwilling to increase wages, so pressure is building up, since for the workers prices rise and wages stagnate. In the present recession, the employers have warned that declining orders will inevitably mean delayed payment of wages. The factory owners have asked for loans on easy terms to maintain salaries.

Mintu operates in a way similar to that of the *gumashtas*, the agents of the East India Company.

At each arang, there emerged a hierarchy of official procurers and supervisors (in fact all those who were involved in the Company's procurement process). Under the gumashta came the *muqim* (supervisor of looms, yarn, etc.), *muhrir* (clerk), *tagadgir, dihidar* (village supervisors), cash-keeper and peons. They controlled all aspects of the cloth investment at the arang level, issuing orders, dispensing advances, supervising looms and receiving goods (Hossain, 2010).

Beneath Mintu an equally complex division of labour must superintend the production of orders for which he is answerable to the company that employs him.

Mintu has been both beneficiary and victim of increased integration in the garment industry. In Bangladesh it used to be simply a question of cutting and stitching designs from elsewhere, but now new designs, patterns and products originate within the country. It makes the business more competitive, since all salaries are paid in Bangladeshi taka and not in Western currencies. This gives Mintu opportunities but also new insecurities. His working hours are long and unpredictable. He cannot relax, and spends less time with his young family than he might wish.

Mintu is to visit the company headquarters in Manchester for two or three days. He will fly directly to Manchester, and will spend forty-eight hours in meetings, drawing up reports, signing contracts and agreeing to targets. His performance and evaluation are under constant scrutiny. So far, he has been successful. He will then return to Dhaka, and resume work the following day.

Swapan, Mintu's brother, is in the hotel industry. He went to London in 2000 to study catering. This cost the family dear. In Britain, Swapan, made to work twelve hours a day, found it impossible to survive. I have a vivid memory of meeting him in London at the time. He wore a knitted balaclava helmet against the cold and a cheap plastic jacket, and as we sat in the food concourse of Euston station, he presented a desolate picture of misery and exile. I lent him a little money, since he was finding it impossible to live on his earnings as part-time waiter. Later, in defiance of his visa restrictions, he took a second hotel job, working fifty hours a week for about £1.5 an hour. He got up at 5.30 in the morning, worked illegally from six until mid-day, went to college from noon to 5.30, then waited tables in the restaurant from six until midnight. When his course finished, he had a debt of £3,000. He stayed on for six months simply to clear what he owed. He had paid £5,500 for his 'qualification', the value of which, he says, was negligible. He says of his time in London that it was wasteful and exploitative: the college where he studied reminded him of free-enterprise private schools in Bangladesh, which claim to be English medium, but whose personnel are tongue-tied in the presence of a native speaker of English. Swapan returned with relief to Dhaka. He now works for an international hotel chain, receiving guests at the airport and ensuring they reach their destination in safety. He gets up at 4.30 to go to work, and rarely reaches home before eight or nine in the evening. He sees little of his wife and baby, and although he provides for them with a generous salary, he asks what is the point of supplying the family with money instead of his loving presence.

Home for the two young men is still Barisal. Their grandfather had land, but lost his home to water seven times during his lifetime. He invested in the education of his children, sending them to Dhaka and Kolkata to become doctors and lawyers. Their parents' house is now in Barisal City. The family no longer owns land. Their security now depends upon a lucrative, but fragile, garment industry, and those who travel from Europe and the US to oversee it.

In March 2011, I visited the family in their new apartment in Bailey Road, close to the commercial district of Dhaka. It is a spacious high-ceilinged unit, with cool tiled floors and wide windows. The only problem is that it is so close to adjacent high-rise buildings that neither light nor air can circulate freely within the apartment. Electric light burns for most of the time— the building has its own generator against the constant power failures; and the air conditioning must run for nine months of the year. So densely packed is Dhaka that even the most privileged residents live in airless semi-darkness.

Barisal is far from the somnolent parochial place it appears to be. Its displaced and marginalized, victims of erosion and loss, occupy the decrepit township, awaiting deliverance into the industrial alternative—that generator of pollution and global warming, which intensifies the lethal turbulence of the Bay of Bengal, submerges more land and sends more people to seek shelter from the violence of storms, the natural and human-made having become indistinguishable.

Barisal also exemplifies the serial injuries of imperialism, colonial expropriation and globalism. What a harsh dilemma it is, for those caught between monetary gain borrowed from a used-up future, and growing hunger, which every day abridges the lives of thousands of people. How can the people of Barisal, poised between the rising ocean and the polluting brickfield, be expected to resolve contradictions which baffle even the most powerful, the owners of the wealth of the world, the zamindars of globalism?

It is an unstable resting place for people trapped between a perishing tradition and an unsustainable modernity, ousted from self-reliance by a combination of the harsh exigencies of nature and no less savage human activity. The hope of its inhabitants is the road to a more prosperous elsewhere—the steamer beneath a towering architecture of cumulonimbus clouds in the watery landscapes that will deliver them to Dhaka by tomorrow morning. Barisal is an entrepôt, where poverties are traded—a frontier of one of the most fateful boundaries in the world, where the ability of human beings to procure food and create shelter by their own labour on their own land is finally lost. The tragedy of Barisal is that this is perceived, not as a measureless privation, but as the chance to grow rich.

Urbanization without industry makes of Barisal only a kind of holding centre, a refugee camp, from where people will expect to move on to the factories of Dhaka or Chittagong. It is far from how the new inhabitants of the raw industrial towns of Britain saw their migration into the urban centres. They had no conception of becoming rich; for them, the move offered, with luck, only a chance to become a little less poor. Even so, there are conspicuous similarities in the crush of humanity besieging Dhaka, and the one-way migration of the people of Britain into the miserable tenements and back-to-back houses of the industrial revolution.

Part III

Dhaka

Dhaka was rated in 2013 by the Economist Intelligence Unit as one of the world's least liveable cities, just above war-stricken Damascus. It is now one of the most congested cities on earth. Its population more than doubled in the decade after the Liberation War in 1971. By 1981 there were over three million people in the city. In the following ten years it doubled again. For the assembly-line culture of its garment industry, rural migrants enter the city on a scale that overshadows any other rural–urban migration in the world. Each day, hundreds of newcomers are jostled and pushed in the overcrowded streets, and more cycle rickshaws—the most easily available form of employment—take to the streets: fragile, even delicate craft, with their painted hoods like Victorian bonnets. They look like vehicles made for excursions of pleasure, for leisured dalliance—a sad deception, for in reality, each one represents lost land, tragic dispossession, a desperate effort to find a new livelihood in an alien environment.

An outpost under Mughal emperor Akbar, Dhaka became a fortified city and the capital of Bengal, the richest province of the Mughal empire, in the seventeenth century. In 1704, Dhaka ceased to be the capital of Bengal, and after Plassey in 1765, it came under the control of the East India Company. In the nineteenth century it became what it remained until the Liberation War—an overblown country town, conduit for the export of raw materials: jute, indigo, tea, sugar. During the abortive partition of 1905, it was the capital of East Bengal, and after partition, capital of the eastern province of Pakistan. In 1971, it became the capital of Bangladesh, and gradually took on its present shape: a vast camp of captive labour for liberated young countrywomen, suffocated in the endless drudgery of turning cloth into apparel for the markets of the world.

Dhaka, like all cities, is haunted: conditions in which its two million garment workers labour recall terms on which the East India Company once secured its 'investment': driving down wages, posting spies outside weavers' dwellings to ensure they dealt with no other merchants. For, during the garment rush, Bangladesh's equivalent of gold, more than three thousand factories were set up in Dhaka.

The growth of the garment industry has produced an extensive middle class, and a construction boom has evicted hundreds of thousands of slum dwellers, sometimes in the name of the 'beautification' of Dhaka, one of the ugliest cities on earth. With the rising price of land, the poor are subject to increasing *compression*. Ponds have been filled in, people removed and buildings erected randomly. Many urban poor are now stacked in concrete dwellings, one family to a room in dilapidated flats. Others have been dumped on the far periphery. Many sleep close to their workplace: some workers rest beneath their factory machines; some in a garage with rented rickshaws; others share with strangers a room without running water; women and girls working as domestic servants shelter on verandahs.

Even new high-rise apartments are in permanent darkness, because neighbouring buildings are so close you can almost touch them. Electricity burns all day, and air conditioning is essential most of the year. Poverty, overcrowding, pollution: Dhaka is a claustrophobic place, its traffic stalled, sometimes for hours on end. Adjacent suburbs can be reached only after epic journeys; business appointments are cancelled, since nothing moves on roads built when Dhaka was a provincial town in Bengal. The planning of Dhaka has been subject to the most effective form of deregulation: corruption. Bangladesh has been named for years as one of Transparency International's most corrupt countries, and corruption over the years has contributed significantly to Dhaka's chaotic overbuilding.

Thirty years ago, the new migrants to Dhaka lived around *jheels* or ponds, natural waterbodies. On what was then the periphery of the city, they built huts in the country style— of chetai, bamboo poles and wood. Some of these structures were ingenious, an aerial geometry of dwelling spaces in small areas, wooden walkways linking precarious structures over the turbid water. Other remnants of its somnolent past include the aforementioned cycle rickshaws: 400,000 of them ply the streets, each a symbol of lost land and decayed rural livelihoods. A century ago, Dhaka was criss-crossed by rivers and canals that permitted navigation to the heart of the city markets. It would be hard to say where the city's heart now lies, or whether it has one at all. Dhaka has transformed from a watery, deliquescent place into an island of hard concrete and metal: its waters vitrified and raised into cascades of glass; white light from factories soaring above the slums; malls eight storeys high, where bangles, toys, fabrics, shoes, television sets, refrigerators, mobile phones— made in China—jostle for the attention of the newly affluent.

With the dredging of rivers and canals, over-construction, abandonment of water transport, Dhaka risks death by drowning: built on quicksand, with dark monsoon clouds perching on high-rise buildings, like ragged vultures waiting for the end of this 'unliveable' city, which fifteen million people nevertheless call home.

Dacca was the centre of one of the most flourishing textile industries in India. Bengal muslin had been produced by generations of artisans for the high officials and aristocracy of the Mughal court. It was also exported all over India to the princely states, and to other countries: Dacca muslin was traded in Persia, Arabia, Armenia, China and Sumatra.

In 1665, during the reign of Aurangzeb, François Bernier, traveller, physician and ethnographer, visited Bengal. He wrote in his *Travels* (1670):

> There is in Bengale such a quantity of cotton and silks that the kingdom may be called the common store house for those two kinds of merchandise, not only of Hindusthan or the Empire of the Great Mogul only, but of all the neighbouring kingdoms, even Europe... In describing the beauty of Bengale, it should be remarked throughout a country extending nearly an hundred leagues in length on both banks of the Ganges, from Raje-Mahal to the sea, is an endless number of channels cut in bygone ages, from that river with immense labour, for the conveyance of merchandise, and of the water itself, which is reported by the Indians to be superior to any in the world. These channels are lined on both sides with towns and villages, thickly peopled with gentiles; with extensive fields of rice and sugar, corn and three or four sorts of vegetables, mustard and sesame for oil; with mulberry-trees, two or three feet in height, for the food of silk-worms.

Weavers produced for the imperial court and for the

international market the celebrated *jamdani* weaving, which became known as muslin. Jamdani is a Persian term, from *jam*, flower, and *dani*, a vessel or container. It is believed to be a fusion of ancient Bengal cloth making and the muslin produced by Bengali Muslims from the fourteenth century. Bengal produced a range of cloth:

> *mulmul* (thin plain muslin), *tanjib* (ornament of the body), *abroan* (thin texture, its transparency was compared to that of limpid running water), *alabalee* (very fine, a muslin of close texture), *nyansook* (thick muslin), *buddun khas* (fine muslin, its weft not so close as that of *nyansook*), *sarbati* (semi-transparent like sherbet), *terindam* (clinging to the body), *sarkar ali* (manufactured for the use of the Nawab's court), *jamdanee* (flowered muslin; in the time of Md Reza Khan in 1776, some were woven at 450 rupees a piece), *hummum* (a cloth of thick, stout texture), *doorea* (striped muslin). One of the best varieties of muslin was called *jungle khasa*. Perhaps the pellucid muslin was described as 'evening dew'. When spread over grass it could not be distinguished from the dew on it (N.K. Sinha, 1962).

The quality of the cotton was determined by the special *kapas* that flourished in the soil of Bengal; and this created the special quality of Dacca muslins. The climate and geography of the region also made their contribution to the unique quality of the fabrics. A temperature of 28° Celsius, combined with high humidity, was favourable to the weaving— a long, labour-intensive process—of the finest muslin. Weavers worked in the early morning and in the evening to avoid the high temperature of the middle of the day. The period from May to August was the most favourable; and in hot dry weather vessels of water were placed beneath the looms so that the evaporation kept the threads moist and prevented them from snapping. The newly gathered cotton retained moisture; after two or three months it became elastic and could be drawn into delicate threads suitable for the finest cloth. Although coarse material of the customary size—20 x 1 yards—could be produced in a matter of days, the very finest pieces could take up to ten months to weave.

Observers were astonished at the refinement of the goods which emerged from the crudely made looms at which the weavers worked. "The explanation lies in the fact that the Bengali weaver was endowed with a fine sensibility of touch, a nice perception of weight and he also had a singular command over muscular action" (Mitra, 1978). I once spoke with some older people in a Delhi slum whose parents and grandparents had been weavers. They said, "The fingers and the heart remember, even when people forget."

Much of the material went to the Mughal court, although by the eighteenth century European traders and companies had become more significant buyers. The total exports from Dacca in 1753 were worth 2,850,000 Arcot rupees. Of this 100,000 worth went to the emperor at Delhi; 300,000 to Murshidabad for the use of the nawab and the court; 150,000 to Jagat Seth, the banker of Murshidabad; 500,000 went to Armenian merchants for markets in the Arabian Sea; and 350,000 to the English Company for Europe (N.K. Sinha, 1970).

In the eighteenth century, as many as 8,000 looms in Dacca were producing muslin for the court and the international market (Smith, 1920). Professor of history at Dhaka University, Sirajul Islam, who is president of the Asiatic Society of Dhaka, says it is not known how many people were involved in weaving. "One census of 1786 by an East India Company survey of the textile sector estimated that there were six million people—one million families—who depended upon textile production." This may well be an underestimate, for almost every household was both an agricultural as well as a manufacturing unit. They cultivated cotton and wove, as well as produced food crops. Most had this dual role, although there was a specialized class devoted entirely to weaving the finest muslins. The weavers were scattered, and their work was collected by banias, the trading community, from their homes and taken to the city, either for consumption locally or for export.

Dhaka's varying fortunes, the ebb and flow of its people, have been, to a great extent, controlled by its textiles. Professor Islam described to me the history of the city:

> When Dacca—which became Dhaka in 1983 under the military rule of General H.M. Ershad, who believed that the more recent spelling is an accurate reflection of the way the word is pronounced in Bengali—became the Mughal capital of Bengal in the early seventeenth century, it was a city of settlers, highly militarized, an enclave of foreigners. The Mughal rulers posted their officials and representatives in Dacca. The army and the cavalry had to be provisioned as well as their accompanying livestock. Everything had to be carried by animals—horses, elephants, bullocks were the main bearers of men and material in wartime. There were no roads.
>
> Imagine how many people and animals were required for the supply of a whole army. There was a big department procuring fodder for cattle and elephants. Many of the people who did this work came in the supply line of the Mughal army. Many were highly specialized and came from north India, Bihar, UP [Uttar Pradesh], and some ethnic and caste specialists from Orissa and elsewhere, whose work was with the sustenance and care of certain beasts.
>
> The people of Dacca were not Bengalis, since these remained in the villages. The peasantry flourished under Mughal rule, communications were good, security was improved. The people in the rural hinterland were generally contented, although Dacca remained an alien Mughal enclave. People spoke a mixture of languages, Bengali, Arabic, Urdu, although Persian was the language whereby people measured their superiority. Dacca was predominantly a Persian-speaking city, with Urdu and Hindi its secondary languages.

Dacca had been made the capital of Mughal Bengal in 1610. There was a long power tussle between the nawab (the emperor's representative in the province) and the diwan (the revenue collector), which ultimately resulted in the removal of the exchequer to Muqsadabad by Murshid Quli Khan, a diwan, who renamed the town Murshidabad. When Murshidabad became the capital of Bengal in 1704, some of the administrative structure went, some stayed in Dacca, which remained a *niabat*, a sub-capital or sub-province of Bengal. Revenue was still collected, and justice dispensed, from Dacca, but the main functions went to Murshidabad. The desertion of Dacca by both the nawab and the diwan robbed it of the extensive establishments of both; and with the departure of the army and its servants to Patna, the first decline of Dacca began. This was not complete, since the deputy nawab was allowed to function from Dacca, and his army and establishment, although smaller, checked what would have been a steeper decline.

Dacca's first decline was halted by the coming of the European trading houses, in the late seventeenth century, to the city and to Calcutta. To Dacca came the Armenians, Portuguese, British, French and Dutch, who all had settlements and 'factories'—or depots. They exported Bengal products on an enormous scale. Their business, apart from textiles from Bengal, also involved saltpetre from Bihar, hides and skins, tobacco and sugar.

The city's second decline began with the growth in the East India Company's power following the Battle of Plassey in 1757.

Before Plassey, there was no monopoly and until the days of Siraj-ud-Daula there was the Nawab's administration, however corrupt, to appeal to. Alivardi (Nawab in 1740s) treated all the European Companies on the same level and if anybody had done an act of injustice to the other, the Nawab punished the wrongdoer... Competition amongst the purchasers was much to the advantage of the weavers because it resulted in an increase of the prices that were offered to them (

This changed after 1757, as the Company ope
increasingly coercive policy, gradually eliminating its riva
tethering weavers to its own system of procurement which
them less and less autonomy and with declining rewards. The
Company passed stringent laws governing their terms of work
and quality of the goods they produced—laws enforced through
a network of agents and middlemen—with the result that
weavers became dependent on the Company, unable to work for
its competitors and subject to loans and advances which further
impoverished them.

The Mughal emperor conceded the *diwani*—the collection
of revenue—to the East India Company in 1765. Additionally,
with the decay of Mughal power, the old centres of weaving for
the luxury trade of the Mughal princes and their dependants fell
into decline.

With the industrial revolution spurring the growth of the
textile industry in Britain, Bengal textiles and Dacca's prosperity
were under serious threat. The British misused their power to
prohibit the normal production of textiles in India, and by 1820
they had succeeded in displacing the cotton goods of Bengal.

...produced in Bengal had had no easy passage into Britain.

Between 1802 and 1819 duties on imports of Indian textiles for the British market were increased on nine separate occasions. At the highest point, in 1813, the duty on calicoes was 85 per cent. So rigid was the enforcement of the rules which prevented calicoes being printed, stained or dyed and also silk goods from being used in this country and being made into apparel that passengers arriving from India in London found that these goods were taken out of their baggage. Even napkins etc. which contained a coloured stripe, however small, were considered to be prohibited (Marshall, 2006).

And when British textiles began to gain momentum, the textiles of Bengal had no chance. The orotund phrases of self-interested British observers were calculated to put a favourable gloss on the indefensible; and in their words, the genesis of the myths of imperialism may be discerned as they evolved.

When British influence was first established in Bengal, the country was literally crowded with manufacturers and artisans of all description. The various officers of the Mogul Court and the subordinate principalities and governments, with their numerous retainers, occasioned an immense consumption of every article which luxury could devise or the ingenuity of the country produce; and some of these, on account of their beauty and costliness, formed the basis of a considerable export trade. But on the substitution of a comparatively economical

European government, the demand for productions of this nature almost entirely ceased; the industry everywhere met with a sensible check; and the finishing blow was put to many of these manufactures, for which India had been so long celebrated, by the fabrics of Europe being made to rival them in delicacy of workmanship, and even to surpass them in cheapness. Nothing was then reserved for the industry of the natives but such articles as were too coarse or too valueless to excite competition; and the great increase of this import trade soon converted India almost exclusively into a market for raw produce (Young, 1829).

The Ninth Report of the Commons Select Committee on the Administration of Justice in India, in 1783, clearly admitted that the Company had

adumbrated and advanced a perfect plan of policy, both of compulsion and encouragement, which must in a very considerable degree operate destructively to the manufactures of Bengal. Its effect must be (so far as it could operate without being eluded) to change the whole face of that industrial country, in order to render it a field to the producers of crude materials subservient to the manufactures of Great Britain.

The stories of the British cutting off the thumbs of weavers are quite untrue, except as metaphor, for their thumbs were rendered useless by the ruin of their craft and their ability to sell what they produced. This dramatic image probably originates with William Bolts (1772), who referred to the self-mutilation of workers: "Winders of raw silk have been treated with such injustice, that instances have been known of their cutting off their thumbs to prevent their being forced to wind silk."

Stories are notorious migrants; and many legends that surround the cruelty of the British have origins in an older indigenous tradition, as a friend pointed out to me. The tale is told in the Mahabharata of the warrior Ekalavya of the Nishada tribe, who managed to outperform Arjuna, the brilliant kshatriya pupil of brahmin guru Dronacharya. When Drona confronts Ekalavya, and demands to know where he acquired his skill in archery, Ekalavya replies that, as a lowly tribal, he would never be able to learn the skill from a brahmin guru like Drona. He therefore made a clay idol of Drona, and taught himself archery. As *gurudakshina* (the fee paid to a master by his pupil), Drona demands Ekalavya's thumb. Ekalavya agrees and forfeits his thumb, thereby permitting Arjuna to regain his status as the best archer. This is the victor's version of the story. In dalit and adivasi narratives, the brahmin guru and the kshatriya forcibly and by deceit remove the thumb of the more talented archer; for why would a forest-dwelling tribal need to surreptitiously learn archery from the brahmin city-dweller, Drona? The myth informs the story of weavers who cut their own thumbs: it is, in fact, an emblem of the thwarting or destruction of their skills by more powerful others.

The East India Company, playing Dronacharya, captured the market with the inferior Manchester cloth (Arjuna) by neutralizing the genius of the local weavers.

The most dramatic impact was on Dacca.

Of all the textile centres, Dacca was the most vulnerable to the collapse of European exports... In 1781, the weaving of muslins commenced in Britain ... and this soon attained great perfection there. From the year 1781 to 1787, the British cotton manufactures increased in value from 2 million pounds to 7.5 million, and in the year 1785, 500,000 pieces of muslin were manufactured which appear to have rivalled the common qualities of Indian muslins. From this time, the foreign trade of Dacca began to be affected, and from the heavy duty of 75 per cent which was afterwards imposed upon its staple, it declined in proportion as the manufactures of Britain increased in volume, until at length in the year 1817 it entirely ceased... (Taylor, 1840).

Although a majority of households alternated, according to the season, between the plough and the loom, the most skilled weavers knew no other occupation. When the Company closed its factories in Bengal in the early 1820s (the Dacca factory closed in 1818), the repercussions were felt far and wide: those thrown out of work included weavers, cotton growers, spinners, dressers, bleachers and people employed to salvage muslin damaged during the bleaching process, embroiderers. The Resident at Sonamooky found most of them were "thrown at large on the world, some becoming *sannyasis*, some *byragis*, others coolies, very few agriculturalists and some mechanics... A vast number had died."

Some thousands of workmen of the Luckipore arang, on learning that the Company's factory would close, said,

> We who are Jogees and weavers are not able to perform any other profession besides that of weaving cloths. By this, we have supported ourselves and lived within the Company's territories paying revenue from year to year and if owing to our misfortune the factory should be abolished and the making of advances ceases, we shall have no means whatever for discharging the Company's balances. We are possessed of no property and are reduced to great distress.

Professor Sirajul Islam says British textiles made local production impossible, except among the very poor who continued to weave their far coarser 'country-made' cloth for local use.

As a direct result of the Company's closure of all its cloth establishments in Bengal in 1825, the Board of Trade estimated that the number of those thrown out of work "may fairly be calculated at 500,000 souls". But the Company only ever employed about one-third of the weavers of Bengal; so to that number should be added the loss of the labour which had been employed by private traders and other European companies.

N.K. Sinha (1970) estimated the number at about one million; and if each family consisted of an average of six persons, some six million were affected, or approximately 16 per cent of the population of Bengal.

The loss of highly skilled weaving for export in India was not, as has sometimes been reported by imperial economic historians, simply because of the superior quality of machine-made Manchester goods. It was the outcome of a long and unequal struggle, in which the weavers of Bengal were increasingly dominated by the demands of the Company, which systematically restricted their freedoms and reduced their earning power. Nor was it that English-made goods were superior: their lack of durability compared with items made in Bengal was a frequent object of comment; but they were preferred by the newly rising classes as objects of prestige.

By the 1820s, British exports had ousted the textiles of Bengal from European markets, and were increasingly taking over its markets in Asia. The first great de-industrialization of the modern world had begun. It coincided with, and indeed, was created by, the industrial technologies of Britain. N.K. Sinha says, "On the threshold of the nineteenth century, Bengal's economy became fully subservient to that of England." The loss of the export trade was one thing; but the displacement of the weavers' work locally by large-scale imports from Britain led to unparalleled misery and loss.

The women employed in spinning fared the worst. They were severely disadvantaged by the ending of the Company's business, and even more by the export of thread from England. Less has been written about their fate than about the loss to the male weavers, although their work was scarcely less vital than that of the men.

The work of women was laborious and highly skilled. Theirs was an intricate—and scarcely acknowledged—contribution to the much-admired muslin.

> The cotton, as *kapas*, is cleaned and prepared by the women who spin the yarn. The wool adhering to the seed is carded with the jawbone of the *baoli* fish. To detach the fibres from the seeds, a small quantity is placed upon a small flat board, upon which the spinner rolls an iron pin back and forth with the hands so as to separate the fibres without crushing the seeds. The cotton is then teased out with a small hand bow formed of a piece of bamboo with two elastic slips of the same material inserted into it and strung with a cord of catgut, silk or twisted plantain or rattan fibre. This reduced the cotton to a light downy fleece that was spread out and wrapped around a thick wooden roller, and on the removal of the latter instrument, it is pressed between two flat boards. It is next rolled round a piece of lacquered reed and lastly is enveloped in the soft and smooth skin of the *cuchia* fish which serves as a cover to protect it from dust and from being soiled, while it is held in the hand during the process of spinning... The spinning apparatus which is contained in a small, flat work basket comprises the cylindrical

roll of cotton, a delicate iron spindle no thicker than a needle, and a concrete piece of shell embedded in clay... The spinner sitting on a low stool holds the spindle in an inclined position, with the point resting in the hollow of the piece of shell, and turns it between thumb and forefinger of one hand, while at the same time drawing out the single fibres from the roll of cotton held in the other hand, and twists them into yarn upon the spindle... (Sharma 1998).

The making of fine thread called for unique skills.

To make superfine thread a quickness of sight as well as great pliancy of the fingers was necessary. At an advanced age women were not therefore so capable of spinning well as in their youth. The thread used for muslins of all kinds except the stripes of the *dooreas* was to be spun by the hand spindle that required peculiar expertness and flexibility of the finger. It was turned with the thumb and forefinger, the lower end resting in a bit of shell. With this hand spindle the spinners produced the finest thread in the world (N.K. Sinha, 1956).

William Wroughton, Collector of Mymensingh district, gathered the following information about the preparation of the finest thread:

Before the spinners are set to this work they are presented a particular diet as such will keep their body cool and temperate and such medicines are daily administered as are supposed to assist and clear the sight. When the spinning commences a large pan of clear water is placed before them which by magnifying the thread prevents that detriment to the sight which must naturally have resulted from eyes being continually fixed upon so very small an object. A situation is chosen when no wind whatever can come to them and where a strong even light is reflected equally on the water. Two hours in the morning and two in the evening is the time limited, but which varies agreeable to the ability of the spinners; during the time of this work they occasionally use some soft refined *chunam* which is rubbed between the finger and thumb of the right hand and so careful are they of these useful spinners that till the quantity wanted is completed they are not suffered to do any part of the drudgery of the family (quoted in N.K. Sinha, 1956).

Women continued to spin for the weaving of coarse cloth after the decay of the export industry, since they had no economic alternative to spinning; as agricultural and all other labour was closed to them. We found a sad echo of this in New Delhi in 2010, when women who were working as domestic servants said they had left West Bengal since their husbands did not think it proper for them to perform such labour at home, but that in the anonymity of a distant city, their work as servants was not stigmatized by neighbours and kinsfolk to whom it remained invisible.

Following the decline of weaving in Bengal, which retreated to the domestic sphere, new economic activities were tried with varying degrees of success. These were imposed coercively on the ryots; the British, their agents and middlemen reaped the greatest advantage. The system of 'advances' continued in most occupations in one form or another, so that cultivators or workers never quite became free of debt bondage.

a) Indigo

Indigo grew naturally almost all over India, and had for centuries been used for dyeing; but it had not become an object of export, since there was no process whereby it could be made solid enough to transport over long distances. Early attempts by the Company to procure indigo were not successful, and it was only in the last decade of the eighteenth century that free merchants and servants of the country began to invest seriously in indigo, and to set up factories that would produce indigo in solid form ready for export. Before the turn of the nineteenth century, evidence appeared of what was to follow: the forcible diversion of peasant land to the production of indigo. N.K. Sinha (1956) cites an example from 1796, when Vakil Rahamatullah submitted a petition to the court on behalf of a widow dispossessed of her land. An indigo manufacturer had forcibly taken possession of twenty bighas of land, which the poor widow disputed. The indigo manufacturer sent two of his henchmen to apprehend the woman, who, for the sake of her reputation, fled. She remained for a time in the house of a peasant, but in the end, bowing to the inevitable, abandoned her homestead, since all the labourers who cultivated her land had threatened that they would run away if they were coerced to produce indigo. The petitioner, seeing no remedy, travelled a long distance to complain to a high official, hoping he would convey a request to the present judge in Calcutta, directing him to guard her land against the violent incursion of the indigo manufacturer, just as the judge's predecessors had previously protected her.

The East India Company brought planters from western India and settled them in selected districts of Bengal. The Company's officers were also allowed to trade. The industry grew rapidly in the next fifty years, and by 1850 indigo was one of the most important exports.

The advent of the indigo planter introduced a new element in rural life: European adventurers' bid for wealth in direct contact with the peasantry (N.K. Sinha, 1956). The British indigo planters conducted themselves with feudal arrogance, and the condition of the peasants in the indigo tracts was worse than of those in other parts of the country. "The system on which indigo was cultivated was not strictly a plantation system. It was only rarely that the manufacturers of indigo cultivated their own lands by means of hired labour" (Gadgil, 1938). The usual system was to enter into contracts with tenants of other zamindars of lands over which the planters themselves had acquired zamindari or *talukdari* rights, to sow a certain portion of their land with indigo, which was sold to the planter at a certain fixed price. Advances were generally made at the beginning of the agricultural season to the peasant to grow indigo, and many a time they were forced upon him. The ryot, once he took the advances, was ruined.

Macaulay said in his essay on Lord Clive, 1840: "That great evils exist, that great injustice is consequently committed, that many ryots have been brought, partly by the operation of the law, partly by acts committed in defiance of the law, into a state not far removed from that of partial slavery, is, I fear, too certain." The uprisings of peasants in Lower Bengal in the late 1850s caused particular concern in Britain, coming so soon after the events of 1857. The movement against indigo led to the setting up of the Indigo Commission in 1860. The Commission's report confirmed the link between cultivation of the crop and extreme repression. Its findings also sadly confirm and prefigure the continuing attitude of the colonial authorities, the subsequent Pakistani overlords and the present-day rulers of Bangladesh towards the poor.

The Indigo Commission Report of 1861 said: "It matters little whether the ryot took his original advances with reluctance or cheerfulness, the result in either case is the same; he is never afterwards a free man." In view of the large areas of Bengal and Bihar under indigo, this extract of the Report is enough to condemn the entire system under which cultivation was carried on. The language of these commissions is always lofty and sometimes opaque.

> Even the most advantageous statement made on favourable suppositions shows but a slight profit derivable to the ryot from indigo, and it is quite clear from statements as to the production of rice, not to speak of the higher kinds of produce, that indigo as a paying crop must stand very low in the scale. Only one inference can be drawn from this, even apart from the direct evidence of coercion produced before the Commission, and that is that indigo cultivation was carried on in a system which had no connection with the welfare of the peasant. Such was the system of indigo cultivation, and such it remained.

Following the fall in the price of indigo on the international market in the late 1840s, the planters forced the ryots to continue production, even at the expense of their own food crops. In a long-established tradition, the planters compelled the peasants to sign contracts that they would cultivate indigo. They used their henchmen to loot and destroy the houses of those who refused, and compelled them to bring their most fertile land under cultivation. They seized their property and draught animals if they failed to comply. The planters cheated on the contracts, and contrived to keep the peasants indebted to them. Police and magistrates regularly colluded with the planters against the cultivators. Similar observations could be made of other crops or products, substituting for indigo almost any other commodity which has been the source of livelihood to the people of Bengal, whether opium, tobacco, jute or garments.

William Vansittart, MP for Windsor, spoke on the issue in the House of Commons in May 1860:

> There had been great discontent for a very considerable period on the part of the ryots against the indigo planters of Lower Bengal. They accused the planters of great tyranny and oppression, and that charge had been fully proved by the Colonization Committee of which he (Mr Vansittart) was a Member. That evidence proved that the indigo planters of Lower Bengal were a very different class of gentlemen from those residing in Tirhoot and the Upper Provinces, and that they had been in the habit of keeping in their pay Latteals, or bludgeon-men, in order to coerce the ryots. The ryots also complained of the very arbitrary clauses which the planters were in the habit of inserting in the Cabooleeut, or contract-deed, on making advances of money for the cultivation of indigo, by which clauses they reserved to themselves the power of sending to the fields their own people to weed, reap and cart the indigo. The consequence was that it mattered not how favourable the season might be and how abundant the crop, the ryots could not fulfil their engagements, because on their bringing to the planter the specified number of bundles of indigo the planter produced a counter-statement of the expenses incurred in weeding, reaping and carting. And thus he kept the ryot on his books as a defaulter. When he (Mr Vansittart) was in India

a ryot told him that, do what he would, he could not liquidate the debt incurred by his father twenty-three years previously, and it was a remarkable fact that, the more industrious the ryot was and the better he cultivated, the greater were the exertions made by the indigo planter to keep him on his books as a defaulter (*Hansard*, 4 May 1860).

Synthetic indigo was used from the late 1880s, and the area under cultivation diminished after 1891. Exports of indigo of 166,308 hundredweight in 1895–96 fell to 10,938 hundredweight by 1913–14.

b) Jute

Jute, too, had been long cultivated and was an important item of trade since the early days of the East India Company. It was originally used in the making of cordage and ropes, but by 1840 it was used by the Dutch for the transport of coffee from Java. Until about 1830, the making of gunny bags and jute cloth had been carried out solely by handloom weavers in Bengal. Jute was particularly important in the region for providing cord and rope to moor fishing boats. By the 1830s a significant flax industry emerged in Dundee in Scotland, and since the Crimean War interrupted the supply of flax from Russia, the mills of Dundee were converted into jute mills. The establishment of the industry in Dundee effectively destroyed Bengal's jute handlooms.

The manufacture of jute by machinery was established in India in 1854. The first jute mill was opened at Serampore. In the following decade only one more mill was built; but from the early 1860s, the industry grew significantly. Manufacture was, of course, far cheaper in Bengal, and by 1870, in anticipation of later economic relocations, Dundee had lost a good proportion of its trade. By 1882, of the twenty-two jute mills operating in India, eighteen were in Bengal, seventeen of them close to Calcutta. By 1900, the export of jute made up almost one-third of the export trade of Bengal, and this was the only significant manufacturing industry. With the First World War, demand for raw jute increased, since it was used for making sandbags to protect soldiers in the trenches, and to carry grain. Between 1880 and 1940 the number of jute looms in Bengal (mainly Calcutta) increased fourteen-fold, and well over a quarter of a million people were employed in the industry.

In the nineteenth century, the durable jute cloth produced in Calcutta was a caricature of the cotton goods produced in Manchester, since this was a coarse, functional product, as it were, suitable for manufacture in the imperial hinterland.

With independence, virtually all of the jute mills were in West Bengal, and the then East Pakistan had to start afresh. More than two-thirds of the mill owners were from West Pakistan, and with the Liberation War in 1971, the Bangladesh Jute Mills Corporation was formed to ensure continuity of production. At this time, the use of jute was in sharp decline, since plastic soon overtook jute as the principal packing material for goods. The industry was privatized, and made significant losses. But in recent decades, jute has been revived as an environmentally acceptable material, unlike the non-biodegradable plastic bags, which had begun to choke the waterways and rivers of Bangladesh. They were banned in 2005. Jute is now a major export of Bangladesh, used for carpet weaving, wall coverings, shopping bags, canvas, handicrafts and containers for perishable goods.

West Bengal still has sixty-one of the seventy-eight jute mills in India. Jute provides livelihood for about four million families, and employs 400,000 workers in India. Although the industry in India produces 1.4 billion bags a year under compulsory packaging norms, in January 2011, Coca-Cola, Cadbury, Nestle India and GlaxoSmithKline rejected the use of jute bags for sugar since, they argue, the fibres have been contaminating the sugar they use in their products.

c) Opium

It is, perhaps, misleading to talk, as many historians have, of the 'de-industrialization' of Bengal. Not only did the majority of people in Bengal move between weaving and agriculture, but the materials with which they worked—cotton, jute, indigo, and of course, opium—were all processed and transformed into industrial commodities. Opium cultivation by peasant farmers had existed in India, operated by merchants and traders, who were able to get around the ban on it by the largest opium using country, China, by bribing the Cantonese authorities (a weakly enforced law was promulgated in 1729, and the import of opium was prohibited in 1799). In 1773, the Company established a monopoly, reserving the sole right to produce and process opium (which took place in its factories in Patna and Benares); and both the Company and its more formal imperial successor promoted the export of the drug, in the process fighting two wars with China in order to open up its markets for opium and to balance the 'triangular trade' between Britain, India and China.

Earlier, the problem for the Company was that Britain had nothing to sell to the Chinese, so the trade in tea had to be paid for by the export of bullion from London. With the 'opening up' of the Chinese market, the export of opium provided the resources to pay for the exports of tea to Britain. By the 1820s, more than £20 million of Indian opium and cotton to China was balanced by the export of tea to Britain, and the export of a similar—or slightly greater—value of British textiles and machinery to India. In 1831 Bentinck doubled the area under cultivation of the opium poppy in Bengal to about 175,000 acres. By 1900, this area had become half a million acres along the Ganga Valley. China was forced by the Second Opium War to legalize the trade in 1858. In 1860, opium accounted for about one-third of the value of the country's exports (Habib, 2006).

Nor was this commodity unconnected with the condition of the people of Britain. Throughout the nineteenth century, narcotics became an increasing part of the daily life of the labouring classes of Britain. The consumption of caffeine, especially in the form of tea, nicotine and indeed opiates, greatly increased during the course of the nineteenth century. Opium was incorporated into many patent medicines, including remedies for diarrhoea and stomach ailments, of which, given the state of public health and nutrition, there were many. Laudanum was widely used as a sedative and sleeping draught, and was often fed, in small doses, to children, to keep them quiet. The use of opium-based medicines increased seven-fold in the half century after 1850. It is not idle speculation to wonder whether the Bengali peasant, compelled to grow opium instead of grain, might not have contributed not only to the impoverishment of his own family but also to the alleviation of the pain of the Lancashire millworker, whose life—with her constant child-bearing, her alcohol- and tobacco-addicted husband—was made slightly more bearable by a tincture of the product he was compelled to grow at the behest of others. Much produce from the empire was used in this way—to render the experience less harsh for the disaffected, and sometimes mutinous, workers of industrial Britain. When Marx observed that religion was the opium of the people, he was already partly in error, since opium itself had become an object of salvation for many of those oppressed workers for whose wretchedness he had in mind other prescriptions of liberation.

Dhaka, with its markets and waterways, has always been the focal point of an extensive rural economy. It has expanded and contracted, attracted people and then expelled them. There has been confusion and clamour, the rough male energy of a military city at the time it became the capital of Bengal under the Mughals in the seventeenth century. At its zenith, it was reported to have had a population not far from one million. With the decline in weaving, by 1800, this had shrunk to 200,000.

Thirty years later, the city reached its lowest point, with fewer than 50,000 inhabitants. (In contrast, Calcutta was growing: it had more than 200,000 inhabitants by 1800, and more than 300,000 thirty years later.) Dacca had become a provincial town.

The dereliction of Dacca continued for a long time, well over half a century. The population of East Bengal was always less urban than that in West Bengal, mainly because the region had no metropolitan city, nothing approaching Calcutta: according to the 1891 census, only 3.9 per cent of the population of East Bengal was urban, compared to 11.4 per cent in West Bengal.

Although the population began to increase after 1850,

in 1869, the assistant civil surgeon of Dhaka, Cutcliffe, reported that there were no proper drainage systems in Dhaka, and for years the rubbish and excrement had accumulated in the streets and doorsteps of people's houses. The water of the wells was polluted, the town was criss-crossed by innumerable dark lanes, which, too, were filled with dirt... The air they used to inhale was polluted, the water they used to drink was like poison. When tap water was introduced in the 1870s, Dhaka still had only four brick roads, and there were no railways; electricity was introduced only in 1901, fifty years after it had appeared in Calcutta (Mamoon, 2010).

Until the 1840s, the people of Dacca district had never seen a wheeled vehicle. It is widely reported that as early as the 1780s, Dacca had become so far reclaimed by jungle that it was threatened by tigers and elephants which used to attack the city at night, and "even in the mid-19th century, tigers used to roam freely around Dhaka city" (Mamoon, 2010). During the time of Warren Hastings, anyone who could submit the head of a tiger would receive prize money. All they had to do was present the head of the dead tiger to the authorities. But the same head was presented so many times, they were compelled to forfeit the head. Dacca was described then as "a city of monkeys". The city of men had become a city of animals by the early years of the nineteenth century.

Part of Dacca was known as *tantibazar*, the weavers' quarter. As the industry declined, the area was opened to other business, including a cattle market and slaughterhouse. Many of the former weavers did not leave the city, but turned to agriculture, even on the site of decayed urban settlements. In any case, rice growing had always been a part of the husbandry of households. In the mid-nineteenth century, Bengal was the granary of India and exported rice to both north and south. Dacca was the centre of rice processing and distribution. In the nineteenth century, rice traders returned to Dacca. A whole new class of women rice huskers was summoned to the city: today's garment workers have their antecedents in the migration of young women to the rice-husking mills. They even spoke their own dialect, which was neither the Urdu of Dacca nor the Bengali of the village. They developed their own particular culture, known as *kutti*, and traces of it remain in Dhaka even today.

The demographic composition of the city was in flux. Until

the end of the eighteenth century it was a non-Bengali city. As it declined, it contained the remnants of the old Muslim inhabitants. But from the first decade of the nineteenth century, the population changed, as Dacca became a great rice export centre. Hindus came, many involved in the export business, especially of rice; the rice trade was almost entirely in the hands of Hindu merchants. They began to settle in the city, and although the population continued to decline, traditional Muslim dominance ebbed. Bengalis from the villages also came to trade, although they rarely settled in the city.

One of the greatest blows to the Muslim population, especially the *ashraf*, or superior classes, was the loss of the Persian language as the means of expression of the ruling elite; it ceased to be the language of the court in 1837. Diwan Kartikeyachandra Ray of Krishnanagar described in his autobiography how this was experienced. "The sorrow we felt at that news [the abolition of Persian as official court language] was akin to that feeling when one is deprived of a cherished treasure, accumulated through hard labour, or loses a son capable of earning money. All that we learnt through industrious application became an illusion and the hope we cherished for earning fame for learning lost all its meaning" (cited by P. Sinha, 1965). The Hindu gentry of Bengal took more readily to English-language education, since they had long been competent in Persian, while Muslims— although Bengali or Urdu speakers—were affected by a sense of bewildering change, which was certainly of no advantage to them.

Professor Sirajul Islam has traced the Hinduization of Dacca as the nineteenth century progressed. In the census of 1882 the population was half Hindu, half Muslim. By 1892 there was a clear Hindu majority, and in 1911, an overwhelming Hindu majority. Professor Islam states that by 1922 it could almost be described as a Hindu city, although the countryside remained predominantly Muslim.

The communal strife following partition did bring villagers to Dacca, but for the third time, the city lost much of its population: since Hindus were attacked and their property confiscated, they departed in large numbers for Calcutta. Many simply fled, abandoning property and possessions, so there were rich pickings to be had. People also came from Bihar to East Pakistan, a very different culture, and the period of 1947–52 was characterized by property grabbing and the further flight of Hindus. By the time of the 1952 census, the Hindu population of the city had become once again insignificant, and Dacca, capital of East Pakistan, was for the first time an overwhelmingly Bengali Muslim city.

Dacca was a Persian-speaking city in the eighteenth century, then Urdu predominated, and it became Bengali-speaking for the first time only later in the nineteenth century. It was a Muslim city, then a Hindu city and is now once more a Muslim city. It has been three times a ghost town: first, when the capital shifted to Murshidabad in 1704, second, when Muslim rule ended at the end of the eighteenth century and the weavers were dispossessed, and third, in 1947 when it became, briefly, an empty city again.

In reviewing the mutability of Dhaka, few people have remarked on what might become a reason for yet another evacuation of the teeming metropolis. But those who have criticized both the filling in of the ponds and waterways and the absence of any structural precautions in the unregulated building frenzy of the past two or three decades, have pointed out that Dhaka is in an area vulnerable to earthquakes. The apparent solidity of a city whose fortunes have fluctuated so wildly might once more prove to be an illusion. The collapse of Rana Plaza occurred without any trace of earth tremors. After this event, surveys suggested that up to 60 per cent of the garment factories in Dhaka may be insecure, and certainly not resistant to a significant quake. The city may yet lose its people once more, this time through carelessness in relation to nature, or perhaps through the revenge of nature, rather than as a result of political or economic upheaval.

The myth of Golden Bengal has deep roots. Bengal was indeed one of the most prosperous parts of the world, although its riches were less inexhaustible than the covetous regard of servants of the East India Company estimated. Its goods were in demand everywhere. Memories of the years of opulence and fabulous wealth lingered; and the dream of recovering them has haunted Bengal ever since. There is no doubt that the Liberation War of Bangladesh in 1971 was nourished not only by resentment at Pakistani rule, but also by ancient stories of past glory. It was believed that an independent Bangladesh would restore the vanished wonders of the distant past. And it was foreseeable that the freedom of Bangladesh, a truncated Bengal after all, would lead to disappointment, if not to the poverty and struggle for life which has become the lot for a majority of the people.

The tormented history of Bengal has left its legacy on the sensibility of the people. Dr Shafique uz Zaman, professor of economics at Dhaka University, says that Dhaka is a city for psychoanalysts rather than historians. Since the people have been subject to so many apparently capricious rulers, they have learned to dissimulate and to hide their feelings, just as they hid themselves from authority, police and spies in the jungles and waterways. Thomas Macaulay, in his 1840 essay on Robert Clive, wrote, "Sometimes they [Bengalis] fled from the white man ... and the palanquin of the English traveller was often carried through silent villages and towns which the report of his arrival had made desolate." William Wilson Hunter (1899) also observed the sense of self-concealment of Bengalis. "Outward, palpable proofs of suffering are often wholly wanting... The Bengali bears existence with composure that neither accident nor chance can ruffle... The emotional part of his nature is strict subjection; his resentment enduring but unspoken."

The villages of East Bengal were also threatened with constant erosion, natural disasters, as well as the oppression of *jotedars* and the agents and employees of zamindars. From river to village there were only tracks, walkways between irregularly shaped rice fields. These were impassable for bullock carts, and in the monsoon, whole areas would disappear under water. In consequence, people consistently changed settlements, and rarely lived for many generations in one place.

Dr Shafique describes how, until the European powers came, the system of labour and production in Bengal was traditional. Most people provided for their own food and shelter. Within the weaving class there was a wide range of skills and accomplishments in which they had learned to specialize over generations. Some weavers cultivated the land in addition to weaving, while others remained constantly at their looms. Imperialism divided the population into clear hierarchies. There were the rulers, then the middlemen or compradors who supported the colonial power, and finally the rest of the people, who were mainly poor peasants. Under the British, the fine muslin that had gone to the Mughal court diminished, and people increasingly retreated to cultivating the land or growing cotton. The practice of producing goods of the finest quality was lost. In Dacca, as the export of muslin was taxed, untaxed English thread replaced homespun yarn. This was economic violence—a concept that has lapsed in the modern world.

There were also what would now be recognized as marketing campaigns, which prefigure subsequent more sophisticated efforts. Tea drinking was introduced by means of offering it free in the beginning, which created addiction and hence, demand. In the same way, British cloth and yarn were on sale at absurdly low, subsidized prices. (Plenty of other British goods were imported at the time. In the nineteenth century, British fashions and shoes were available in Dacca and Calcutta, and because there was always a significant British population, it was even possible to buy Yorkshire ham in Dacca.) In spite of this, old skills survived, although pushed to the margins. Weaving did not die out, but markets were lost as one ruling class was replaced by another, and the patronage which had assured a sale for superior goods no longer existed.

By the 1840s, the colonial authority had already diversified its industrial base: it had introduced a network of railways, shipbuilding, heavy engineering, and had expanded the production of raw materials and cash crops such as tea, coffee and jute. By then, Britain had worldwide markets, so mills were set up, in Bombay especially, many of them modelled on the mills of Lancashire, and indeed, using some of the machinery these had discarded. This dumping of unwanted goods and ancient technologies continues today. The Japanese have flooded the market of Bangladesh with reconditioned cars; they are the biggest 'development partner' with Bangladesh, but are least bothered that no roads exist to contain the cars they sell.

The same kind of dissociation had occurred when Bangladesh was part of Pakistan. All the civil servants came from a shared family background, sons of zamindars or business people; and the bureaucracy of the country knew little or nothing about their own land. Even now, only 10 per cent of the school curriculum of Bangladesh is the history of Bengal. Generation after generation grows up with no study of history. Dr Shafique believes that no nation unaware of its past will ever progress. "Dhaka today is horrible. Yet in Mughal times it was the Queen of the cities of the East. Look at the number of places with the suffix *bagh*, which means garden. How many of them were green and flowering places, and now how overrun with dirt and overcrowding."

Golden ages remembered are, by their nature, beyond

recovery. But among the disadvantages of present-day Dhaka—excessive hours of labour, pollution, the stalled traffic and the tangled wheels of cycle rickshaws, slum accommodation—some compensatory dream is needed, in order to make tolerable such living conditions. Nostalgia is, perhaps, one of the few costless luxuries of the exploited of posterity.

Part IV

Murshidabad

Murshidabad's sojourn as the Mughal capital of Bengal, beginning in 1704, proved relatively brief: by 1772 most of the functions of the capital city had been transferred to Calcutta. Murshidabad was the centre of silk weaving; and this, too, came increasingly under the dominion of the Company.

Winding of fragile skeins was increasingly undertaken in the Company's *filatures*, factories where silk winding was done following European methods that were far more technically advanced than those of domestic winders, since the domestic silk winders produced thread of variable quality. They heated water with cow dung fuel in a small furnace to soak the cocoons and loosen the thread. Of course, much silk remained 'country-wound', as domestic employment. The Company increased exports of raw silk to Britain to be used in the silk-weaving industry there, and the emphasis shifted over time from piece goods to raw silk. In 1772 the Company offered wasteland—of which there was then a great deal, another of the great historical 'clearances', this time by famine and pestilence—rent-free for two years to anyone who would cultivate mulberry. Between 1775 and 1785, the quality of silk was unequalled anywhere in the world, and by 1790, Bengal silk dominated the British market. It was not until the 1830s that the Company ceased to export silk, and this passed completely to private traders.

The slump in Bengal's silk industry was only one of the factors in Murshidabad's almost continuous decline over two centuries. The effects of the famine of 1769–70—when one-third of the population of Bengal either perished or fled—continued to be felt for years afterwards. In June 1770, the Resident at Murshidabad reported to Calcutta: "The scene of misery that intervened, and still continues, shocks humanity too much to bear description. Certain it is, that in several parts the living have fed on the dead; and the number which has perished in those provinces which have suffered most is calculated to have been within these few months as six is to sixteen of the whole inhabitants." It was said that it became necessary to keep a set of persons constantly employed in removing the dead bodies from the streets and roads, and these unfortunates were placed in hundreds of rafts and floated down the river. "At length, the persons employed in these offices died also ... and for a time dogs, jackals and vultures were the only scavengers" (quoted in A.T. Embree, 1958.)

Bankim Chandra Chattopadhyay, influential nineteenth-century Bengali writer, imaginatively reconstructed the scenes of famine in *Anandamath* (1882):

The little crop that was harvested was purchased by the officials for the soldiers. People began to starve. At first, they had one meal a day; then it became half a meal a day; then they began to starve. What could be harvested in the spring was wholly inadequate to meet the requirements of the people. Mohammad Reza Khan, the Minister of Finance, in his eagerness to curry favour with his master, enhanced the revenue by 10 per cent ... People began to beg. Then who could give alms? The people began to starve. Then they fell victim to diseases. They sold their cattle, they sold their implements of agriculture; they devoured their seed grain; they sold their houses and land. They began to sell their daughters, next sons, after their wives. Then who would buy girls, boys, women? Everyone wanted to sell and none to produce. For want of food they ate the leaves of trees and the grass of the field and also weeds. Members of the nomadic tribes and those belonging to the lower strata of society began to eat rats and cats. Many helpless people left their villages. Those who left died of starvation in strange places; and those who did not do so died of disease and as the result of eating unwholesome food. Pestilence broke out—fever, cholera and small-pox began to roam rampant, small-pox being most prevalent. In every household people began to succumb. Who would tend the sick and touch them? No one was attended to—no one was looked after and no one removed the corpse. Beautiful men and women died in their houses and their bodies were left to rot.

Murshidabad district suffered the greatest loss of people. Silk manufacturers, weavers, industrial artisans, boatmen and other labourers died in greater numbers than peasant cultivators. The price of silk rose between 1765 and 1771 by more than 50 per cent. Although by 1772–73 harvests were reported to have been very good, peasants were unable to sell enough grain to pay their revenues because so many consumers had died.

Restoration of life in Murshidabad was impeded by the policies of the Company. Above all, revenues were not permitted to fall. The average income from diwani lands was 1.43 million rupees between 1765 and 1770. The revenue in 1769–70 was 1.37 million, a drop of a mere 4 per cent, even though at least one-third of the people had perished (Mohsin, 1973). The tradition of *najai*, which customarily compelled peasants to make good any deficiency in payment by their neighbours in any village, was enforced by the Company after the famine, even though some settlements had lost half their cultivators. Private remittances to Europe between the Battle of Plassey (1757) and 1766 came to almost £6 million. The Company regarded Bengal simply as a source of revenue; and the wealth that flowed out of Bengal was not matched by any corresponding inflow of revenue: the cost was borne by the peasantry of Bengal. After the award of the diwani, all pretence that the Company was merely a trading operation ceased: the desire to remit the spoils of conquest determined the size and nature of the Company's investment.

Murshidabad shrank as a consequence of the famine, and although in 1821 it still had 40,000 houses, its population had been reduced to 146,000. In the 1760s it had been above half a million. In his 1902 history of the district, J.H. Tull Walsh, army surgeon and physician, writes:

> Much of the land depopulated in 1770 remained uncultivated even nine years later, and indeed the population decreased until 1788. The land became jungle and wild beasts increased notably. Even twenty years after the famine the jails contained many debtors for revenue. Driven by want, the small cultivators sold cattle, ploughs, all they possessed. They ate the little store that should have given them seed for the next harvest. They sold even their own children and were finally driven to eat leaves and grass. Tanks and wells dried up, and to add to the trouble, many homesteads were destroyed by bands of roving incendiaries.

British observers noted the increase in banditry and 'dacoity'—although many of those involved were either soldiers dismissed from the nawab's army by the urgencies of Company retrenchment, or perhaps people evicted or driven out by hunger.

The consequences of famine are always more enduring than the—often brief—time of hunger. Although the famine year was followed by three years of plenty, the people were gone and the country was forsaken, abandoned by one-third of its ten million people. Murshidabad was further damaged by the shifting of many of the functions of a capital city to Calcutta. In 1772, the *khalsa*, or treasury, was also transferred to Calcutta. Many of those dismissed from the household of the nawab—again as a result of reductions by the Company in allowances—sought their fortune in what was effectively the new capital. By 1781, the mint had also been transferred from Murshidabad to Calcutta, which continued to grow at the expense of a city neglected and unpeopled.

The recovery of Murshidabad was not helped by the change of course of the Bhagirathi in 1813. By 1817, according to Tull Walsh's *A History of Murshidabad Disrict* (1902), it was reported "the extraordinary unhealthiness of Murshidabad, which seems to have been becoming worse year after year, has forced most of the European functionaries to seek residence at some distance, and only to repair to the city for the discharge of their duties".

Many inhabitants of the city had been removed by other events which left them with no choice. The famine was followed by a smallpox epidemic, which also devastated survivors weakened by malnutrition. Houses and lands fell into ruin and became waste, and Murshidabad never regained its lost pre-eminence.

The traumas endured by the whole district had other consequences. They reinforced the rich folklore that sometimes merged with
religious traditions which were themselves fluid and syncretic. It
is difficult, at this remove, particularly now that smallpox has
been eradicated, to enter into the mind of the starvelings of the
stricken city and the surrounding district of the time. Smallpox
was a goddess, Shitala, a gold-complexioned woman arrayed
in scarlet, pictured sitting on a lotus or riding an ass. Placatory
rituals were enacted to beg her to remove the disease, and victims
offered gifts that would diminish her wrath.

Meanwhile, mendicants travelled through the city bearing
stones and images of the goddess, demanding that those affected
make offerings of money or food. Water pots with branches of
mango were placed in the room where the sick lay; neem leaves,
turmeric and grasses were pounded into a paste and smeared on
the body; while only old women attended them, since a young
woman capable of bearing children would suffer if she looked
upon anyone suffering from smallpox. Superstition became
rife, since the *ojhas* and *baids*—sorcerers and healers—could do
nothing to halt the spread of sickness among a people already
weakened by hunger. Muslims hung the skin of a goat at the door
to ward off the disease. A bird or an animal offered to Kali would
be set free to take the illness away; or turmeric seeds wrapped
in a rag and thrown down in the street, so that whoever trod on
it would take the disease in place of the sufferer. The transfer of
sickness to others was widely practised: certain articles would

be placed under the head of a sufferer while he or she slept—some rice or dal and turmeric, a knife or other implement—and the following morning would be given to a stranger or a beggar, who, it was believed, would also take away the disease.

The spirit of a pir might inhabit a stone or a tree; and rags were tied to trees to appease female evil spirits living in trees and rocks. A woman who wished to conceive would hang a stone on a pipal or banyan tree, to signify her desire for a weight in her body. When children died, the mother would tie a rag on the branches of certain trees: if the rags disappeared the next child would be spared. Ancient practices of magic, spells and charms which recur in popular culture through time, across geographical boundaries and religious faiths, naturally dominated the lives of people who had been devastated by hunger and disease.

Because life was so hazardous, amulets, charms and rituals were necessary, not so much to prevent catastrophe as to forestall anything worse. Witchcraft was everywhere. A witch could be identified because she or he had no shadow; if salt were thrown, the witch would become paralysed. It remains the practice to paint with charcoal or kohl a circle on the head of a child, since this would make it unattractive to witches and evil spirits. A ladder placed over a threshold effectively barred entry to any evildoer. Children could be protected by cow dung on their forehead, juice of the *najdana* (*Artemisia vulgaris*, commonly known as mugwort) or saliva rubbed on their chest, or by biting the nail of the little finger of the left hand. Protection could be assured by fragments of the root of water yam in each ear; chilli burned beneath the nose of one bewitched would drive out the evil spirit. Distinctions were made between *bhoots* (spirits or ghosts) and witches. Witches left their homes from time to time to ride on wolves, their animal of choice.

Demons had also to be exorcized from those suffering from hysteria, epilepsy or delirium. A possessed or haunted woman (and women were more usually victims) would be placed on a stool, and dust or mustard seeds thrown over her while she was beaten with a twisted cloth or a shoe, and the devil called upon to quit. Evil spirits particularly chose to inhabit the bodies of pregnant women and children. Live birds would be offered to gods and goddesses, and as they flew away, the spirit or fever would fly with them. Mantras were chanted over a rag or thread which was then tied around the upper arm.

A culture haunted by poverty and death is bound to be more concerned with preventing evil than with auguries of good; but if a butterfly settled on a child's head, this was an omen of good fortune. Certain animals are viewed with favour by Hindus, since they are identified with individual gods—Durga is seated on a tiger, Shiva on a bull, Indra an elephant. Tame pigeons were believed to be the companions of the god of fortune; and many people kept them as symbols of hope.

Charms to protect cattle and crops, agents of survival, were widely used: a beehive or the shell of a tortoise protected animals, while in the cattle shed a piece of paper with the name of Arjun was a preventive against theft or disease. A stem of maize painted red and placed in the middle of a field would make the growing crops proof against pests. If a pig were let loose among cows and buffaloes until it was trampled to death, its body would be burned afterwards to protect the cattle. To walk in shoes among vegetables would bring misfortune, and menstruating women should not go near certain growing things. If the crop failed, purification rituals were necessary—the shell of a crab made into a lamp was lighted and placed in the middle of the field on top of a black-painted earthenware pot.

Survivors of the great calamities returned to planting rice and subsistence crops. Silkworm breeders resumed their livelihood in the rearing houses, plastered with cow dung, silkworms fed with young mulberry leaves every four hours on shelves supported by bamboo staves which stood in earthen vessels of water to prevent insects and rats from attacking the worms. Breeders of silkworms continued to watch as the worms shed their skins five times before being ready to spin, as their colour changed from greenish cream to a mellow light orange colour. They regarded their work as an almost sacred duty; and they observed certain rituals to ensure the survival of each crop: the breeders abstained from sexual activity and forbade parturient or menstruating women from entering the rearing sheds. They avoided fish, turmeric, garlic and onions; and placed an old shoe with a bunch of thorns in the entrance to the rearing house.

Superstition and science coexisted. Breeders kept the tiny eggs laid by the adult moth in a calico bag beneath their clothing day and night to maintain a constant temperature for hatching. It was a precarious undertaking; cleanliness was imperative, and since many breeders lost at least two harvests a year, they often turned to cultivating land instead.

After being the seat of the Mughal government for much of the eighteenth century, and the site of the Jagat Seth bankers who financed it, Murshidabad subsequently saw only contraction and the memory of its former grandeur. During its period as Mughal capital, the architecture of its mosques had been in the Islamic tradition, spectacular and distinctive; but by the beginning of the nineteenth century, the nawab was increasingly losing power to the expanding British presence, and the official residence built for him between 1829 and 1837 is like a vast English country house with Corinthian pillars and a ceremonial staircase. Opposite it, the nawab constructed an *imambara*, a congregation hall, also influenced by the European style, symbols of the powerlessness of the receding Mughal empire. The leading zamindars of the region constructed their opulent dwellings in a style heavily inflected by that of extravagant Italianate villas.

The Hazarduari Palace, so called because it has a thousand doors, nine hundred of them illusory, leading nowhere, is sadly symbolic of the closed pathways of the Mughal retreat. An announcement is carved into a stone, surmounted by a chipped lion, that the foundation was laid "by His Highness Nawab Nizam Humayun Jah Bahadur in the presence of the agent of the Governor-General the Commandant of the British troops and a large concourse of natives". The structure, begun under Bentinck, was completed eight years later under Lord Auckland. Inside, rather than a monument to the authority of the nawab, it is a celebration of the apparently invincible might of the British. A vast canvas of the ceremony that transferred the diwani to

Clive from Emperor Shah Alam II sets the tone. Portraits of recent nizams share space with images of Cleopatra, Ariadne and Bacchus, Queen Victoria, and Colonel McLeod Duncan who designed the palace, a van Dyck portrait of the Marquis of Spinola, several images of Cinderella, some cavaliers of Venice and a fairy with infants—all of which suggests a transplant of arbitrary Victoriana calculated to impress imperial subjects. At the same time, there are silver thrones, ivory howdahs, symbols of the magnificence which the British had vanquished. Drawing rooms are furnished with elaborate and uncomfortable wood-carved chairs, brocade-covered causeuses and velvet four-seater square sofas designed for whispered confidences behind ivory fans. There are plates and ceramics, cut-glass flower vases, brass *aftabs* (to pour drinks), and above all, cases of armaments, both British and indigenous, pikes, knives, cutlasses, scimitars, daggers and swords, from which only the blood of those who perished by them is missing.

The imambara—symbol of the nawab's unimpaired religious power, despite his failing control of the material world—looks by contrast diminished and spectral, although it is an even longer structure than the palace. The buildings overlook the Bhagirathi, where, instead of the fishing barques and pleasure craft of the old Mughal capital, a boat full of plastic bottles, collected by an enterprising owner from the garbage discarded by tourists, glides by.

And tourism is one of the few economic activities of a Murshidabad which thrives on the somnolence of two centuries of decline. A long, winding road follows the Bhagirathi, and among the ruins of the old capital people have made their modest dwellings. The bricks of an ornamental arch have been used to make semi-pukka structures, while other people have built their tenements against an ancient wall. Unmoved by the grandeur around them, since Murshidabad district is still one of the poorest in West Bengal, they live in the shadow of history, obscured by forgotten crafts and self-reliant skills—an impression heightened by the bleating of goats and the lowing of cattle, which affirm the supremacy of the living over the dead. Out of the abandoned structures of fallen buildings, walls overgrown with thorn bushes and wild flowers, issues a long lament of loss, privation and insufficiency; this is a place which for two hundred years has sent its victims to Calcutta and Bombay; and from where people are still leaving.

In New Delhi in November 2010, a building collapsed in Laxmi Nagar, and among the seventy people killed were a number of domestic servants from Murshidabad. Among the survivors were those who said they could not go back home because there was nothing there for them: only the implacable monuments and the mansions of zamindars who grew rich on the poverty of others. And this was a city which Clive claimed, on the day of his victorious progress through the capital after his victory at Plassey, was a place "as extensive, populous and rich as the city of London".

The melancholy of life in the shell of departed grandeur is emphasized by the shabbiness of people employed in its aftermath: the security guards subcontracted to protect the Hazarduara Palace sit disconsolately in the early morning sun, the ill-stitched logo on their uniform half-detached, their shoes dusty, trousers frayed. Many of their acquaintances have gone. Their salaries are low, the task they perform thankless. The stalls jostling for tourists on the banks of the Bhagirathi sell metal trinkets, toys from China, photographs of the imambara, shell necklaces, in mimicry of the cowries which were once low-value currency in the district, and pots of brass, the making of which was in the eighteenth century one of the principal crafts of Murshidabad. The young men who work in hotels with their scented gardens full of English flowers conveyed here generations ago—antirrhinums, zinnias and marigolds—sit negligently watching cricket on TV, while guests come and go unattended by them; and they show more interest in the pornographic pictures exchanged on their mobile phones than in the well-being of those they are supposed to serve. Cycle rickshaw drivers ply the dilapidated streets, and professional hustlers waylay the unwary, offering to show them the wasted beauties and overgrown ruins of the derelict capital; while students, eager to follow the long procession of migrants, breathe longings, which seem to have been inspired by the archaic grandeur of the city, to become famous—movie stars, cricketers and celebrities.

Efforts have been made to revive the silk industry, but now only a few solitary weavers make saris for the merchants of Kolkata; for each astonishing marvel of silk they create, they receive 500–750 rupees, and since each item takes ten days of labour they receive only 2,000 rupees a month, and the craft continues its long agony, since their sons would rather drive rickshaws than follow so unremunerative a calling, and the girls have already departed to wait, with self-effacing deference, upon the middle class of Kolkata and Delhi.

I met Sanjay Doogar, tenth generation of a family of Rajasthani Jains who came to Murshidabad in the early eighteenth century to help finance and manage the exchequer of the nawab, which was soon to dwindle away under the control of the Company. Having renovated his own beautiful mid-nineteenth-century villa, with its classical columns, elegant stairwell and luxuriant greenery of fragrant mango and brilliant gulmohar trees, Sanjay Doogar is passionately committed to the revival of the city, its heritage and traditional skills.

When the capital of Bengal moved to Calcutta in the 1770s, many people went with it; beginning an exodus that has continued until today. The basic reason for the loss of handwoven silk is that machinery took over. Handloom weaving still continues in villages in the silk-weaving district of Murshidabad, but the industry is a shadow of what it was. There are no more than three or four hundred still weaving in Murshidabad. The traders that provide the silk get the advantage, and the weavers have no more power than they did at the time of the East India dominance (although Grameen Bank or NGOs now give loans to the weavers). Instead of pride in their unique ability, the weavers feel shame because the next generation does not wish to follow them: there is no incentive for the transmission of ancient manual skills.

Children are still apprenticed, but earlier the weaver took on members of the next generation from within his family. Now, the remaining weaving families, who do highly specialised work, are better off. Their children go to school, so they employ other people's children, from families poorer than they. There was a whole culture that went with weaving, the *jamdani boli*, the song of the loom, the master recited with the shuttle and the boy sang as he did so. There is nothing like some of the descriptions of cloth made in the seventeenth or eighteenth centuries, of gifts that the nawabs gave to the Emperor, a length of fabric that had taken six months to make, and was wrapped in banana leaves to be transported to Delhi.

We also want to renew Murshidabad as a centre of spiritual pilgrimage. Three hundred years ago, Jains came from Rajasthan to Azimganj, where we settled. There are many Jain temples, which belonged to the fourteen families who controlled the land of undivided Bengal. The people from outside came as zamindars and bankers; and set up the hundi system, bills which enabled funds to be transmitted through the countryside when it was infested by robbers and dacoits. We became bankers to the nawabs and the Mughal empire and intermediaries between them and the British. Fateh Chand, descendant of Manick Chand who founded the great banking house, was awarded the title of 'Jagat Seth', banker to the world, by the Emperor Malmood Shah in 1723. When there was famine in Delhi and the coffers of the king were empty, it was these bankers who saved the lives of lakhs of people. Twenty per cent of the GDP of India was controlled around

Murshidabad in the early eighteenth century and 5 per cent of the total product of the world.

Sanjay Doogar has portraits of his ancestors who, arriving from Rajasthan at the beginning of the eighteenth century, are fully attired in traditional Hindu turbans and Rajasthani dress; as the years passed, the headdress and the clothing they wore became more inflected by Mughal influence. His villa, which is an eclectic mixture of Italianate splendour and Indian magnificence, was a kind of official residence where the English and other foreigners were entertained. The family retained its own private haveli, where, of course, no outsiders could be permitted to enter, because of the purdah system and the zenana.

The coexistence of faded splendour, profound poverty and the archaic monuments of a vanished imperialism suggests a possibility of significant economic renewal, although of a very different kind from that which has swept up Dhaka in the vortex of global garment manufacture.

Part V

Kolkata

If I have dwelt on the decline of Dhaka and the provincial cities of Bengal so far, this has been to balance the emphasis that has been placed on the most rapidly expanding city that dominated the moment of high imperialism in the nineteenth century—the colonial capital, the second city of Empire, also a port, centre of industry, and administrative and commercial metropolis. This was originally situated in the late seventeenth century on the three villages—Kalikata, Sutanati and Govindapur—leased by the East India Company's Job Charnock from the Mughal government. Sutanati was even at that time a thriving thread and fabric market. European traders were granted permission to defend themselves, and this resulted in the construction of Fort William, completed in 1707. Although the 'writers'—unmarried clerks—stayed within the fort, married officials constructed their houses outside, and this gave rise to a recognizable city settlement, including spectacular mansions along the banks of the Hooghly.

In 1717, the Company obtained the right to buy a further thirty-eight villages; and in view of the Maratha threat to the west of Bengal, settlers sought safety in the area around the Fort. In the adjacent 'Black Town', it is believed that almost 200,000 people were living by the 1850s. In 1756, Siraj-ud-Daula attacked the English and took possession of the Fort; and his imprisonment of more than a hundred prisoners gave rise to the so-called Black Hole of Calcutta, an event that haunted the imperial imagination of the British for generations. Even in my childhood, our primary school headmaster told us with relish (this in 1946) a fable of innocent Britishers incarcerated and suffocated in a small airless cell by people who were strangers to clemency and humanity alike; a tale initiated and magnified by Zephaniah Holwell, surgeon employee of the Company, who recorded an account of the event, a version later questioned by historians. This was used to justify almost every British atrocity in India of the following two centuries, as well, incidentally, to inculcate a sense of horror of 'natives' in children in British schools as late as the mid-twentieth century.

Alexander Hamilton (1744) reported that the salt water lake about three miles south-eastward "overflowed in September and October and then a prodigious number of fish resort, but in November and December, when the floods are dissipated, the fishes are left high and dry and with their putrefaction affect the air with thick stinking vapours which the north-east wind bring with them to Fort William that there cause a yearly mortality."

The perils of the site did not inhibit urban growth. As Calcutta displaced the old capitals of Dacca and Murshidabad, it attracted agency houses, merchants and dealers, buyers of opium and indigo, bankers, bill brokers, insurance agents, shipping and freight agents for silk and cotton piece goods, saltpetre, opium, indigo, sugar and other produce that was so swiftly spirited away from Bengal. Into the Black Town poured displaced weavers and cultivators, the evictees of imperialism and the violence of nature in the Bay of Bengal, as well as opportunists, the capable and the ambitious. By 1822, the population of Calcutta was close to 180,000, by 1831, over 200,000. Howrah Station was built in 1854, and the Kidderpore docks, constructed earlier in the century, could, from the 1880s, provide berths for steamships.

It was "a very noble city, with tall and stately houses ornamented with Grecian pillars, and each, for the most part, surrounded by a little apology for a garden" (Heber, 1829). The European section of Chowringhee was described by observers as a series of houses, each with a considerable piece of ground, with an average of ten rooms, designed to display the luxury of the owner and to allow the free circulation of air. The architecture of this Calcutta was hybrid: mosques, temples, churches in traditional style, public buildings and the houses of the rich a combination of European and oriental, furnished after the European style with "elegant chandeliers, pier glasses, couches, chests of drawers, writing desks and two or three hundred chairs". While the Indian section of the city was "deep, bleak and dingy, with narrow crooked streets, huts of earth baked in the sun, or of twisted bamboos, interspersed here and there with ruinous brick bazaars, pools of dirty water, cocoanut trees and little gardens" (Heber, 1823).

Many accounts have reached us of the life of the gilded expatriates—the makers of fortunes of the East India Company, often behind the backs of their ostensible employer, remitting their gains home by means of French, Dutch or Danish merchants. Their appetite for food matched their love of money; and descriptions of what they actually ate represent marvels of consumption, unrivalled even by the heroic excesses of the obese and overfed of posterity. After copious repasts, an independent woman traveller and letter-writer, Mrs Eliza Fay, wrote in the early 1780s, that

> the custom of reposing, if not sleeping, after dinner is so general that the streets of Calcutta are from four to five in the afternoon almost as empty of Europeans as if it was midnight. Next come the evening airings. To the Course everyone goes, though sure of being suffocated with dust. On returning from thence, tea is served, and universally drunk here even during the extreme heats. After tea, either cards or music fill up the space till ten when supper is generally announced.

The ostentation of Calcutta overwhelmed visitors who, like Lord Valentia (1811), exhibiting a patrician approval, declared:

> The town of Calcutta is at present worthy of being the seat

of our Eastern Government, both from its size and from the magnificent buildings which decorate the part of it inhabited by Europeans... The esplanade leaves a good opening, on the edge of which is placed the new Government House erected by Lord Wellesley, a noble structure although not without faults in its architecture, and on the whole not unworthy of its destination. The sums expended upon it have been considered as extravagant by those who carry European ideas and European economy into Asia; but they ought to remember, that India is a country of splendour, of extravagance and of outward appearances; that the Head of a mighty empire ought to conform itself to the prejudices of the country he rules over, and that the British in particular ought to emulate the works of the prince of the House of Timour, lest it should be supposed that we merit the reproach which our great rivals, the French, have ever cast upon us, of being alone influenced by a sordid mercantile spirit. In short, I wish India to be ruled from a palace, not from a counting-house; with the ideas of a Prince, not those of a retail dealer in muslin or indigo.

Their concerns were with the order and precedents of Britain, and bore no relation to the people of India, inhabitants of the Black Town, the streets of which, according to the same writer, "are narrow and dirty, the houses of two stories, occasionally brick but generally mud, thatched, *perfectly resembling the cabins of the poorest class in Ireland*" (emphasis added). Other writers, preoccupied with the purposes of their fellow countrymen, observed: "It must be remembered that every Englishman in India has something to do; it is not like London, where many have only to *spend* fortunes; *here* we are all busy making them" (Henry Roberdeau, Assistant Collector of Mymensingh, 1805). In 1835, while Alexis de Tocqueville was expressing his admiring horror of a Manchester transformed by the textile industry, Emily Eden, sister of Lord Auckland, who had just been appointed Governor-General of Bengal, enthused about a Calcutta that belonged to a different world from that of cotton manufacture.

> Depend upon it, Calcutta is the finest place in the world. I know there are towns with far larger and grander buildings; but then they are not half as clean and new and beautiful as this bride-like city. I have been standing on the roof of the house for the last half-hour for air, as it was midnight, had an opportunity of seeing all the gay company returning from an entertainment at the government house, and I assure you I never witnessed anything that could compare with the splendid exhibition.

Of course, she was describing the imperial showplace, and not the Native Town, nor indeed the nascent industrial city, since Calcutta, in addition to its role as colonial capital, also shadowed Manchester: by 1855, the first jute mill also opened some distance outside the city. Jute, widely used for making sacks and containers for goods, matting, and cheap clothing, was the principal occupation of Calcutta until the mid-twentieth century.

The stories of the British rarely reflected the lives of 'natives', except insofar as these served as servants or curiosities. When the Welsh travel writer Fanny Parks' sircar told her, "You are my mother and father, you are my God", she reproved him severely for using such terms. Their status gave them the power to pass capricious judgements on people. "They say that, next to the Chinese, the people of India are the most dexterous thieves in the world"; "Sleep seems to follow every repast. From this drowsiness I conclude that there is but little reflection or occupation of mind among them; their actions, customs, and all, seem indeed, entirely animal." "The idleness of the natives is excessive; for instance, my ayha [sic] will dress me, after which she will return to her house and eat her dinner; and then returning, will sleep in a corner of my room on the floor for the whole day. The bearers also do nothing but eat and sleep when they are not pulling the pankha."

'Natives' were banned from the White Town at certain times of day. An order of the Governor of Fort William in 1821 declared:

It having been represented to the Most Noble the Governor of Fort William that considerable inconvenience is experienced by the European part of the community who resort to the Respondentia [a walkway along the Hooghly] from the crowds of Native workmen and Coolies who make a thoroughfare of the Walk. His Lordship is pleased to direct that Natives shall not in future be allowed to pass the Sluice Bridge ... between the hours of 5 and 8 in the morning and 5 and 8 in the evening (cited in Bannerjee, 1989).

Although contemporary observers noted the sharp contrast between the Black and White Towns, Pradip Sinha (1978) suggests there was a significant Grey Town, which formed a buffer between the two and consisted of a highly cosmopolitan population: Persians, Arabs, Armenians, Parsees, Jews, Greeks and Gujaratis. Jews had come mainly from Baghdad; the poorer among them dealt in rosewater, horses, Persian ware, and some were 'box-wallas' or pedlars. A police census conducted in 1837 found Calcutta to be a predominantly Hindu city, with 156,000 'up-country Hindus' and 56,000 'up-country Muslims'. There were 3,138 English, 3,181 Portuguese and 19,000 unspecified 'lower orders'. Significantly there were 4,746 'East Indians', which was the term that had supplanted the eighteenth-century *kala feringhi* (black foreigners)—a category that subsequently mutated into Eurasian, and thence into Anglo-Indian. The pseudonymous Griffin (a term used to indicate a newcomer from Britain to India), in his *Sketches of Calcutta* in 1848, wrote:

If a European lady were to marry an East Indian, she would lose caste among her acquaintances and be discarded by them, though his wealth would enable her to sparkle with diamonds... European bachelors are not always as inflexible as European ladies toward the East Indians, and some of them have condescended to marry East Indian females who have heavy purses, and a few have condescended to marry those who have light ones, but in both cases, these alliances may be regarded as 'marriages of convenience' (quoted in P. Sinha, 1978).

Calcutta was shaped by imperial occupation and equally, by the banias and diwans who served the British, and by indigenous merchants and traders, who also created their opulent buildings in the Bengali city. By the 1830s, leading Bengali merchants had lost their principal specialization in cotton piece goods; well-to-do Bengalis were increasingly investing in both rural and urban property, and this was reflected in the fabric of a city that, by the 1850s, covered eighteen square kilometres. Some had acquired zamindaris, localities they never, or rarely, visited, and they built their conspicuous establishments in Calcutta with the proceeds. These people, "rentiers-turned-aristocrats" (P. Sinha, 1978), became the most dynamic force in the city; and the houses of prominent families, masonry houses of the middle class—subordinate officials, physicians, small landowners— grew alongside the more showy structures, which towered above thatched or tiled huts of those who served them. Dealers along the riverfront dealt in bamboo, straw, timber, grain, oil and gunny bags.

Significant families—of Sobharam Basak, Nabakrishna Deb, the Mallicks, Dattas and Tagores—left great fortunes to their descendants, who spent lavishly on marriages and *sradh* (death) ceremonies, often quarrelling and dissipating much of their wealth. Sinha describes the squabble that broke out among the heirs of Nemai Charan Mullick over his sradh, which the older sons claimed cost 600,000 rupees, while the younger claimed it cost only 200,000: a lawsuit was filed in the Supreme Court at Calcutta in 1807, and the appeal was still awaiting a hearing at the Privy Council in Britain in 1831.

The city owed much of its physical character to the preference of urban real estate owners as represented by the banias and dewans, and the original banias, the Subarabaniks, the Setts and Banaks. The existence of rented lands, bazaars, storage spaces, rented houses, gardens, open spaces and ponds in and around Calcutta gave the city not only a visual but also a deeper quality of urban growth which continues tenaciously to this day (P. Sinha, 1978).

Urban gentry moved from the immediate area around Calcutta into the city, driven by opportunities to earn a livelihood, and sometimes in response to fevers and plagues in the large villages and small urban centres in which they had lived leisurely lives, superintending their estates, following the observances of their caste, and regulating the lives of their families.

Calcutta was indeed the site of significant migration—almost half the population were migrants by the end of the nineteenth century—but the growth of the city had none of the features of Western urbanization associated with the abandonment of the rural hinterland and the growth of an industrial proletariat. Millworkers in Calcutta and the surrounding mill towns were primarily from Bihar and the United Provinces. Biharis and Oriyas worked in jute mills, dockyards and railways. In the census of 1901, Calcutta had almost as many immigrants from the Hindi-speaking north as from Bengal.

As a consequence of its imperial functions, and of the interaction between the representatives of the Company and its servants and Bengalis, Calcutta was the site of a unique experiment in the mutual exchange of intellectual, moral and political ideas. By the second half of the nineteenth century, Calcutta had become the centre of intellectual, educational, cultural and political activity, of a middle class that had undergone English education and, from time to time, reacted violently against it. From the appearance, in 1815, of Rammohun Roy, who foresaw a synthesis between a Hinduism shorn of its idolatry and priestcraft, and the moral teachings of a Christianity from which its miracles and wonders were excluded, Calcutta was the nucleus where the interaction between British progressive and reactionary thought and Bengali fascination with, and revulsion against, their rulers was played out; where ideas were formulated, political, literary and spiritual struggles were engaged in. Conservatives, reformers and radicals in Bengal both looked towards Britain and turned away from it, to find a tolerable intellectual resting place between tradition and modernity, between subordination and liberation.

For a century Calcutta was the site of acceptance of new ideas. Traditional conservatism had been shaken by Rammohun Roy's efforts to create a Hindu monotheism, and even more by the wilder exultations of Young Bengal, their fierce flouting of taboos, particularly under the influence of Henry Derozio. Derozio (who died at the age of twenty-two) was of Indian and Portuguese descent, a poet and a radical, a charismatic individual who profoundly influenced his peers with what were then iconoclastic Western views. The Hindu reformist movement spearheaded by Rammohun Roy, Brahmoism, which sought to assimilate rationalism and Western liberalism without abandoning its Hindu roots, encouraged people anxious to improve themselves to attend meetings and lectures and embrace a thoroughly Victorian faith in progress. The sometimes tormented interplay of Indian and Western cultures gave rise to a unique flourishing of poetry, novel writing, social criticism and drama of what became known as the 'Renaissance' of Bengal. The Brahmo movement, however, split between radical and moderate adherents; and indeed, splitting seems to have become something of an occupational hazard of being Bengali, since social and religious movements, reforms, politics and social organizations exhibited a tendency to throw up schisms and breakaways—a tendency exploited by the British in their effort to separate East from West Bengal in 1905.

The literary and cultural humanism of Bengal made Calcutta the most vibrant city in India. It was here that radical ideas were formulated, movements were founded, and where the Bengali bhadralok assumed for itself the moral and intellectual leadership of a nationalism that didn't distinguish too clearly between that of Bengal and of India in general. When the Indian National Congress was founded in Bombay in 1885, the rival movement in Calcutta was astonished and perturbed to find it had been bypassed; and they consoled themselves with the thought they were the bearers of a deeper-rooted and more radical form of national consciousness than that expressed by the more temperate considerations emerging from Bombay.

Bhadralok was the name given to genteel, intellectual and educated Bengalis, overwhelmingly Hindu: it implied an aristocracy of mind, cultured manners and an interest in literature and social progress, although this could also be allied to a tenacity of tradition. Indeed, as the nineteenth century progressed, the tendency for social conservatism became more pronounced. The growth of purdah, child marriage, dowry and restrictions on widows were the social manifestations of an insecure middle class, seeking to maintain its dignity between colonial overlords and the helpless mass of the poor, Hindu as well as Muslim.

For the Bengali elite the sanctuary of the home was where the colonized elite sought refuge from collaboration and negotiation with the colonizers. This became part of the nationalist discourse. Women were custodians of this sacred space. Middle class men had to define tradition against the intrusion of the colonial state and also to redefine it to meet the new compulsion of professional and service employment (Sen, 1999).

The distinction between the bhadralok and the chotolok, literally the small folk, was sharp and remained so: the bhadralok lived in a different world from the workers in jute mills and the port, who worked as coolies and labourers. The lives of the Calcutta working class—of manual workers, Muslim peasants and low-caste Hindus—intersected the lives of the bhadralok principally in serving them, in the elaborate and artificial construct of employers and servants. Employers sometimes exhibited a fascination with the exotic qualities of those who came and went, sometimes inexplicably, to administer their domestic organization. The bhadralok were often charitable towards them, paying them in kind—mainly in leftover food and discarded garments—above their official remuneration, but social separation survived, which the metropolitan atmosphere of the second city of empire did little to dispel.

But, on the whole, the bhadralok were as anxious to distance themselves from the poor as they were to be acknowledged by the imperial occupiers, and little was known of the nineteenth-century poor of Calcutta, either to the British or to the respectable Hindu middle class. Accounts of the city sometimes give a passing glimpse of their lives, self-effacing servants who fled the presence of those who scarcely observed them anyway.

The original inhabitants of the swamps of Calcutta were agricultural and fishing communities, with a sprinkling of 'falconers and snake-catchers' forced to the eastern periphery by the growth of the city. It was observed (P. Sinha, 1978) that the practice of dumping the city's waste in the eastern *dihi* served as a means of living to the very poor, through rummaging in the garbage—a practice that is still a major source of livelihood today. In the eighteenth century, palanquin bearers, of the Bengali bagdi caste, constituted a significant category of employees; their descendants still draw the shafts of painted rickshaws of spare elegance, in spite of this work having been banned as degrading labour by successive governments. There were burners of shells who made *chunam* (lime); Muslims provided table servants, boatswains, bookbinders, butchers, tailors and others who served the Europeans.

Most accounts of nineteenth-century Calcutta list the variety of occupations available in an expanding division of labour: potters, bamboo workers, blanket weavers, butchers, carpenters, herbalists, coal-dust cake makers, bookbinders, dealers in hides and buffalo horn, diamond cutters, printers of Arabic and Persian books, zari makers and embroiderers, engravers, ornament makers. There were also coach and palanquin makers, stable keepers, washermen, vegetable sellers, painters, fishermen and fish vendors, cobblers, bullock transporters, as well as entertainers, jugglers and makers of toys, while in a city of male migrants, prostitution was a major industry, which in the early twentieth century was estimated to be a significant employer of female labour in the city. In addition, there were scavengers, cleaners and servants of all kinds, as well as the floating population of frauds and tricksters, thieves, counterfeiters, the hirelings of moneylenders and landlords. Many occupations are commemorated in certain neighbourhoods of the city from which they have largely vanished: Kumartoli (potters), Colootola (oil pressers), Jelintola (fishermen), Goaltoli (milkmen), Domtoli (scavengers), Sankaritola (conch shell workers), Chootapara (carpenters) (Thomas, 1997).

What is, perhaps, astonishing is how many of these occupations have survived in the 'informal' economy of present-day Kolkata. In this sense, although there was a significant organized sector, the poor of Calcutta were more likely to be self-employed than their counterparts in Manchester. By the ingenuity they showed in creating work for themselves, the urban poor of Calcutta in the nineteenth century were more like their London counterparts than the majority of working people who entered into the organized cotton industry of Manchester.

Of the mass of people living in the Native Town, through which Chitpur Street was the main thoroughfare, most accounts dwell on the squalor, the absence of sanitation and drainage, and on the 'indifference' of the inhabitants to the noxious effluvia, dirty water and decaying offal around them. Baron Dowlease wrote in the *Calcutta Review* in 1860:

Bustees are generally large spots of ground belonging to a

particular individual, and let out in small portions to the poorest class of the native community. The tenants build their own huts and pay only ground rent to the owner of the locality. The particular spot on which the hut is erected is generally taken on a lease of twelve months, at the expiration of which the lease may be renewed, or the tenant is at liberty to remove the hut, provided he has paid the ground rent due by him. In the majority of cases, the tenant is in arrears, and his miserable hut is forfeited to the landlord. No difficulty ought to exist in clearing such bustees for the special purpose of opening new squares, and it is in such localities where the much needed improvements might be carried out at a very moderate expense (cited in P. Chaudhury and A. Mukhopadhyay, 1975).

The imperial characterization of slums as places of squalor, dirt and disease, which had to be removed, without regard for the people living in them, set a long precedent from which the leaders of free India and independent Bangladesh have scarcely deviated. The poor are a different kind of human being from persons of sensibility (that is, ruling castes and elites), and this led an official of the Raj to pronounce: "The disgusting spectacle of persons bathing in open streets would not be tolerated in any other city under a Christian government."

Clearances of people who are an encumbrance to progress, amenities, hygiene, the beautification of the city, are seen as a legitimate means of town planning. Where those to whom these sites of squalor are home should go, is not of interest, and is even now only of vestigial concern to those who would have them removed. Clearances of the poor began as early as 1757, with the rebuilding of Fort William, and have continued without interruption for the following two and a half centuries.

The poor are constantly displaced, for the building of ghats or temples, or simply to remove them from the sight and smell of the well-to-do. They have been ousted not only by city expansion and beautification projects, but also by altered technologies, the falling into disuse of handicrafts, skills and trades, the death of old crafts and the growth of new ones—palanquin bearers displaced by trams and motorcars, brass and bell-metal workers superseded by crafts in enamel and aluminium, coarse-sugar makers by factory-made sugar, conch shell workers by plastic bangle makers. In 2010, I met many workers in plastic who were making chappals, who had displaced chamars and leatherworkers; and who in turn were awaiting their own redundancy, as a consequence of even cheaper machine-made footwear imported from China. There is also a considerable industry that has grown up making counterfeit substitutes for internationally branded goods—scent and cosmetics, handbags, footwear and clothing, falsely labelled with exclusive logos, as well as illegally copied films, both Hindi and Western.

The city is a place of perpetual mobility and change. The only constant has been the embarrassment of the poor, whose persistence is seen as an encumbrance and obstacle to progress or development. They have existed largely as two-dimensional figures in the landscapes of others. In 1860, thirty-six people out of every thousand died of cholera, kala-azar or malaria. Waterborne diseases scythed through the population much as they did in the Manchester of the period. Until the 1870s, the poor people depended upon polluted tanks, a degraded version of village wells; by the 1880s, some insanitary tanks were filled in, piped water was extended to some bustees, but the provision of services never caught up with the growth in population. Even as late as the 1950s, Calcutta was known as the 'cholera capital of the world'.

The wraith-like presence of the destitute becomes visible only at times of great upheaval: during the famine of 1943, when they came to die, unmourned, on the pavements of Calcutta. People picked out undigested seeds from cattle dung, parents abandoned babies outside the homes of the wealthy. In the years after Partition 4.2 million came from East Pakistan, while in 1971, 7.5 million reached West Bengal, of whom about 1.5 million remained after the establishment of Bangladesh.

Generally, the city's poor had to await their 'discovery' by Western philanthropy in the late twentieth century. Then they reappear dramatically through the figure of Mother Teresa, who lifted them from the streets of the city to recover—or more frequently, to die—in her refuges for the destitute. It is significant that it required the charity of a Christian nun before the plight of the most impoverished was 'recognized'; and although the Missionaries of Charity no doubt removed much of the distress from the streets, they also failed to treat the curable or to rehabilitate those who might have lived to lead productive lives had they not been transported to the mercy of these charitable antechambers of death.

There is a sad and ironic afterlife of Bengal's textiles in the common term 'ragpickers', which is used, especially of children and women's work, and it means collecting waste materials in general, but refers in particular to shreds, chiffons, leavings, small pieces of cloth and fabric, a debris of consumerism, to be recycled, unpicked, restitched or used again. In a growing consumer society nothing is thrown away and nothing wasted but the bodies of the people who undertake the work of rescue of metals from electronic goods, medical waste, plastic, copper, wire, glass, wood, iron, paper and cardboard. 'Ragpickers' has become almost a generic term for the poor, those who live off the city's waste—objects of charitable and humanitarian 'rehabilitation' by NGOs. There are tens of thousands of them in the Muslim slums of Kolkata, captives of waste, bent over a penitential labour of sorting, cleaning, selling discarded garments to middlemen, which, after having adorned the bodies of the well-to-do and clothed the poor before they reached the destitute were finally passed on as rags to provide a living of sorts for the city's destitute, the inconsolables of development.

The most significant group of workers in late nineteenth and early twentieth century Calcutta were employed in the jute mills—an occupation the structure of which prefigures the contemporary garment industry of Dhaka; at the same time, there are suggestions of both convergences and differences between the industrial workers of Manchester and those of Bengal.

While there were decidedly rural echoes in the lives of the early migrants to the cotton towns of Lancashire, these faded within a couple of generations, since the rural hinterland had become for the majority little more than a memory. Agriculture as an occupation in Britain dwindled throughout the nineteenth century, and what remained became more and more mechanized, so that by 1900 it employed only 10 per cent of the working population. The countryside was depleted, and although nostalgia for a rural past remained, the traditions, festivals and customs on which this was based ceased to be a living, organic element in the lives of the people.

It was very different for the workers in the jute mills of Calcutta. The industry was an offspring of the Dundee trade, which had turned to jute as a substitute for traditional flax; when the Russian flax crop failed in 1834, Dundee became the destination of imports of raw jute from Bengal. It was then only a matter of time before the processing was transferred to Bengal, close to both the raw material and the cheap labour that would work it. The first jute mill was set up on the Hooghly river near Calcutta in 1855. Jute spinning machinery was brought from Dundee, and by 1869, five mills were operating in Bengal—much of the industry supervised and managed by expatriate Scots, who brought with them both working practices and prejudices from their homeland. The second half of the nineteenth century saw the fall of Dundee and the rise of production in Calcutta, and by the early twentieth century 200,000 people were employed in the mills of Calcutta, the largest industrial workforce in the city and the least well paid.

Dipesh Chakrabarty (2000) discusses the complacency of the Indian Jute Manufacturers' Association, which enjoyed substantial profits, using simple technology and cheap labour. They had little concern for their workers—a situation paralleled today in Bangladesh. Labour was drawn from the vast rural hinterland of Bengal and Bihar, and represented a culture that had no experience of capitalist production, and was feudal and hierarchical. There was little sense of a common predicament, because loyalties were determined by religious, kinship, caste or linguistic ties, and disputes between groups of workers arose more readily than a sense of shared grievance against employers; although this did occur from time to time, and strikes flared up, unions were formed and disbanded as soon as the immediate problem was settled. Chakrabarty observes the paucity of information on working-class life: "Bengali intelligentsia seldom, if ever, produced social investigators like Henry Mayhew."

Production in the jute mills involved mechanical processes similar to those in cotton mills, and as the demand for jute increased, especially the need for sandbags at the time of the First World War, managements saw no good reason to alter what was already an archaic technology. The government of Bengal was always anxious to conciliate the mill owners—a characteristic shared by the present-day government of Bangladesh in relation to its garment producers. The outlook of the workers remained to some degree that of the peasantry. They had little understanding of the machinery, which ran continuously, without regard for the safety of the operatives. Accidents were frequent, as workers had to clean moving parts while they were still running. It was not uncommon for clothing, especially that of women, to get caught in the machine; an occurrence also recorded in the early days of the Lancashire mills. According to the report on the workings of the Factory Acts in Bengal, "Many [women] died because the work was decidedly arduous, bangles on their arms or wrists and anklets on the feet have on several occasions been the direct cause of fatal accidents" (cited in Sen, 1999). In 1898 a woman died in Clive Mill when jute became entangled with her bangles and drew her arms into the rollers of the machine softener. Another was killed in Shibpur when the jute fibres around her feet pulled her into the machinery. It was no wonder that the workers feared the machines and attributed supernatural powers to them. Chakrabarty says people revered tools, "which were endowed with magical or godly qualities. They would sacrifice a goat at Diwali, offer sweetmeats and incense."

Workers were replaceable. They came and went, and often lived in the mill compound, so that they remained a constant supply. The sewing of gunnysacks by hand was piecework, and women could come and go more or less as they pleased. They would leave the mills to feed their babies, to do household chores and then return to work. By 1926 the number of people employed in jute mills was almost 390,000, but these did not create a settled urban community. Migrants from the United Provinces and Bihar sustained the flow of labour; and Bengalis were increasingly displaced by cheaper 'upcountry' workers. Corruption was an integral part of the system—*sardars* were contractors who supplied labour, and they often had to be paid if the worker was to keep his job. The 'time-babu' checked attendance: the names of ghost workers were added to the list, and the money they received was shared between the babu and the sardar. Village relationships—the giving of gifts, traditional customs of ingratiation with powerful headmen—all this simply replicated in the city the practice of the countryside.

Between 1921 and 1929, there were over two hundred strikes in the jute mills. With the rise of nationalism—and later, Bolshevism—the owners began to take a greater interest in the lives of the workers. Paid spies were placed in the mills to give information to the Intelligence Officers—a procedure widespread in Bangladesh's garment sector today. If there was an outbreak of violence or rioting, this would be blamed on 'outside agitation'; just as the leaders of Bangladesh see the hidden hand of a foreign power (India) in any unrest that breaks out or any sabotage that occurs in the factories of Dhaka.

By the 1920s, the bhadralok, perhaps under the influence of Western political impulse, began to display a concern for workers; but this still replicated relations of dominance and subordination which subsisted between managers and workers. Managers sometimes prided themselves on a paternalistic interest, which infantilized workers, treating them with 'fairness' but 'firmness'. Managers embodied authority, and in the event of grievances, anger would be directed against them; and they did not hesitate to assault, and even beat to death, recalcitrant workers. Chakrabarty cites one nineteenth-century engineer who was fined fifty rupees for beating a labourer to death.

The industrial dynamism of Calcutta was sustained by the workers in the jute mills, overwhelmingly male, and the burden of these in turn was borne by women and children working for the most part in the rural economy. Women supported male migrants who, even if they retained only a few bighas of land, had a buffer against absolute destitution. These female workforces performed largely unpaid labour or labour paid in kind—gathering fuel and fodder, making dung cakes; in agriculture, sowing, reaping, weeding, threshing; selling ghee, curd and fish. With growing industrialism many poor rural families saw the work of women—in spinning and rice husking—increasingly passed over to mills. But women rarely occupied even one-fifth of the jobs in the jute mills.

Most city employment for women was in domestic service, the carrying of earth and bricks, sweeping, retailing, ancillary artisanal occupations (pottery and textiles) and prostitution. Women rarely migrated alone into the city, unless all possibility of sustenance had been exhausted in the village, or unless they were barren, widows or 'truant' women who had violated caste or kin rules.

Women provided up to half the necessities of the household, although their work was constantly devalued. The "wages of jute were insufficient to maintain a family in the city, or even a man in the city and a family in the village" (Sen, 1999). Most workers were in debt, and moneylenders would queue up outside the mill on payday.

Although many strikes occurred in the jute mills, there was no enduring sense of solidarity. Militancy was brief and intense, but soon passed. Trade unions rose and fell, and depended—just as in the garment factories—upon the charisma and power of this or that leader. There was no organization, no constitution, which led to splits and factions, breakaway groups that were largely ineffective.

Thus, while the bhadralok came to form a distinctively identifiable class, the labouring poor, although a majority, remained divided and isolated. If poverty gave the workers a common identity, the sense of solidarity was always liable to be fractured along communal, caste or linguistic lines. "Calcutta's lower orders were a fragmented lot, owing to linguistic origins (the palanquin-bearers who went on strike in 1817 paralysing the city's transport system were Oriyas) as to regional affiliations and to caste–occupation loyalties" (Bannerjee, 1989). The idea of a self-conscious 'working class', even in the cultural sense, as described by Richard Hoggart in the *Uses of Literacy* (1957), in his native Yorkshire, was rudimentary. What remained strong were traditional values of custom and honour, of dominance and subordination which were rooted in village life; and many people continued to move between city and country without the sense of radical rupture that was forced upon the irreversible migrations of a decayed British peasantry in the early nineteenth century.

It is a uniquely Calcuttan twist that the Communist Party—largely of idealistic bhadralok origin—should come to power only in the last quarter of the twentieth century, at a time when the old industrial base of Calcutta was itself in the process of dissolution, which the workers' party furthered with great bombast and empty rhetoric. The party of the poor and oppressed achieved power only at the moment when that power—in the shape of industrial organization—was wasting away. Its ebb left few traces of a working class, but did reveal once more the human debris of poverty.

A late September Sunday evening in Kolkata. It seems the rain has been falling forever; an air of melancholy pervades a city where nothing remains dry; the clothes in the cupboards are covered with mould, metal utensils are tarnished, the electric light flickers where the damp has penetrated the wires through the plaster. Torrents of water gouge craters in the surface of the road, collect in sagging pools in the canopy of cycle rickshaws, and blur the reflection of the scarlet rear lights of stalled traffic. A funeral procession parts the crowds, a small group of mourners on their way to Neemtalla, men splashing barefoot through the puddles, carrying aloft the body of an old woman in drenched cerements: emblem in the pre-festival moment, despite the dramatic rise in life expectancy in India since independence, of the exile from eternity that is life. I thought of Maria Graham, two hundred years earlier, who wrote in her *Journal of a Residence in India* in 1813, "returning last night from my evening's drive, I passed the English burying ground for the first time. There are many acres covered so thick with columns, urns and obelisks, that there scarcely seems room for another; it is like a city of the dead. It extends on both sides of the road, and you see nothing beyond it; the greater number of them buried here are under five and twenty years of age."

Yet Kolkata seethes with life just before Durga Puja: gorged stores spill promiscuously onto the sidewalk, bolts of damp cloth spread in a lavish splash of crimson and gold, and if there is a synthetic commercialism in the anticipation, perhaps this is because of the spurious goods on sale—flacons of counterfeit perfume, fake brands of wristwatches, falsely labelled shoes and handbags, pirated DVDs, iPods, TVs and mobile phones, the showy desirability of which call out to crowds louder than the cries of salespeople.

A warm damp air spreads kleptomaniac fungal fingers across the stained concrete, penetrating the secure blue-washed interiors where white strip lighting throws a harsh radiance on still frugal utilitarian furniture: a wooden table, metal almirah, a bench with a damp bedroll behind rusty window grilles. The dampness has blistered walls and peeled varnish, rusted ornamental balconies whose cracked masonry threatens to subside at any moment into the crowds beneath.

Although it is only eight o'clock, the homeless are already sleeping on ledges outside shops, on verandahs, in the shelter provided by stone walls, the noiseless slumber of total exhaustion. Men play cards by the light of kerosene lamps, while women are kindling faint orange flames from damp firewood. Vegetable stalls take the earnings of labourers whose families live only a day's work from hunger. The dim streets are peopled by wraiths, sharp-eyed children, lean pickpockets and flashy hustlers, the go-betweens and middlemen of quick sex and fast money, the supplicatory murmur of accomplished beggars. Are these the same people the Company's servants called "importunate vendors of books, sandalwood boxes, fans made of peacock feathers and oriental curiosities"; described as 'servile', 'indolent', 'ingratiating'; "the native who attached himself to me entreating my patronage", the "host of native servants unemployed and on the lookout for a situation"? And are they descendants of millworkers, returning to the mill lines, where women in 'temporary marriages' await them, or to the room they share with half a dozen other men from Bihar, where cooking fires fill the one-room houses with choking smoke, and only sacking on bamboo sticks affords some small privacy? Did the grandparents of today's servants and labourers rise at four in the morning to be in time for the mills, and did they take their children with them as they sewed gunny bags, watching infants who lay on sacking, breathing in fibres of jute, and did they pause in their work to give them the breast? In 1921, one-third of the children of women millworkers were actually born while they were at their machine—a time when for every thousand births in Calcutta, 386 died.

In spite of the great slabs of new apartments, this austere city seems made for the punishment of its inhabitants, guilty of being the inheritors of a defunct prosperity that was never theirs. Hope is no longer inscribed in the archaic Leftism which for a season assumed governance of Kolkata, banished now by the privatized bright lights of a resurgent capitalism: hospitals with names borrowed from classical mythology or a colonial history— Apollo or Gleneagles, advertised on illuminated panels whose muddy reflection shimmers in the waters of the Hooghly; high-rise apartments called Mayfair Towers or Blenheim Heights, malls through which people shuffle in awe and wonderment at exotic brand names.

The taxis, Ambassador cars, giant wasps, smelling faintly of the drivers who spend twenty-four hours in them, sleeping at night with their feet extended from a half-closed window, skid on the tramway tracks and bump on the exposed cobbles of ancient infrastructure; the elevation of a flyover rises like a weal on the face of the wounded city, speeding the traffic jam a further three hundred metres down the road. A music of glass bangles follows the young women who slide like serpents through the tightly packed bodies on the streets.

The decayed splendour of the Raj is barely detectable through crumbling facades, where shrubs and flowers grow out of the cracked masonry. Inside the buildings some of the derelict of the city take shelter, the non-labouring poor, who chase the dragon with a match light beneath a square of silver paper, in places where, only the day before yesterday, according to accounts from long-dead imperial exiles, *khidmatgars*, dressed in white livery, held extravagant dainties high on the flat of their hand, distributing the choicest viands to the glittering midnight assemblies, or serving "tiffin moistened by a glass or two of good claret".

The glare from the shops gashes the gloom with orange and lemon, and illuminates the thin arrows of rain. Shopkeepers sweep out ochre-coloured floodwater, thick as sweet tea, from the dark interiors, while in the slum along the glassy canal, whole families crowd onto a wooden bedstead, waiting for the water to subside. The electricity, taken illegally from loops of cable, has been extinguished by the wet; clothes stick to skin and bone, and sleep is a refuge before another day's livelihood—a group of women squatting before bamboo baskets at the foot of towering mounds of garbage, men renting a portion of the gutter adjacent to the jeweller's shop to prospect for tiny particles of gold, sorting fragments of unconsumed coal from burnt ash and clinker to sell as fuel. Four rough men, dressed in saris, climb into an autorickshaw after their night's work as imaginary women for labourers in the Tangra slaughterhouse.

Kolkata is a city scoured to the bone by the passage through it of so much money, its streets worn conduits of the wealth of others. The toxic dumps of labour camps, informal settlements as the bearers of development call them, sit beside rivers of sewage and the poisonous crimson and silver effluent of factories. The labour of these places gives them the air of penal colonies, where the convicted must expiate the social crime of their poverty, without hope of remission or release. Ragpickers here have a symbolic role in a West Bengal where even the social fabric is frayed, urchins and young girls, bony women and lean old men pluck at the remains of clothing, textiles, garments, apparel, stuff to be reused, darned and stitched, or synthetic materials to be burnt for fuel, and which smoulder as they are reduced to a pool of dark liquid.

Waves of modernization break over the city, in a work of constant displacement and eviction: ancient counting houses are disappearing, where flimsy invoices fluttered on rusty spikes, and squeaky ceiling fans, whiskery with old cobwebs and lamps dim with dust shed their pale light on greasy desks in rooms where the day never penetrated, and ancient hierarchies lingered and clerks received their tea in clay vessels. In their place are shimmering screens from a distant elsewhere, the shadowless lighting and rubberized floors, the indestructible plant life that has known no other climate than that of the artificially cooled air and the electronic hum of a knowledge culture that produces its own castes of knowingness and ignorance. The mournful middle-class elderly, with mouldy black umbrellas, slide on the algae spreading its green slime in treacherous puddles, while their wives, pinched and graceful in handwoven saris, issue instructions to elderly maidservants on whom they have become utterly dependent; and the young men with American accents sit through the night in narrow cubicles, guiding puzzled Westerners through the arcana of the service sector, and women with degrees in engineering and public administration try to explain to their parents why they are working and their sons-in-law are changing nappies.

But nooks and crannies of the city continue to shelter remnants of the past. Gracie is the great-granddaughter of an officer "from Epsom". At seventy-six, with her meticulous English and harrowing cough, she is still working as a telephonist, to keep herself and her eighty-four-year-old husband. There are other lives of genteel poverty, like those of the Anglo-Indian women in the old age home on Lenin Sarani, who went to Britain in the 1950s, and were so shocked by the rudeness, the immorality and chill welcome of the British that they couldn't wait to get back to Calcutta. These are the women of whom the memsahibs, such as Emma Roberts, said: "The English language has degenerated in the possession of the 'country-born'; their pronunciation is

short and disagreeable, and they usually place the accent on the
wrong syllable … the mother, or rather father-tongue has lost all
its strength and beauty…"

Kolkata remains the site of perpetual crimes against its
people. Impoverished by the predations of the East India
Company, straitened and repressed by Victorian Puritanism,
nourished by the exaltations of freedom fighters, dominated for
three decades by an austere and bureaucratic Left, and now, ruled
by the unmerciful forces of globalism. Traces of all these remain:
elderly servants of the British, regretting the vanished discipline
of colonial administrators, embittered dreamers of a freedom,
fought for with such passion and self-sacrifice, which has reached
only the rich, officials monitoring the most trivial infringements
of a labyrinthine code of regulations, while extortionists and big-
time criminals ride freely in their Mercedes to gated colonies
located in a new Kolkata of fantasy with aristocratic names
like Blenheim Heights, Chelsea Towers or Marlborough Green.
Elderly babus with dhoti held between thumb and forefinger,
silvery stubble on their cheeks, pick their way through the offal
in the gutter, returning home to indifferent grandchildren: it was
all to have been so different, for they had pictured themselves
surrounded by loving descendants, who would listen eagerly
to stories of heroism against the imperialists, the bomb at the
racecourse and the burning of British goods; but the heads of the
young turn aside, drawn to the eerie light of the TV screen and its
urgent promises of tomorrow, which have eclipsed the memories
of yesterday.

It is a city of apprentices in deprivation too: students from
Odisha and the North East, young men waiting for the arranged
marriage and the unarranged labour, running between rumours
of work, carrying their tattered biodata, the cybercafé and the
porn video clip their only road to participation in a global
economy. A city of security guards, summoned into existence
by a class of people whose possessions have made them feel

unsafe, half-educated country boys in uniforms, midway between servitude and officialdom; what do they dream of in the twelve-hour vigil patrolling the stone corridor or the gate of the compound, opening and closing the glass door to the jewel house, with its ugly clusters of gold nestling on velvety imitations of the necks of privilege? A city of maidservants, travelling into the city by train before dawn, or sleeping on a mat in the kitchen, listening for the cry in the night of the mistress who has forgotten where she is and whose identity has also been eroded by the mildew of too many monsoons.

The image of impoverishment and squalor has pursued the city through the years, and was reinforced in the twentieth century by writers such as V.S. Naipaul, Günter Grass and film-maker Louis Malle. The long communist years saw neglect of the city and the extinction of its old industrial base, and then an effort to renew its economy by attracting the IT sector, outsourced call centres and back-office work for international entities, financial services and utilities. The name was changed to Kolkata in 2001; and a measure of vitality has been restored, but this is once more primarily in the area of real estate. Great stone menhirs of apartments have displaced slum populations; projects with idealized artists' impressions of the final structures look balefully over polluted canals, a threat to the poor who, although scarcely diminished in number, have nevertheless been forced into a more restricted part of the city area. Kolkata has ceded to Mumbai, Bangalore and Delhi the economic power which has continued to drain away in step with other decaying cities in the old imperial heartlands of Britain.

By 1911, when the British moved the capital to Delhi, Calcutta had already passed the height of its prosperity, and its fate was a slow subsidence throughout the next third of a century. It became a worldwide emblem of intractable urban poverty. This was reinforced by the Bengal famine of 1943, in which an estimated 3 million Bengalis died and new waves of dispossessed people sought asylum in Calcutta. Its association with deprivation persisted with the flow of refugees after the partition of 1947, when East Bengal became the eastern province of Pakistan. This was given a further impetus by the great shift of population that came during and after the Liberation War of Bangladesh in 1971.

Dignity of a kind was restored to the poor of West Bengal with the election of the communist government in 1977, and although its rule was contested by extreme-Left Naxalites and social disturbance, it galvanized the hinterland with its land reforms; and the benefits to former landless, sharecroppers and marginal farmers earned the government a gratitude that saw it returned to power for over three decades. Rural crowds were conveyed regularly into the city, where they shouted themselves hoarse and waved their fists at the impassively decaying imperial structures of the city; while the well-to-do complained bitterly about the traffic jams and the inconvenience of a city possessed, even for a day or so, by skinny and ragged militants who, if they chose, might commit who knew what mischiefs. One consequence of the thirty-year rule of the Left was that the existing industries in Calcutta were closed down or moved out of the city, creating a belief that West Bengal was irretrievably sliding towards bottomless impoverishment. Amit Chaudhuri (2013) evokes the dying breath of the Leftist culture, shortly before the election of Mamata Banerjee's Trinamool Congress in 2011:

> The eighties confirmed Calcutta's economic decline under the Left Front government, its (to use the word Joyce once used of Dublin) 'paralysis'; but they also announced that the sort of lyricism Calcutta represented, with its central paradox—that life and the imagination would hover most palpably over decay and dereliction—was now unviable… [Calcutta's] long history and aura of failure, cherished and even metamorphosed into something vital by the Bengali imagination, ceased to be intellectually or artistically instructive or illuminating. Without

the transforming effect of imagination, decay is just decay, despair plain despair. That is what happened to Calcutta in the eighties.

But the poor continued to dominate the landscape of Calcutta, both as humanitarian catastrophe and social blight; and it was under nominally communist administration that they were put *back in their place*, that is, in the invisible spaces between the construction boom that followed liberalization of the Indian economy in 1991. For the past twenty years the poor have been in retreat; not necessarily numerically, but the physical spaces they occupy have been more and more constricted, so that veils have been drawn over their presence, a vast stone burka of concrete and brick. Extensive new 'colonies', apartment complexes, living spaces have expanded from Salt Lake and stridden across the city, compressing the poor, confining them in slums and ghettos that are scarcely detectable from the traffic jams on expressways and circular roads that gird the city. And a new renaissance has been declared in Kolkata, which coincided with the last days of the Left and the first non-Left government in three decades: IT, biotechnology and call centres have replaced the tanneries, oily workshops and engineering sheds, while Tangra, district of the tanneries, many of them run by the significant Chinese minority in the city, has seen an astonishing resurgence in the form of Chinese restaurants, perhaps the most incongruous of the multiple metamorphoses in the city.

But, again and again, the past impinges on the present. In Kolkata, the wheel turns, not the charkha, but the slower revolution of the years, so that ancient colonial voices are reincarnated in the imperious orders of the wealthy, who have inherited both idiom and bearing from their former aristocratic masters.

The places of public resort and amusement in Calcutta are the course, the ball-room and the theatre. The course in a fine broad road, which leads out to the suburbs of the city, and on which the fashionable figure in the evening; here, landaus, coaches, chariots, curricles, phaetons etc., press forward in closed ranks, full of gentlemen and ladies well-dressed; on every side you behold equipages, horses, ostrich feathers and dandies ... resembl[ing] Hyde Park, wanting only the cool breezes of England to make it equally agreeable... Public balls are given at the Town hall ... [where] the lustre of chandeliers, dress, address, dancing and music animate the dullest tempers. The public dances are in an elegant style, and attended by the fashionable and accomplished, as persons in humble circumstances seldom make their appearance there (Huggins, 1824).

In the gilded salons and marble halls of the rich, in the hotels which reconstruct the palaces of the Raj, parties and balls evoke the fluttering of fans and the dancing of quadrilles, the swirl of the waltz and fumes of Madeira and claret from Europe, the glint of spurs on the parquet and the flirtation on the stairs, the sumptuous table and the thoroughbred horse—evocations of two centuries ago are brought to vivid life in the contemporary scene, so that it is possible to mistake today's ruling elite for the alien oppressors of the day before yesterday. These are the inheritors of the Raj, whose lordly progression through time follows the same trajectory as their sometime rulers.

The same observer quoted above—a former indigo planter, writing of Calcutta in 1824, and referring to the 'writers', employees of the Company—says:

These young gentlemen, generally the sons of respectable families, have received the rudiments of a good education at home; perhaps the height of their ambition and extent of their means in England was to purchase a dandy coat and strut upon the flags; or on a journey to the country, to travel in a mail-coach. But in India, how altered!—Arabs, English blood-horses, Pegu ponies, curricles and phaetons come prancing before them with most bewitching fascination. Their pay, 300 rupees a month, is quite sufficient to keep them respectable, but not at all sufficient to purchase all these fine things.

Of course, today's privileged young make the journey in the opposite direction—to California, London or New York—but their conspicuous consumption is identical. Only the technologies and venues have changed: the fast cars and hand-crafted shoes, tailored suits and designer brands; shopping malls and luxury hotels, international sporting events, first nights and parties of a less decorous nature than those at which exiled beauties hoped to ensnare a military husband. Of course, their lives are not shadowed by cholera, typhus, malaria or the unknown sicknesses of early nineteenth-century Bengal; but they are, perhaps, prey to other fevers: the rage to experience everything, drugs, alcohol, the dangers of fast cars on slow roads, the morbid passions of excess.

What this gilded youth of a country emancipated not only from alien rule, but equally from the constraints of tradition, have in common with their forebears is a revulsion against all who do not share their way of life, the excluded majority, their imitators and aspirants to the style of living to which they have become so swiftly addicted. Just as the servant classes of the Raj were treated with disdain, so all those who, like the bearers of palanquins of cosseted European flesh, carry aloft, by their labour or service, the privilege of the contemporary rich, are objects of similar arrogance. Confides Mrs Fenton (1901) to her journal:

> I had declined the service of Mrs Cleland's ayah, who with her attendant of low caste, always appeared to stand at your side to *put on* and *take off* your clothes—a ceremony which nothing could ever induce me to comply with. I could not endure their hands about me; the oil which forms a part of their toilet, the pawn [a primitive imperial transliteration of paan] they eat,

renders them so offensive that I could not bear them in my room; they are so insatiably curious; they try to make it appear they are indispensable to your comfort, and follow a thousand contrivances to keep always in your way, and a perpetual watch on what you do. They attend you with the most disgusting servility if they have any end to attain, then perhaps decamp with whatever they can strip you of.

Their reflections on the characteristics of those who serve them accurately prefigure the prejudices of today's indigenous employers of domestic labour; so much so that it often seems that the Indian middle class speaks of its subordinates with voices from beyond the grave, the cadences and tones of long-defunct memsahibs. They dilate on the indolence and idleness of those in their service, their incorrigible dishonesty and unknowable mentality. They are unreliable, inert and wanting in initiative, unless it is to steal your jewellery or to empty a whisky bottle negligently left on the side table. Careless and incapable of carrying out the most elementary instructions, they have no sense of loyalty and take not the remotest pride in their work.

What Henry Roberdeau wrote of the British rulers anticipates the sensibility of the rulers of contemporary India: "The Character of an Englishman undergoes some change by a residence in the East. An Englishman in India is proud and tenacious, he feels himself a Conqueror amongst a vanquished people, and looks down with some degree of Superiority on all below him." He goes on: "Independent of the climate, we could not descend to any manual labour, for almost all of us being in high official situations it is necessary to support a kind of Dignity in the Eyes of the Natives, which would be entirely lost were we to make such an exertion."

Even the consumers in the malls, in thrall to the names with which they, like the goods they purchase, have been branded, have been here before: the women crowding over the box-wallas with their trumpery or venturing into the market—only then, they were enchanted by the produce of India; while India's rich are under the spell of the same showy merchandise emanating from the manufactories of their former masters. Mrs Fenton, in ecstasies over the products she found in Burra Bazaar in 1828—the native bangles, necklaces of coral and cornelian, the specimens of boxes, lacquer work, playthings, shells of all possible variety and hues, miniature casts of native gods and sacred animals, feathers, flowers, china, silks, chintz—declares she would like to fill a wagon indiscriminately with all the treasures on offer, which would amuse her for fully a year. How, it might be wondered, does she differ from her true descendants, who are, as well as the inheritors of independence, "a class of persons Indian in blood and colour, but English (or perhaps, now American) in tastes and opinions" foreseen by Macaulay almost two hundred years ago?

The first attempt by the British to divide Bengal occurred in 1905, when Lord Curzon devised plans for the breaking of Bengal, Bihar and Orissa, which had constituted a single state since 1765. Although that was the time of the greatest prosperity of industrial Calcutta (it was estimated that more than 20 per cent of Calcutta's economy was by that time industrial), East Bengal, predominantly Muslim, was mostly rural and the proposed capital, Dacca, still a somnolent provincial town. The proposal was seen as an act of aggression against Indian nationalism, which was more assertive and passionate in Bengal than in the rest of India, and it had the effect of uniting the people, and led to mass disturbances and demonstrations and the Swadeshi movement, which boycotted British goods. In 1911, the capital was moved by the British to Delhi, and Bengal was reunited. The partition of 1947 that accompanied India's independence from British rule split up Bengal again, East Bengal becoming the eastern province of newly formed Pakistan, and finally, with the Liberation War in 1971, the new nation of Bangladesh, with Dacca as capital.

Travelling the short distance between Kolkata and Dhaka now provides a sharp shock. It isn't only the religious cultures that divide the two great cities. Between them there is a curious estrangement, a sense of familial alienation: both sides maintain a virtuous aloofness, as though each were convinced of being the injured party in a quarrel between kinsfolk.

The most obvious difference between the two is the age profile of the people. Kolkata has become a middle-aged city, with an increasing proportion of elderly. Dhaka, by contrast, teems with exuberant, and sometimes dangerously volatile, youth. Kolkata has seen its best days, and indeed has not been averse to seeing the remnants of them fall into ruins. The energy of Dhaka is absent from the resigned enervation with which the people of Kolkata pursue their daily business. The material fabric of Kolkata speaks of the past, stone tenements and imperial relics suggest the heavy burden of time; while the buildings of Dhaka, raw, functional, unadorned, garment factories, malls, new blocks of luxury flats, suggest the fast fortunes of money in a hurry.

In both cities, public spaces are dominated by men. But Dhaka, for a brief period each day—in the early morning, and again late at night—becomes a city of women; a continuous procession of young girls and women, luxuriant, multicoloured with only here and there a dark burka, transform the landscape and kick up clouds of dust with their chappals on the margin of the road, before they are swallowed up in the factories which claim their energy twelve or fourteen hours a day.

Sometimes, it seems, Kolkata and Dhaka have changed identities. Dhaka, a placid backwater at the time of partition, is now a restless, overcrowded metropolis; whereas Kolkata, the sometime byword for uncontrolled city growth, the great wound of Bengal through which its wealth poured, is now stagnant, sedate, melancholy in its decline.

Dhaka still attracts its eager migrants from all over Bangladesh, much as Calcutta was at one time the destination of rural migrants from Bengal, Bihar, Orissa and the North West Provinces, drawn to the jute mills, service and the port. Kolkata's population has stabilized, although waves of economic refugees from Bangladesh continue to find shelter in its Muslim slums.

Kolkata is still richer than Dhaka, and has a more ample and established infrastructure: many middle-class people from Bangladesh go to Kolkata for medical consultations and some— who cannot afford the US or the UK—go there for higher education. Kolkata is a more settled city, while Dhaka still gives the impression of an extensive and improvised labour camp. In any case, the rickshaw drivers, garment workers, labourers and domestic servants of Dhaka are still closer to their rural origins. Nearly everyone in Dhaka still identifies with a village or region. The people of Kolkata have become more truly urban; and their dream is no longer of the countryside or a return to their roots. They are looking for a more secure place in the city, and although land ownership still tugs at the heart, they perceive the social and economic advancement of their children to be a result of modernization. Paradoxically, Kolkata appears more *enclosed*, despite having been laid open to the world by an extractive imperialism. It is as though it has turned its back upon the rural hinterland, as though agriculture and food production were beneath the dignity of its pretensions to technological supremacy.

Kolkata also sees itself as the true guardian of Bengali culture, and regards Dhaka as an upstart without roots. In other words, Dhaka is a product of contemporary globalization, whereas Kolkata sprang from an older version, the global imperium of Britain. Perhaps because so much of the wealth of Bengal flowed through Kolkata it exudes a sense of exhaustion, even of indifference, towards the world. Dhaka is now the extractive conduit, for labour as for garments, the more so since millions of its people abroad now sustain whole areas of the country with remittances that amounted to $11 billion in 2012, according to the World Bank.

Kolkata is less hospitable than Dhaka, not so ready to open its doors or its heart to strangers. The people of Dhaka say Kolkata is a stingy place. "If they invite you, they say, 'Come to our house having eaten', they don't want to give you anything," is a common perception of a Dhaka that prides itself on its hospitality, even though so many are without resources. And there is no slum dwelling so poor that people will not somehow borrow some teacups and provide a packet of biscuits to offer some small welcome to others. Kolkata appears to have little curiosity about outsiders, while Dhaka is all smiles and eagerness; of course, the smile may have ulterior motives, but its absence in Kolkata is remarkable. Kolkata has become like all long-established cities: crowds who do not see the individuals within them; dogged, weary, anxious only to get home at the end of the day. Kolkata gives the impression that it has seen everything; it knows the world and expects little good of it. The young people of Dhaka still marvel at the vast, congested monstrosity of their city, in which their dreams are still intact. The dreams of Kolkata are more staid, elderly, less ambitious, befitting the "abandoned, unimportant city" Amit Chaudhuri maintains it has become.

Kolkata was neglected by the long years of Leftist rule; its rich heritage offers the spectacle of moth-eaten elegance, probably too far gone even to be successfully marketed by its rulers. Dhaka has the vitality of youth.

Both cities are oppressive in their way. The long shadow of Kolkata's past is an almost tangible weight over the city, with its memories of famine, struggle and impoverishment. With street names like British India Street, Free School Street and Ripon Road (only recently changed to Abdul Hameed Street, Mirza Ghalib Street and Muzzaffar Ahmad Street, respectively), and thoroughfares that still commemorate the identity of former colonial functionaries or international historical figures— Shakespeare and Lenin—Kolkata has been overtaken by the lassitude of its own history.

Dhaka has nothing of this. But its pollution, the indiscipline of its traffic, the tension and political violence, the relentless exploitation of its workers severely diminish its attractions. If Kolkata exhibits the melancholy sobriety of a maturity that no longer expects much from life, it is difficult to believe that Dhaka's exuberance will, with time, yield greater satisfactions than a city which, however long ago it now appears, was the centre of a vibrant culture and a major source of opposition to imperial dominance.

Part VI

Industrialism

In the early years of the East India Company, the British took the unrivalled materials produced in Bengal—the muslin of Dhaka, the silk of Murshidabad—and introduced them to a wider world. Although the materials were greatly sought after, their distribution had the misfortune of being introduced into Britain in the period immediately preceding the industrial era.

From the earliest years of the East India Company, there had been complaints in Britain against the import of Indian fabrics. The impact of the variety of Indian textiles is attested by the number of Hindi words that entered the language: calico, gingham, taffeta, chintz, khaki, pyjama, seersucker, satin, shawl, etc. As early as 1678, a pamphlet was published by woollen manufacturers, called *The Ancient Trades Decayed and Repaired Again*. By 1700, dissatisfaction was so great that Acts were passed which prohibited the introduction of printed calicoes for domestic use, either as apparel or furniture, under a penalty of £2,000 on the wearer or seller. Cotton goods were then smuggled into the country, in defiance of one of the first trade barriers erected by a country which subsequently became the principal proponent of the virtues of 'free trade'.

But not yet. Britain protected its own manufacturing system in the early days of industrialism. If it had not done so, Indian fabrics would never have been displaced by Manchester cottons. Britain's conversion to 'free trade' coincided with its capacity to impose it coercively upon the world: by the 1820s, the weavers of India had been reduced to misery, and no longer posed any 'competition' to Lancashire.

The fashion for wearing Indian calicoes and printed linen became a source of serious disturbances in 1719. A mob of several thousand Spitalfields weavers paraded through the streets of the city, attacking all women they could find wearing Indian calicoes or linens and sousing them with ink, *aqua fortis*, and what were, perhaps euphemistically, called 'other fluids'.

In 1720, an Act was passed prohibiting altogether the use in Britain of "any garment or apparel whatsoever, of any painted, printed or dyed calicoes, in or about any bed, chair, cushion, window curtain or any other sort of household stuff or furniture". In 1774, a law was passed sanctioning the manufacture of purely cotton goods, but still prohibiting the import of such goods, officially protecting the infant industry from foreign competition. Throughout the eighteenth century, improvements in machinery, and the availability of cotton from plantations in the US, gave a powerful impetus to the cotton industry within Britain: in 1733, Kay's flying shuttle; 1767, Hargreaves' spinning jenny; 1785, Cartwright's power loom. British cotton manufacturers also later argued for the imposition of higher duties on the imported cotton goods which threatened them, thus effectively excluding them from, and protecting, the English market.

It was the controversy over calicoes that presented in an acute form to people and parliaments the choice between protectionism and free trade, and ultimately, after a protectionist phase, led to the adoption of those doctrines of free enterprise and laissez-faire, which dominated English theory and practice for many generations. By the mid nineteenth century, highly contrived 'competition' from British manufacturers was significantly responsible for the decay of Indian handicrafts. The quality of Indian goods remained supreme, but in the question of price, the mass-produced, machine-made goods displaced local production; a process assisted by the fascination of a newly emerging Indian middle class for all things foreign and exotic. The imposition of tariffs also protected the nascent industries of Britain, since Indian goods could have been sold at half the price of fabric made in England. India became increasingly a supplier of raw cotton to the Lancashire industry; while jute from Bengal provided over half the workforce of Dundee in Scotland with employment, making the packaging for imported and exported goods; and by the last decade of the 19th century, Dundee had a virtual global monopoly of jute processing (Alvares, 1991).

The import of Indian cotton goods to Britain reached a peak in 1798. Even thirty years after the transformation of textile production in England, Indian textiles remained cheaper than machine-made goods. In 1813, Indian cotton goods were 50–60 per cent cheaper than those made in England; in consequence, the latter were protected by duties on the former of 70–80 per cent of their value. A century later, in 1898, India was receiving £28 million worth of imported cotton goods from Britain, while its exports—mainly raw cotton—came to about £14 million. Cotton was no longer available to weavers in India.

There were some voices of dissent. Critics of British commercial activity in India were largely animated by outrage that a 'Christian' or 'civilized' country should exploit its subject peoples. Robert Montgomery Martin, in his précis (1838) of Dr Francis Buchanan's epic survey of Bengal conducted between 1807 and 1814, states:

We have done everything possible to impoverish still further the miserable beings subject to the cruel selfishness of English commerce... Under the pretence of free trade, England has compelled the Hindoos to receive the products of the steam-looms of Lancashire, Yorkshire, Glasgow etc. at mere nominal duties; while the hand-wrought manufactures of Bengal and Behar, beautiful in fabric, durable in wear, have had heavy and almost prohibitory duties imposed on their importation into England; so Birmingham, Staffordshire and domestic wares have ruined the native artisan of the East, who endeavoured to compete in their accumulation of wealth and steam-power in England.

The plunder of Bengal by the British, and the erasure of the most skilled muslin weaving, should not be understood simply as an assault upon what they regarded as 'lesser people'; for nothing the British practised in the extensive territories they annexed all over the world had not already been tried and tested within the British Isles, or at least, was taking place at the same time as ideological and social experiments abroad. It would scarcely be an exaggeration to say that the imperial adventure was a projection on to a wider world of policies of which the people of Britain had been the first victims. Later, of course, the labouring poor would benefit from the incursions of their 'betters' into the lands of others, but not before they had been the object of tests and trials, the 'success' of which emboldened their rulers to pursue them in the remote corners of Empire.

Evictions of the poor, enclosure of common lands, famine, the destruction of cultures (the clan system in Scotland), the bloody penal code, use of the gallows for trivial offences, transportation or exile as deterrent, both to criminals and to dissent—the story enacted within the British Isles would be repeated wherever the British took their buccaneering spirit and their piratical enterprise.

In 1746, after the Jacobite rising (the last attempt to restore the House of Stuart to the English and Scottish thrones) was crushed at Culloden in Scotland, the English soldiery set out across the Highlands, looting and killing, leaving a trail of devastation. Not content with removing the threat to the throne, they laid waste the landscape, scattered the people and prepared the way for the destruction of the Highland clan system. They ruined a culture which they perceived as barbaric, backward and brutal. In order to ensure the extinction of that way of life, the government in London enacted vengeful legislation that struck at the heart of that way of life: a law was passed against the wearing of Highland dress: the tartan plaid and kilt were banned. The skills of weaving patterns and making dyes from the herbs of the hills fell into disuse. "The clans were no more, their true identity had gone with the broadsword and their chiefs... The banning of their dress took from the clans their pride and sense of belonging to a unique people. The abolition of the hereditary jurisdictions of their chiefs, which followed, destroyed the political and social system that had held them together" (Prebble, 1962). The Act of Proscription of 1747 banned the wearing of the tartan, the teaching of Gaelic, the right of Highlanders to their ceremonial gatherings and the playing of bagpipes in Scotland.

In the late eighteenth and early nineteenth centuries, the Highlands were subjected to further violence. Landlords of the estates systematically drove the local people from their homes in order to replace them with more profitable sheep. These 'clearances' chased people from their ancestral dwellings; and many took to emigration ships bound for the colonies, or went to settle in rocky coastal areas. The crofters of the Highlands, proud and independent, had been small cultivators, with a little arable land and pastures for cows. The most brutal evictions occurred in Sutherland, the northernmost part of the country. Of those who boarded ships for North America, many suffered from typhus and cholera, and never reached their destination.

Since the reign of Elizabeth I, former common and 'waste' land had been enclosed, partly for sheep and the wool trade, and partly to create or expand estates. This process accelerated in the time preceding the industrial revolution, much of it ostensibly in pursuit of agricultural 'improvements', but also to make parks and hunting land for the aristocracy, and not insignificantly, for those who had made fortunes with the East India Company. By these actions of privilege, many poor villagers lost their rights to graze animals, to collect fuel, gather wild fruits and nuts, hunt rabbits and birds, and to cultivate the small strip of land which augmented their meagre income as agricultural labourers. They were denied access to small resources which made the difference between bare sufficiency and hunger. Most land was enclosed by Acts of Parliament, introduced by MPs on behalf of individual beneficiaries of the proposed enclosure, against which the poor had little opportunity to protest; and which they were not well enough informed to contest.

During the eighteenth century, draconian laws, mostly relating to property, turned more and more offences into crimes punishable by death. Robert Hughes, in his account of the convict colonies of Australia (1986), wrote:

> The most notorious of these laws, passed in the 1720s, and known as the Waltham Black Act, passed by the Commons without a murmur of dissent, prescribed the gallows for over two hundred offences, in various permutations. One could be hanged for burning a house or a hut, a standing rick of corn or an insignificant pile of straw; for poaching a rabbit, for breaking down the 'head or mound' of a fish-pond, or even cutting down an ornamental shrub; for appearing on a high road with a sooty face.

Public hangings were festivals of death, which the ruling classes believed would serve as a deterrent spectacle to potential wrongdoers, even though the ceremonial route from Newgate prison to Tyburn gallows often turned into a macabre fair, where the crowds expressed their sympathy with the condemned. However repressive the legislation, crime continued to increase; criminals were detained in 'hulks', disused ships lying offshore near the great seaports. Even these became inadequate to hold their cargo of misery, and this led to the introduction of transportation: between 1788 and 1868 at least 160,000 'felons' were consigned to the dungeons of memory at the other end of the world.

Transportation also encompassed a wider range of political 'criminals'. The first ship to carry political prisoners, members of the Society of United Irishmen, was from Ireland in 1795. Many more went in the wake of the Rebellion of 1798. Hundreds arrested during the agricultural riots of the 1830s, including the Dorsetshire 'Tolpuddle Martyrs', guilty of an attempt to set up an agricultural trade union in 1834 (they were charged with uttering 'unlawful oaths'), were also forced into exile. Transportation failed either to abate crime or suppress radicalism—facts that did not interfere with the imperial way of exiling, criminalizing or jailing dissenters, freedom fighters and other perceived threats to British rule in the wider world. Efforts were continuously made by the British to stigmatize those fighting for liberation as terrorists. As late as the Second World War, during the Quit India movement, more than 80,000 people were imprisoned, to prevent their activities from disrupting the war effort.

The common experience of the poor of the British Isles and the colonial subjects was noted throughout the nineteenth century. John Cobden (1853) is explicit. Writing of India, he said:

> The burden imposed upon the Hindoos are precisely of the character and extent of those that have reduced Ireland to poverty and her people to slavery. Besides the enormous rents, which are sufficient of themselves to dishearten the tillers of the soil, the British authorities seem to have exhausted invention in devising taxes. So dear a price to live was never paid by any people except the Irish.

The city to benefit the most, industrially, from imperial protectionist tactics was Manchester. The population of Manchester (with adjacent Salford) was only 25,000 in 1772, just after famine had partly emptied Dacca and Murshidabad. In Britain, the production of cotton had already overtaken the historic staple, wool, even though ships of the East India Company in their voyages to Asia had been hopefully stocked with British woollen goods, for which they, perhaps not unsurprisingly, found negligible demand in the tropical regions for which they were bound.

By 1800, 95,000 people were living in Manchester, a time when Watt's rotary steam engine had been installed in over five hundred mills and factories in Britain. The first quarter of the nineteenth century saw the erection of many of the mills, imposing and ornamented, which were to dominate the landscape for the next century and a half, including the Redhill Street Mill. This Tocqueville described as "a place where some 1,500 workers, labouring sixty-nine hours a week, with an average wage of eleven shillings, and where three quarters of the workers are women and children". The mills were the wonder of the world: six or eight storeys high, with iron frames, cast-iron columns and sheds with six hundred or more looms; furnished with gaslighting as early as 1810. They soared over the slums, houses packed close to sites of labour to minimize the energy wasted by operatives in travelling to and fro: most people could be at work within two or three minutes of leaving home. The great buildings shed their

chlorotic light on polluted canals and waterways glittering with
waste chemicals—much as today's factories of Dhaka tower over
and illuminate with their even, white light the tenements and
huts of the people who work in them. The Manchester–Liverpool
railway was opened in 1830, to expedite exports; and from here,
many of the cotton goods were dispatched to flood the market
of Bengal. Tocqueville wrote of Manchester in 1835: "A sort of
black smoke covers the city. Under this half-daylight 300,000
human beings are ceaselessly at work. The homes of the poor
are scattered haphazard around the factories. From this filthy
sewer pure gold flows. In Manchester civilized man is turned
back almost into a savage."

Angus Reach, a journalist writing in the *Morning Chronicle* in
1849, described it thus:

> The traveller by railway is made aware of his approach to the
> great northern seats of industry by the dull leaden-coloured
> sky, tainted by thousands of ever-smoking chimneys, which
> broods over the distance... You shoot by town after town—
> the outlying satellites of the great cotton metropolis. They
> have all similar features—they are all little Manchesters.
> Huge, shapeless, unsightly mills, with their countless rows
> of windows, their towering shafts, their jets of waste steam
> continually puffing in panting gushes from the brown grimy
> wall. Some dozen or so of miles so characterized, you enter the
> Queen of the cotton cities—and then amid smoke and noise,
> and the hum of never ceasing toil, you are borne over the roofs
> to the terminus platform. You stand in Manchester.

There is a smoky brown sky overhead—smoky brown
streets all round long piles of warehouses, many of them pillared
with stately fronts—great grimy mills, the leviathans of ugly
architecture, with their smoke-pouring shafts. There are streets
of all kinds—some with glittering shops and vast hotels, others
grim and little frequented—formed of rows and stacks of

warehouses; many mean and distressingly monotonous vistas of uniform brick houses.

The operatives of Manchester are frequently described as 'stunted' or 'stooping'. Their complexions are 'sallow' or 'sickly', their clothing 'fustian' trousers for men, shawls and skirts for women, clogs for both. No greater contrast could be imagined than with the present-day workers of Dhaka, who flood the streets with their vivid colours, their radiant youth and vitality. The regimented tramp of feet on the cobblestones of Lancashire is different from the noiseless and graceful movement of young girls going to their place of work in Bangladesh. Perhaps it is because the certain misery of the early nineteenth century has been exchanged for the—perhaps deceptive—smile of hope in a century that promises so much more to its workers, and certainly assures them a longevity unknown to the weavers of Lancashire.

By the 1850s, with over one hundred cotton mills, Manchester was the greatest industrial city in the world. By 1913, it processed about two-thirds of the world's cotton. The city's population continued to grow from about 400,000 in 1851 to 563,000 in 1891 and to three-quarters of a million in 1921. The languor and depletion of the Mughal cities of Bengal must have offered a wretched contrast to the dynamic energy of Manchester in the period from the mid-nineteenth to early twentieth centuries.

It is difficult now to imagine the desolation of Dacca following the loss of its export handloom fabrics, particularly if we look at the present headlong rush into the urban agglomeration. In the early nineteenth century, the inhabited area of Dacca was reduced, and the people of the city were forced back upon subsistence agriculture. It is hard to conceive of the de-urbanizing—or 're-ruralizing'—of what had been a capital city.

We, who have only seen cities grow, can have little idea of the desolation of living places deserted by those to whom they no longer offer refuge or livelihood. How swiftly jungle vegetation must have invaded even brick-built buildings, while strips of woven bamboo were swiftly blown away in the monsoon, and the *mati* dwellings of the people returned to the earth out of which they had been made. How quickly the former settlements of weavers must have been reclaimed by water from the overflowing ponds, clumps of clattering bamboo, palms, arum lilies and reeds. The *Gossypium herbaceum*, the local cotton plant, which was different from the common cotton plant of Bengal, with its long fine staple, softer than other cottons, was neglected, its seeds blown away on the monsoon winds.

"Two-thirds of the vast area of Dacca are filled with ruins, some quite desolate, overgrown with jungle, others yet occupied ... [only about] 300,000 inhabitants ... yet roost like bats in these old buildings and rear their huts and their desolate gardens..." (Heber, 1829).

The town presents symptoms of decay corresponding with the diminished population, and reduced circumstances of its present inhabitants. A great number of houses are unoccupied or in a state of ruin. Drains, ghauts, lanes and bridges are neglected from the want of funds to keep them in repair. The suburbs are overrun with jungle, while the interior of the town is filled with stagnant canals and sinks, containing refuse animal and vegetable matters, which taint the water of neighbouring wells. Disease prevails, as may be supposed, to a great extent, throughout all classes of the community, but especially among the poorer inhabitants in whom it is aggravated by their impoverished diet. It is chiefly dependent however on locality for its development, and has its origin in the unwholesome water and the numerous muddy canals and stagnant pools above mentioned. These sources of malaria are extending widely every year, and whilst impure exhalations thus generated, affect the great body of the people with disease, incurable maladies and infirmities of the most humiliating character, are every where presented to our view in a crowd of wretched, helpless objects, who procure a precarious subsistence by begging in the streets (Taylor, 1840).

Apart from some officials and administrators, the most competent and able people must have long departed. Whole families deserted the city, going in the opposite direction of today's irresistible lure of the choking megacity. They may have taken a goat, some chickens, a few clay vessels, an *ektara* they had played in moments of relaxation from their intense labour, ruined eyesight and a head full of stories of ruined livelihoods and sudden penury, perhaps also some unsold specimen of the rare fabric which had been the wonder of the world. Where did they find a homestead in the countryside, how did they adapt to the coarser weaving of the country people, what feelings of injury had they suffered from the decline in trade and the British desire to protect and expand its own nascent textile industry in Lancashire? What did they say when they first saw the machine-made imported cloth from Britain, what scathing comment did they pass on items untouched by human hands?

Who can imagine their grief that skills which had been passed down generations were no longer required; what happened to the songs and tales they had told as they sat at the looms, producing material fluid as water, diaphanous as the evening mist, flowered like meadows, each design spun from memory, that precious storehouse in which the wisdom of millennia had been stored, the children set to work by a master—a high honour for those selected for such a calling? By what foreign witchcraft had their lives been overturned; what spirits had been sent to call them out of their house into a darkness from which they never returned? What shadowless ghosts, their feet facing backwards, had set them under an enchantment which caused the fabulous fabric they wove to turn to rags?

The baton had been passed—or rather, wrenched out of their hands to be passed—to the people of Lancashire.

Although the commercial prosperity of Dacca had been in a declining state for some time prior to its acquisition by the English, yet there can be no doubt that it received its most severe blow from the introduction of mule twist [machine-spun yarn] in 1785. From 1788 to 1803 is considered the golden age of the cotton trade in Britain, and while her manufactures increased in extent under the magic influence of steam, were improved by mechanical invention and fostered by a protecting duty of 75 per cent, those of Dacca, from this imposition of high duties acting as a virtual prohibition of their importation to England, declined year after year, until at length, they ceased to be an object of commerce... The commercial history of Dhaka presents but a melancholy retrospect. In the space of 30 years, its trade with England, which amounted to many lacs of rupees, became extinct... The manufacture of thread, the occupation in former times of almost every family in the district is now, owing to the comparative cheapness of English thread, almost entirely abandoned, and thus the arts of spinning and weaving, which for ages have afforded employment to numerous industrious population, have in the course of sixty years, passed into other hands that supply the wants not only of foreign nations, but of the rivalled country itself ... many families who were formerly in a state of affluence are now reduced to comparative poverty, while the majority of the people belonging to the lower classes, are from want of work in a very destitute condition, and are glad to procure any employment, *however unsuited to their previous habits*, to enable them to earn a subsistence for themselves and their families (Taylor, 1840, emphasis added).

This was a lesson also being learned in England, particularly in Lancashire, where weaving remained a scattered semi-domestic occupation, as well as a rapidly growing industry. The vast output of yarn from spinning factories increased the material available to the weaver, so that more and more people took up the work. Spinning had become highly mechanized, with the result that yarn was plentiful.

It was said in the last decade of the eighteenth century that "... every lumber-room, even old barns, cart-house and outbuildings of any description were repaired, windows broke through the blank walls, and all were fitted up for loom-shops. This source of making room being at length exhausted, new weavers' cottages with loom-shops rose up in every direction" (Thompson, 1963).

Small farmers and labourers turned to weaving, and a more than modest prosperity was enjoyed by handloom weavers at the very time when their counterparts in Dacca were losing the means of their survival. The houses of British weavers were described as clean and neat, each house was furnished with a clock in a mahogany case, handsome tea services in Staffordshire ware, while many families had their cows or raised pigs. They grew vegetables for home consumption, and exuded a sense of modest contentment.

This well-being was not to last. Wage reductions, particularly during the Napoleonic Wars, reduced both the status and income of handloom weavers. Although the emergence of power looms was blamed, and outbreaks of violence did indeed occur against their use, E.P. Thompson points out that the status of the weavers had been destroyed by 1813, a time when only 2,400 power looms existed in Britain, a number destined to grow a hundredfold by mid-century. Thompson argues that the cheapness of hand labour actually retarded the mechanization of weaving. Because so many had entered the industry, they came to form an army of underemployed labour, unable to prevent continuous depreciation of their wages. The degradation of the cotton weavers of Lancashire (and of the wool weavers in Yorkshire) was swift and brutal. John Fielden, giving evidence to a Parliamentary Committee in 1835, declared that a very great number of the weavers "could not obtain sufficient food of the plainest or cheapest kind; were clothed in rags and ashamed to send their children to Sunday school, had no furniture and in some cases slept on straw; worked not unfrequently sixteen hours a day, were demoralized by cheap spirits, and weakened by undernourishment and ill-health" (Thompson, 1963).

Evidence given to the Select Committee on Emigration in 1827 evokes the position of the handloom weavers in relation to factory power looms. The quality of the article being so nearly the same, and the cost of the manufacture being so much less by the power loom than by the handloom, the question posed to Major Thomas Moody was, "Is it your opinion that hand-loom weaving must soon cease in this country?" He replied, "I think it a fair inference, and that mere cottage hand-loom weaving must give way to the cheaper manufacture by machinery." The same report also conveys a poverty almost as bleak and unendurable as that experienced by the weavers of Bengal, or indeed, the starving of Murshidabad:

Mrs Hulton and myself, in visiting the poor, were asked by a person almost starving to go into a house. We there found on one side of the fire a very old man, apparently dying, on the other side a young man about eighteen with a child on his knee, whose mother had just died and been buried. We were going away from that house, when the woman said 'Sir, you have not seen all.' We went upstairs, and, under some rags, we found another young man, the widower; and on turning down the rags, which he was unable to remove himself, we found another man who was dying, and who did die during the course of the day. I have no doubt that the family were actually starving at the time...

So, the extreme contrast between the desolation of the weavers of Dacca at the turn of the nineteenth century and the long-remembered 'golden age' of the Lancashire handloom weavers gave way to a convergence in their fate, as the brief spell of affluence in Britain was followed by the rapid impoverishment and exploitation of weavers. They were eventually forced to enter—or send their children into—cotton mills. The handloom weavers of Britain numbered about a quarter of a million in the 1820s; thirty years later, these had been reduced to a handful of people who could scarcely subsist on their meagre earnings.

The exodus from the disintegrating cities of Murshidabad and
Dacca in the early 1800s was quite the reverse of the flow of the
people of Britain towards the new manufacturing and mining
settlements of industry.

Did the people undertake the journey back to distant villages
by country boat with few possessions and discarded skills, back
to land unoccupied as a result of depopulation and flooding, in
the coastal areas of the Bay, in places exposed to storms and
cyclones? How swiftly they must have floated downriver on rafts
of palm and banana leaves, debris on the rain-swollen Meghna
or Buriganga, as they sought out villages which had long been
submerged or kinsfolk who had no memory of them, or carved
out land for themselves from overgrown plots abandoned by the
dead.

Taylor (1840) evokes the dereliction of Dhaka. The drenched
landscapes had been reclaimed by edible plants and fruits: arum
and other water roots which had been scarcity food; Indian plum,
guavas and litchis; the jungle *khajoor* (wild date palm) and mango
trees; medicinal herbs, trees the bark and roots of which were
known as remedies for fevers and the spitting of blood, ringworm
and dysentery. Monkeys, house bats and roussettes (fruit bats as
small and brightly coloured as butterflies) flitted in and out of
the thatch, while brushwood covered the tracks and mounds
of earth which alone marked the site of once-populous villages.
Leopards and tigers re-established themselves in the jungle, and
became such a menace that the government offered rewards for
the pelts of tigers that had been killed. Snakes sheltered in the

abandoned dwellings of Dacca, while the wild buffalo and the jackal shared territory with the sunbird and weaverbird, and hunched vultures surveyed tracts of land in which the human voice had been stilled. People, affected by loss and pestilence, returned to "the malaria-haunted hamlets of the moribund delta or the flood-swept settlements of the active delta" (Mukerjee, 1938).

To what kind of life did they turn, the disemployed of weaving, the cast-out of the city by a failing export trade, those whose markets among the court of the Nawabs and of the privileged of Europe had been disrupted by the interests of the Company?

During the second half of the eighteenth century, settlement was expanding in East Bengal, whereas West Bengal was declining, as a result of a significant shift that had occurred in the river system of Bengal. The main body of water from the Ganga ceased to find its outlet to the sea in the western part of the delta, since this had become silted up; and there was a marked tendency for the water to create channels for itself in the east (Marshall, 2006). The increasing volume of water in the east made the land more fertile at the expense of West Bengal. The population of Bengal was, in any case, much reduced by the famine of 1770. A significant amount of land remained uncultivated, 'waste' and unoccupied; and some of the victims of the loss of the weaving industry almost certainly took possession of terrain that remained unclaimed. Zamindars sometimes offered inducements to peasants to take over unused land. Heber (1829) estimated that in 1826 waste or uncultivated land occupied a quarter of the land of Bengal.

Mobility and adaptability characterized the people of Bengal, reflecting, perhaps, the features of constantly shifting landscapes. Migrations, from place to place, from Dacca or Murshidabad to rural areas, and from village and isolated farmstead to towns, from west to east, from east to west, have a

long history in Bengal: a constant displacement of people in step
with the continuous movement of the elements. Land and water
were constantly changing places in the eastern part of the delta;
and then, as now, land was continuously being created as well
as destroyed. In the late eighteenth century, one British colonial
official reported from the district of Bakerganj:

> At the present time, the Meghna is cutting away its West bank
> very rapidly in *thana* Mendiganj, and the estuary of the Meghna
> is doing the same with the East side of Dakhin Shahbazpur...
> There is something very desolate in the appearance of the
> country near these large rivers where the force of the streams
> begins to be directed against any particular tract. The
> peasants make haste to remove their houses, to cut town their
> groves of betel and coconut trees; as the diluvation advances,
> nothing is to be seen near the bank but stumps of trees, the
> earthen foundation of houses and the broken walls of tanks.
> The irruption of the Meghna into the tanks is perhaps the most
> melancholy of such sights; for Dakhin Shahbazpur and Hathia
> have many large tanks which must have been constructed at
> much expense and labour. They are surrounded by high walls
> of earth in order to keep out the salt water, and when a breach
> is made in them they become useless, and whole villages suffer
> in consequence. When the peasants are thus driven away by
> the rivers, they sometimes move further inland; but when they
> cannot find fresh land, they are obliged to go to new *chors* or to
> distant parts of the country.

New chors, islands, were also emerging from the unquiet
waters; and peasants could often find alternative settlement
elsewhere.

What kinds of livelihoods did the former weavers of
Dacca find in the villages? Mostly subsistence cultivation. Dr
Sharifuddin Ahmed, of the Centre for Dhaka Studies at the
Asiatic Society in Dhaka, says, "Some of the people became
dacoits and bandits. Others went to cultivate land in the rural

areas, some followed the growing power at Murshidabad or Calcutta. Since the weaving of coarse cloth remained unaffected by the British, some returned to the weaving of coarse cotton for domestic and local use."

While the weavers and spinners of Dacca were being reduced to want and retreating to subsistence agriculture once more, in Lancashire country people were fleeing overburdened villages, abandoning cottages to spiders and rats: the extinguished ash mouldered in the grate, the flags and opaque windowpanes of horn became dusty, as the birds nested in the thatch, and willowherb and buddleia took root in gaps between the stones, and moss covered the unvisited yards. They wheeled their handcarts, piled not very high with rush-bottomed stools, chairs and wooden beds, a change of clothing and household utensils, and made their way along muddy cart tracks to the road that led to the town. The evening sky was red, not with sunset, but with the flares from chimneys; and thick smoke clouded the horizon. As they approached the settlement, where until recently, market day had seen the only bustle and activity, the air was filled with flakes of soot, a dark snow shower, and it smelled, a sour, damp odour of spent coals and cinders.

Children, who had stood barefoot in the stony fields, scaring the crows from the green blades of wheat and barley; who had carried pails of freezing water in their numb fingers; who had enviously watched the sheep as they went about their peaceable lives of perpetual eating; who had been cut by the flail on the threshing floor and beaten by their father's strap for nibbling at the piece of raw bacon that was to serve as Sunday dinner, ran beside the carts, dreaming of a future that would never be theirs.

Although the journey may not have been more than twenty kilometres, many people had never before left their village or gone further than a walk might take them; culturally and socially, it was a migration. If they thought they had left behind the thin diluted milk, crumbs from burnt toast infused with water to make an imitation of tea, the swede stolen from the store of cattle food, the potatoes frozen in the pits where they were stored, they also left sweet chestnuts taken from the trees, horse-mushrooms with the August dew still on them, and were to discover that the diet awaiting them was devoid of nutrients: flour adulterated with chalk, the offal of cows or sheep that had died of disease, water from polluted wells. They had left the tumbledown cottage with its crumbling stone, the unlatched window creaking in the wind, the cobwebby ceilings and draughts that sent the flickering rushlight chasing shadows across the walls; and exchanged them for sunless courts and alleys, where blood-coloured houses had been thrown up, to receive a family in each room, dark insanitary places, heated only by the breath and bodies of the occupants and smoke from stony pieces of coal. The life of the countryside where they had slept when darkness fell and risen with the dawn so as not to 'burn daylight', had been a time of persistent labour, where children had worked as soon as they could walk, and the earth constantly stood open to receive its daily tribute of cold clay, where the seasons imposed their unending burdens of cutting and clearing, manuring and sowing, tending and harvesting, storing and watching over crops that failed to replenish the energy spent on the cultivation of them. They did not know that the city gaslight would dispel darkness and extend even further the working day, so that a winter night, far from keeping them close to the fireside, would exact their presence among machines that imposed a different kind of rhythm, for unlike horses and cows, they needed neither rest nor fodder, but only the unflagging attention of operatives to see to their continuous running.

They also brought with them a country knowledge of the ways of survival—a rural language and lore that had helped to make sense of lives often swiftly abridged, where to be fifty was to be old, and that was rich with the accumulated wisdom of time—a knowledge to which young hearers had listened attentively, since they knew that their own well-being depended upon what elders—that sparse and durable remnant—had to tell them. As in all agrarian societies, the meaning of life still depended on connections between the natural world and human destiny, the march of the seasons, natural disasters and inclemencies, the rituals and repetitions of the countryside: whatever formal religious beliefs people had assumed, there remained a sediment of ancient animism, not completely eliminated even after centuries of Christianity.

The secrets they brought with them to the mushroom towns of industry naturally enough had no place and no root there. Unlike the later experience of the millworkers of Calcutta, a whole knowledge system was instantly superseded, quelled by the artificial skies of smoke of industrial Lancashire and the vegetation of brick that covered the cities. If the echoes of an older culture—to which many people imagined, at least in the early years, that they would return—remained in the cellars of memory, they would perish there, as it dawned upon them that the brief but wrenching journey was irreversible, that they could not go home again; or if they could, it would be only in the brief intervals from their labour, when all they had left behind became infused with the glow of loss, when they might take some brief holiday and savour the sweetness of time never to be recovered.

This mentality was destined to languish, and be reshaped as the sensibility of a working class. This should not be understood as a political entity—although it did produce leaders and people who were committed to social change and uplift of the people—but rather, as a way of perceiving the industrial world, and a means of surviving it: a kind of philosophy, as well as a practical means of getting through. People readily recognized the sameness of the plight of neighbours and kin, and realized that the pooling of resources would make these go further than any attempt to amass money or goods for personal use.

Just as the industrial revolution called forth a new kind of human being, in the form of the industrial worker, so contemporaries recognized that the colonization of Bengal also created new classes of people in Britain. Macaulay, in his essay on Clive, observed: "The plunder of Bengal called into existence a new class of Englishman, to whom their countrymen gave the name of Nabob. These persons had generally sprung from families neither ancient nor opulent; they had generally been sent out at an early age to the East; and they had there acquired large fortunes, which they had brought back to their native land." The history of the cleansing of money is an ancient one; and the corruption and peculation of the Company's servants in Bengal were miraculously transformed into the elegancies of late Georgian or Regency Bath and Brighton, as well as contributing to the reconstruction of country houses—Sezincote, Daylesford, Styche Hall. When Clive was constructing his country house, Claremont, near Esher, Macaulay observed: "The peasantry of Surrey looked with mysterious horror on the stately house which was rising at Claremont, and whispered that the great wicked Lord ordered the walls to be made so thick in order to keep out the Devil who would one day carry him away bodily." This suggests the Nabobs inspired almost as much awe in the rural poor at home as they did in the ryots of Bengal—equal, perhaps, in measure to the revulsion they provoked in the longer established aristocracy of Britain. Cheltenham, Bath and many other eighteenth-century towns remain as testimonies to a primitive form of money cleansing, since their genteel elegance was acquired by means of profits repatriated by servants of the Company.

As the money remitted from Bengal promoted the architectural harmony of late Georgian construction for these parvenus (as they were seen by 'old' wealth), much of the old aristocracy of Bengal was devastated, ruined by famine and taxes.

> The Raja of Burdwan died miserably at the end of the famine, leaving a treasury so drained that his son, a boy of sixteen, had to melt down the family plate, and when that was exhausted, to beg a temporary loan in order to perform his father's obsequies... The aged Hindu Raja of Bishnapur pawned his household god and was still unable to meet government demands. He was sent to a debtors' prison, and released only to die... The youthful Musulman Raja of Birbhoom was hardly suffered to attain his majority before he was confined for arrears. The ancient houses of Bengal, which had been semi-independent under the Moguls, fell into ruin; two-thirds of the old aristocracy of Bengal were ruined (Ghose, 1944).

Simultaneously—as in Britain—new classes arose in Bengal out of the debris of old privilege; in Britain, they coexisted with the existing upper class, and were absorbed into them. Ghose says a new set of zamindars appeared on the scene, "establishing themselves on the ruin of their predecessors, but they could not claim any influence as natural leaders of men, and [did little to contribute to] the traditions of the aristocracy that tenderly entwined themselves around works of public utility—the tanks, ghats, roads, temples and mosques, the remnants of which we still find in almost all parts of Bengal".

Whatever disdain or nostalgia the mutability of elites may have inspired in observers, horror and fear greeted the circumstances in which the industrious classes of Britain were compelled to live in the years when they took on the making of cotton goods after the collapse of the industry in Bengal. The prevailing impression of the manufacturing districts of Lancashire, described by Friedrich Engels, inscribed itself indelibly on the sensibility of Britain; graphic and tenacious, it has proved hard to dislodge from public memory, even though the Manchester of today bears no resemblance to its moment of primitive industrialism, except perhaps in the fugitive glimpse of an untouched Victorian corner or a view from the railway which reveals a ruinous tenement or a workshop that has escaped demolition. Engels' evocation of Manchester and its surrounding towns remained the archetype; and indeed, it is still suggestive today in relation to some of the hastily erected slums of urban South Asia. "Every scrap of space," he wrote, "has been filled up and patched over until not a foot of land is left to be further occupied." Describing the prospect of the River Irk close to the centre of the old town of Manchester, he says:

> The south bank of the Irk is here very steep and between fifty and thirty feet high. On this declivitous hillside there are planted three rows of houses, of which the lowest rise directly out of the river, while the front walls of the highest stand on the crest of the hill in Long Millgate. Among them are mills on the river; in short, the method of construction is as crowded and

disorderly here as in the lower part of Long Millgate. Right and left a multitude of covered passages lead from the main street into numerous courts, and he who turns thither gets into a filth and disgusting grime, the equal of which is not to be found—especially in the courts that lead down to the Irk, and which contain unqualifiedly the most horrible dwellings I have yet beheld. In one of these courts, there stands directly at the entrance, at the end of a covered passage, a privy without a door, so dirty that the inhabitants can pass in and out of the court only by passing through foul pools of stagnant urine and excrement. This is the first court on the Irk above Ducie Bridge—in case anyone should care to look into it. Below it on the river there are several tanneries which fill the whole neighbourhood with the stench of animal putrefaction... Above the bridge are tanneries, bone-mills and gas-works, from which all drains and reuse find their way into the Irk, which receives further the contents of all the neighbouring sewers and privies.

Engels was echoing the words of Sir James Phillips Kay-Shuttleworth who, in a pamphlet of 1832 on the *Moral and Physical Condition of the Working Classes Employed in the Cotton Manufacture in Manchester* (that 'moral' precedes 'physical' suggests his priorities), had also been appalled by the scenes from the same vantage point, at Ducie Bridge, overlooking the Irk. Kay-Shuttleworth wrote: "The Irk, black with the refuse of dye-works erected on its banks, receives excrementitious matters from some sewers in this portion of the town—the drainage from the gas-works, and filth of the most pernicious character from bone-works, tanneries, size manufactories &c." Of the cotton operatives, Kay-Shuttleworth observed:

Prolonged and exhausting labour, continued from day to day, and from year to year, is not calculated to develop the intellectual or moral faculties of man... The population employed in the cotton factories rises at five o'clock in the morning, works in the mills from six to eight, and returns home for half an hour or

forty minutes for breakfast. This meal generally consists of tea
or coffee, with a little bread. Oatmeal porridge is sometimes, but
of late, rarely used, and chiefly by the men; but the stimulus of
tea is preferred, and especially by the women. The tea is almost
always of a bad, and sometimes of a deleterious, quality; the
infusion is weak, and little or no milk is added. The operatives
return to the mills and workshops until twelve o'clock, when
an hour is allowed for dinner... At the expiration of the hour,
they are all again employed in the workshops or mills, where
they continue until seven o'clock or a later hour, when they
generally again indulge in the use of tea, often mingled with
spirits accompanied by a little bread.

Kay-Shuttleworth was a doctor, and he describes the skin
of operatives as becoming "sallow, or of the yellow hue which
is observed in those who have suffered from the influence of
tropical climates".

He further notes:

... the wages of certain classes are exceedingly meagre. The
introduction of the power-loom, although ultimately destined
to be productive of the greatest benefits, has, in the present
restricted the state of commerce, occasioned some temporary
embarrassment, by diminishing the demand for certain kinds
of labour, and consequently, their price. The hand-loom
weavers, *existing in this state of transition*, still continue a very
extensive class, and though they labour fourteen hours and
upwards daily, earn only from five to seven or eight shillings
per week (emphasis added).

He did not conceal his prejudices: he claimed that Ireland
"had poured forth the most destitute of its hordes to supply the
constantly increasing demand for labour". The "barbarous
disregard of forethought and economy" of the Irish had had a
deleterious effect upon the British. "Debased alike by ignorance
and pauperism, [the Irish] have discovered, with the savage,

what is the minimum of the means of life, upon which existence may be prolonged." In keeping with the temper of the 1830s, Kay-Shuttleworth also expands on the damaging nature of the poor law, which he says "retains all the evils of the gross and indiscriminate bounty of ancient monasteries. They also fail in exciting the gratitude of the people, and they extinguish the charity of the rich."

In other words, the cotton operatives suffered not only from dirty and dangerous living conditions and insalubrious work environments, but also from the conviction of a majority of their betters that these circumstances reflected, or at least created, their moral worth. While the British authorities viewed their own people as another caste, a class apart, what Disraeli later diagnosed as "the two nations", it was unlikely that they would have any great tenderness for those whose lives they had turned upside down in distant imperial provinces: a response with which the inheritors of the free countries of India, Pakistan and Bangladesh have shown a considerable degree of continuity.

Early nineteenth-century Britain had called into existence the industrial worker. At first, these people, bewildered migrants from impoverished villages and abandoned rural homesteads, had little understanding of the altered conditions of existence into which they had been coerced. It was inevitable they should be disoriented, since the environment in which they lived—or perished—was inimical to health. In 1841, life expectancy in Manchester was 26.6 years, in Liverpool 28.1, in Glasgow 27. This was, for Manchester, an improvement of almost ten years since the second decade of the nineteenth century. No wonder apologists for child labour were not wanting, as Andrew Ure (1835) wrote of the "tendency to employ merely children with watchful eyes and nimble fingers, instead of journeymen of long experience, [which] shows how the scholastic dogma of the division of labour into degrees of skill have been employed by our enlightened manufacturers". The keen eyesight and nimble fingers of children were no doubt prudently employed, since their owners would soon be dead.

It is not difficult to imagine the state of mind of villagers trapped in back-to-back houses, labour camps become cities, with contaminated food and poisoned water. These settlements were thrown up promiscuously, without foresight or planning, and without thought for the consequences for humanity packed into small spaces devoid of facilities for hygiene, or the disposal of human, or any other, waste. Present-day Dhaka, with its scenes of poverty and puzzlement, of resilience and acceptance, recalls the cities of Lancashire as they were.

Looking at the similarities between nineteenth-century Britain and contemporary Bangladesh, it is tempting to conclude—superficially—that Bangladesh has reached a necessary stage in its development, and that it, too, will pass, more or less automatically, following the evolution of Britain and other Western countries, into increasing prosperity, if not exactly into greater social justice. Paradoxically, the convergences serve as a reason to do nothing, but to let economic growth and expansion take their necessary—and, it is assumed, benign—course.

The situation is not the same; and the past experience of Britain resembles only superficially what is taking place in much of the 'developing' world today. First of all, the leave-taking of impoverished villages in Britain was more frightening to those who departed in the early 1800s than today's journeys to Dhaka or Chittagong. Although most people in Britain travelled only a short distance from their home, the uprooting was unfamiliar and hazardous. The parliamentary acts of settlement, which in theory tied people to the parish in which they were born, were repealed only in 1834, although they had already ceased to inhibit the growth of industrial towns. But in the pre-industrial period, mobility was widely regarded with suspicion—indeed was often adjudged a crime.

When villagers entered the smoky jerry-built towns of early nineteenth-century England in search of work, they did so with even heavier hearts than the young women arriving in the glittering metropolis of Dhaka in the 1980s, 1990s and even 2010s; since the latter were undertaking journeys of hope— sometimes justified, often misplaced—whereas their industrial forebears in Britain had left the impoverished villages for destinations that promised little but a spare subsistence, in an environment alien to them, since never in history had there been such a thing as a town or city based upon the production of a single commodity. Into what aberrant human society had they wandered—those who had known nothing but village life? The migrants of posterity know what the city is; they are familiar with what they should expect there. They can anticipate its excitements and know in advance its pitfalls; while the displaced of early Victorian Britain had never been exposed to the grim agglomerations of labour into which they were to enter.

Migrants went to nearby towns and cities, with their scanty bundle of belongings, travelling by carrier's cart, people for whom even those at twenty miles' distance were strangers, who spoke a different dialect, and were sometimes said to be unintelligible in their speech. Some, of course, driven perhaps by a deeper despair, went as indentured servants or farmhands to distant colonies, a far more final break; and significant numbers went involuntarily, as transported felons, to penal settlements on the other side of the world.

In Bangladesh, the many and rapid forms of transport between Dhaka and even the remotest areas make the upheaval of departure less of an epic undertaking than that which hit migrants in Britain. In the early days of the garment industry—just a little more than thirty years ago—many travelled by launch on the rivers that flow into the Bay of Bengal. Since then, roads have been extended and widened, so the most usual means of conveyance is now bus or truck. What development economists call 'urban–rural linkages' are a reality and remain strong. At Eid-ul-Fitr, Dhaka dramatically loses population: streets, normally blocked by traffic for much of the day, are almost empty, recalling, although perhaps only for historians, earlier, more traumatic losses of population. The ease of journeying is also reflected in the rapid turnover of workers in the factories: they come and go, change jobs frequently, and in any case, units themselves constantly close down and open under another name, especially if there is a 'troublesome' workforce.

One of the great differences between workers in cotton mills and those in garment factories is the far greater life expectancy of today's labourers. Although child and maternal mortality remain high in Bangladesh, there is nothing like the grim bills—officially published record of deaths—of infant mortality in the industrial cities of England in the nineteenth century. A few basic drugs—especially antibiotics—have ensured a life expectancy in Bangladesh into the sixties, while even at the time of the independence of India and Pakistan it was about forty. Death does not hover with the same ubiquitous menace over the sites of industry as it had done in Victorian Britain; as a consequence, the pleasures of the poor are not snatched with the same heedless voracity that characterized the meagre spare time of the cotton operatives, where alcohol and opium derivatives offered instant oblivion, and it used to be said the quickest way out of Manchester was through the door of the nearest pub. In spite of this, the consumption of cheap (and forbidden) narcotics is scarcely unknown in Bangladesh: 'yaba' tablets, Phensedyl—a cough mixture containing an opium derivative, which is a common source of forgetfulness—smuggled from India, and home-brewed liquor (to which battery fluid and other powerful adulterants are sometimes added)—take their toll of both urban and rural poor.

Perhaps the greatest distinction between Britain then and Bangladesh today is that a national division of labour was established in Britain around the turn of the nineteenth century. Almost every town and city was identified with the making of some useful or necessary article of daily life, and places were synonymous with household artefacts: Sheffield meant cutlery and steel, Stoke-on-Trent teacups and lavatory pans, Manchester cottons, Dundee jute, Leeds woollens; Leicester was associated with hosiery, Birmingham with metal goods, Nottingham with lace, my hometown of Northampton with footwear. Glasgow was where ships were built, and into the great ports of Liverpool came the produce of plantations and slavery; while a subterranean people laboured underground in the mining districts to provide power for mills and factories, and coastal towns were devoted to fishing or became, like Blackpool and Southend, pleasure resorts for the brief holidays which workers were granted from their life of labour. The people of all these places were linked through a sense of shared function; and this produced an astonishingly homogeneous way of life in working communities.

No such conditions exist in Bangladesh. The country depends upon a single industry, and that mainly for export. This has not restructured the psychology of people in the same way that the industrial revolution did in Britain. The fabric and raw materials come from elsewhere, and spend only the briefest time in the country before they are urgently moved on to their destination. Garment assembly is too flimsy an occupation to constitute a basis for identity. People are aware of the transient nature of their purpose, and although proud of their skill, they do not become too attached to what they produce, like foster parents who know that children are entrusted to their care only for a brief spell.

A strong sense prevails in Dhaka of the *provisional* nature of the work in the garment assembly units. For the time being at least, a majority still identify with their village of origin; migration remains, at least in theory, reversible, the hope of buying land—however illusory—still animates them. Many factories employ people from the same area, and the young people of whole villages seem to have been transplanted to the city. Workers are often relatives and acquaintances of supervisors and lower management, who are reliable, because they are dependent, so that labour is a kind of lower-order patronage, whereby the employers are seen to 'give' work, an act of grace which demands reciprocal obligations—not complaining, working long hours, not withdrawing labour.

The garment workers know their livelihood depends on the low level of reward they accept, and fear it could fly away tomorrow to more lucrative sites. There is tension between the need to survive and the knowledge that the means of survival are only conditional and of uncertain durability. After all, the factories arose overnight—rectangular buildings four or five storeys high. Geometrical, rudimentary, without ornament, they were thrown up from the 1980s onwards. Land magically became available in this city of landless people. Whole districts were turned into industrial suburbs, as the poor were evicted from their refuge. When the factories had been constructed, yet more land was conjured out of nowhere for apartments for those grown rich on garments, while the poor were pushed onto diminishing parcels of land, or onto the far periphery of the city, while others were stacked vertically in concrete structures of Dhaka. Some factories have been turned into dwelling places for workers: a friend of mine was living in 2009 in an apartment above the entrance to which was painted INSPECTION UNIT.

The suddenness with which the industry appeared lends it a mythic quality, something not quite of this world, since the experience of people has always been one where feet stand perpetually in the shallow water of paddy fields, watching the tranquilly ripening grain, the red flash of a bird's wing, jute retting in roadside ditches or standing in ghostly pyramids to dry, the rising wind of an approaching cyclone. Garment factories, superimposed on this lasting reality, have barely shaken people's sense of rural belonging, even though their eviction from it has been brutal and, for many, irreversible. They are caught up in a global division of labour, of which they know little and with which they have no contact, unless it is the wondering admiration they extend to toys and gimcrack household articles from China with which the ubiquitous shopping emporia overflow.

This makes it difficult for workers or consumers in the West to express solidarity with the abused young women of Dhaka and Chittagong. The British unions and NGOs which support trade unions hope that, perhaps, they are encouraging the emergence of the militant sensibility that animated the pioneers of industry in Britain. This assumes that 'development' is indeed a predictable process, through which the workers of Bangladesh must pass, just as the people of Britain did, even though the sensibility of the workers has also decayed in the places where it was first conceived. The labour movement in the West has become a kind of ghost dance, performed as much to summon back the vanished dead of industry in Britain; like the Plains Indians in the US who, having been effaced by the power of those stronger than they were, thought they could ritually conjure back their ancestors to rid their lands of the colonialists.

The most striking difference between early industrial Britain and contemporary Bangladesh is that successive governments in Britain could not afford to ignore the social consequences of the new human being—the industrial worker—which their system had created. Not only did they have little understanding of the psyche and sensibility of this creature, never before seen in the world, they could not imagine the extent of mischief he or she might be capable of, if left unchecked. So although the ideology of laissez-faire was, in theory, benignly non-interventionist, in reality it was constantly infringed. There were constant inquiries, committees, investigations and Royal Commissions set up to look into the conditions of the people and their labour; and these duly published recommendations and policies, over time, led to mitigation of the worst effects of industrialism. It has to be said that much of this busy government activity was not solely a consequence of conscience, since it also took place in reaction to the capacity of the cotton operatives and other workers to organize themselves, to set up their own defensive institutions against destitution and exploitation. But the common outcome was not to be disputed: it was one of gradual and hard-headed improvement.

The government of Bangladesh, on the other hand, has shown a greater readiness to suppress workers' organizations and movements rather than to accommodate them. This is, no doubt, because they have taken note of the decay of communism, and of the recent relative docility of workers in the West; and have calculated that Bangladeshi labour—despite its restlessness and capacity for local disturbances—poses no serious menace to wealth and power. Indeed, the eclipse of the labour movement in the West emboldens the powerful of this enlightened age to treat with severity a fractious working class, since it knows how nimble and footloose capital has become, and it is prepared to accept considerable indignities to maintain livelihood, however meagre.

In the very early days of industrialization in Britain, laws had been enacted against 'combinations' of workers, that is, forbidding by law any collective effort to 'demand' or to 'enforce' improvements in their fortune. This was paralleled by anxiety about electoral reform: for as long as the poor remained a majority who had 'no stake in the country', they could not be trusted with the franchise, for they might have achieved in one simple election what their superiors most dreaded: dignity, equality and redistribution of wealth. Even in the 1830s, the Scottish doctor Andrew Ure (1835) was speaking for the manufacturing, as well as the landed, classes, when he expressed himself vigorously on the matter of trade unions.

> It is one of the most important truths resulting from the analysis of manufacturing industry, that unions are conspiracies of workmen against the interests of their own order, and never fail to end in the suicide of the body corporate which forms them; an event the more speedy, the more coercive or the better organized the union is.

With Ure also, the 'savage' was never far from his thoughts. "When the wandering savage becomes a citizen," he declared, "he renounces many of his dangerous pleasures in return for tranquility and protection. He can no longer gratify at his will a revengeful spirit upon his foes, nor seize with violence a neighbour's possessions." When the very predations which the British were then undertaking—subjugating 'savages', in Bengal as in the wider world—were ennobled into 'civilizing missions', it became difficult to distinguish the nature of savagery from civilization.

Although continuous legislation improved the conditions of labour of the poor, it was a slow and arduous process. In 1802, the Health and Morals of Apprentices Act limited the labour of children to twelve hours a day, and made it mandatory that males and females should sleep in separate dormitories. These children were 'poor law apprentices', orphans whose labour cost their employers nothing, so it is understandable that there was resistance on the part of owners—including Robert Peel, father of the future prime minister—to legislation that would ensure their lives would be overseen, and the mills where they worked would be "whitewashed twice a year". In the Cotton Mills and Factories Act, 1819, the employment of children under nine was forbidden, and no child was to work more than twelve hours a day. By the Factory Act of 1833, children under the age of thirteen were limited to a nine-hour day; by 1844 women and young persons were to work no more than twelve hours a day. The Ten Hour Act of 1847 forbade employment of women and young persons for more than ten hours a day. By 1878, no child was to be employed under the age of ten; ten–fourteen-year-olds could be employed for half days, and women's labour was restricted to fifty-six hours a week.

Much is made of the continuous 'progress' of the humanitarian impulse; but the fact that it took three quarters of a century to limit the employment of ten-year-olds to six hours a day suggests there are other ways of reading our history than in the light of British solicitude for the poor or their children. The improvements occurred under the continuing threat of self-organization by the workers themselves; and after the eclipse of Chartism in the 1840s, this task passed to the growing trade unions, the cooperative movement and friendly societies. Collective action by workers was, in the main, both restrained and limited in its extent; but the memory of Luddites, machine breakers, the Plug Riots (in 1842, a strike of miners which spread to many industrial areas), the Rebecca Riots (1939–43 in mid and south Wales) and other great demonstrations of popular power kept alive in the mind of elites a sense of menace from the congested, overcrowded and still squalid concentrations of humanity where the textile workers—and all the others pressed into the service of industrial society—lived and laboured.

Much of the argument in Britain over the effects of early industrialism subsequently resolved itself into academic dispute over whether the standard of living of the labouring poor rose or fell between the last two decades of the eighteenth century and the 1840s. Even if it can be shown that there was an overall increase in wages for the majority of those who worked (with the exception of the depressed classes and those trapped, like handloom weavers, in 'archaic' forms of labour), this does not mean, as E.P. Thompson pointed out, that they did not experience the upheaval and change, the coercive migration and forced removal from village life into the urban areas, the stringent discipline of the factory, long hours of work, as a forfeit of important freedoms. The question was whether an increase in monetary income could also be accompanied by a subjective sense of impoverishment, and whether social, environmental and even spiritual costs might not outweigh the advantages gained by the labouring poor. Of course, such considerations rarely entered the economic calculus of laissez-faire, but it remained part of the subjective experience of the people. And this has taken on a fresh resonance in recent years, as the true costs of 'development' and 'progress' have been questioned. The ideology of economic reason has hitherto largely omitted the costs to society of its majestic progression through the world, and it has, until recently, regarded the ecological costs merely as the incidental expense of 'raw materials'. Only as the resource base of the earth becomes more threadbare do some of its more baleful effects become visible.

The issue of the balance between gain and loss in industrial life has also been widely discussed, at least among the people themselves, in Dhaka as all over the 'developing' world. It has also reappeared in the West; but so accustomed have we become to identifying increased wealth with enhanced well-being that it bursts upon us as a revelation, rather than as a long-suppressed tension within industrial society. The garment workers of Bangladesh are acutely aware of the promise of an income, and the way that promise is persistently undermined by rising costs of food, rent and travel. The 5,000 taka minimum wage still cannot procure a decent subsistence and supply the needs of those they have left behind in the villages. The situation during the early industrial era in Britain was similar:

> The 'average' working man remained very close to subsistence level when he was surrounded by the evidence of the increase of national wealth, much of it transparently the product of his own labour, and passing, by equally transparent means, into the hands of his employers. In psychological terms, this felt very much like a decline in standards. His own share in the 'benefits of economic progress' consisted of more potatoes, a few articles of cotton clothing for his family, soap and candles, some tea and sugar, and a great many articles in the *Economic History Review* (Thompson, 1963).

Again: "The majority of the British people in the first half of the nineteenth century was convinced that the coming of industrial capitalism had brought them appalling hardships, that they had entered a bleak and iron age" (Hobsbawm, 1958).

Such testimonies are heard again among migrants to the garment factories of Bangladesh. Of course, they would rather remain in the village, if economic and social security were possible and livelihood assured. The city is preferable only because it provides an opportunity to work, and a hope of better fortune. The home is a place of certain poverty; nothing unexpected will occur: for the devastating floods, cyclones, threatened harvests and the need to reconstruct fragile shelters against storms are part of the predictable march of the seasons. In the city, there is companionship and excitement; but there is also foul air, respiratory problems, the monotony of labour, the endless hours while the minute hand drags on its way to the hour, and at the end of it not enough, never enough, for the medicine for a brother's TB, the schooling of a clever sibling, the extra nourishment needed by a grandmother. The remittance is always shamefully small, and the young women feel guilt at every taka taken for some necessity—or worse, some small pleasure—of their own: a lipstick or a small bar of chocolate. They wrestle with the same contradictions as their sisters did in the mills of Manchester; but they are also the beneficiaries of a posterity which knows how to prolong life, to provide more enduring consolations for toilsome and wearying hours of labour than gin and laudanum, more palpable pleasures than the music hall and the grisly street ballad.

There is a significant passage in the relationship between Bengal and Lancashire, which was played out in the Bombay of the later nineteenth century. The first indigenous textile mill was set up by the Parsee, Cowasjee Nanabhoy Davar, who in 1854 floated a joint-stock company in order to set up a mill producing cotton yarn. This mill was opened in 1856, using machinery imported from Britain. By 1862, there were four mills in Bombay. Lancashire interests required that duty on yarn and cotton piece goods into India be reduced, which it was; however, the number of mills continued to grow, not only in Bombay, but also in Ahmedabad in Gujarat and Nagpur in central Maharashtra. Although the cotton consumed by Indian mills was only a fraction of that used in Lancashire—less than 10 per cent—the import of machinery from Britain increased. Tariffs on British textiles entering India were lowered and finally abolished by the early 1880s. However, the production of mill-made fabric in Bombay did not diminish. By 1887, there were eighty-seven cotton mills in India, forty-nine of them in Bombay.

Continuous devaluation of the rupee only assisted India's cotton exports. The British, in the previous century, had been converted from protecting their own industries into champions of free trade, and, unwilling to reverse this enlightened position, had recourse to closing down the Indian mints, which increased the value of the rupee by one-fifth in 1898–99. This effectively cheapened the price of British piece goods in India. Textile imports into India from Britain continued to grow, and if mill production in India increased, this was probably at the expense of what remained of the cotton handloom industry.

By 1914, ninety textile factories in Bombay employed over 100,000 people. It is estimated by historian Irfan Habib (2006) that by 1914, industry accounted for the livelihood of about 1.5 per cent of the Indian population. The hours of employment for workers in textile mills were long: it could begin at four in the morning and continue until nine at night. In a faint echo of British legislation, the first Factory Act in India limited the daily work of children below twelve years to nine hours. By 1911, adult males were restricted to twelve hours a day.

A mill manager, in a deposition before the Bombay Factory Labour Commission in 1885, said:

> In ordinary seasons, that is when work is not very pressing, the engine starts between 3 and 4 a.m. and stops at 7, 8 or 9 p.m. without any stoppage during the day. The hands work continuously all these hours, and are relieved by one another for meals. In busy seasons, that is, in March and April, the gins and presses sometimes work both day and night, with half an hour's rest in the evening. The same set continue working day and night for about 8 days, and when it is impossible to go on longer, other sets of hands are procured from Bombay, if they can be found... Both the men and women come to the factories at 3 a.m., as they have no idea of the time, and they wish to make sure they are at the factory by the time it opens, i.e. 4 a.m. I have 40 gins in one of my factories at Pachora and I have only 40 women attending these 40 gins. Have only eight spare women. I never allow these women off the gins. I am not alone in this respect; it is the general system (cited in Habib, 2006, from Buchanan, 1934).

Accounts of mill life in Bombay echo the story of the constancy of the machinery and the fragility of the humanity serving them in industrial Britain. Mills transplanted into India were advantaged by the cheapness of labour; and they hint at the—at that time, slight—threat to Lancashire, despite the remonstrations of Manchester employers. Such stories also prefigure the final act of the textile industry in Britain: bringing labour from the subcontinent, people who would work twelve-hour shifts in order to keep the failing enterprises of Lancashire viable for a few years longer than would otherwise have been the case.

Not only was the industry of Bombay similar to that of Lancashire—even the architecture of the mills, with their ceremonial stone entrances, imposing offices furnished in mahogany, archaic counting houses, their dingy sheds of machinery imported (often second-hand, from the closing mills of Lancashire)—but the millworkers organized in trade unions like those of Lancashire. Initially, as employees of indigenous capital, they could be mobilized against the British; but after independence they became more radical and politically affiliated to Leftist parties. The millworkers were seen as leaders of the modern sector in India, industrially militant—a little like the miners in Britain. By the 1970s the millworkers lived in chawls, industrial tenements, crumbling, overcrowded, without amenities, not dissimilar to the streets of working-class dwellings in the Manchester conurbation.

I was in Bombay in 1982, towards the end of the last long millworkers' strike, which saw the end of the industry in Bombay, the closure of mills, and in another strange convergence with British experience, the end of the old colonial phase of industry in India. As many mills closed, the buildings were demolished, and the area of south central Bombay became some of the most valuable real estate in the world.

The strike was led by Datta Samant, an organizer who had begun his professional life as a doctor in a poor part of the city. He began to organize workers who had not been unionized, and successfully negotiated wage increases for those in engineering, pharmaceuticals and glassware. When he undertook to work on behalf of the millworkers, he was facing an industry already in decline, and rather than bringing new prosperity to the workers, he accelerated their extinction. Mills closed down, others 'rationalized' their workforce, and many were thrown out of work, forced into the vast 'unorganized' sector of what was soon to become Mumbai. As a consequence of this setback, Datta Samant—who had, until then, belonged to no political party—floated his own workers' party. But the moment of labour supremacy had passed. Into the power vacuum flowed the energies of Shiv Sena, the Bombay-based Hindu communalist party led by Bal Thackeray. Its resentment of Muslims, migrants to Bombay from other parts of India—north and south—fed the xenophobia of Marathi speakers, those who were from Maharashtra, and felt they were being overtaken by newcomers to the city. In this way, Mumbai maintained a caricature of its 'vanguard' position, anticipating the religion-based fundamentalism that was to follow.

Mumbai underwent its own version of de-industrialization, at almost the same time as Manchester and Kolkata. With the decline of labour in the production of the material necessities of clothing and other manifestly useful goods, a vacancy was created for baleful ideologies of fantasy, both secular and other-worldly.

The lifting of the ambiguous curse of industrialism from the people of Britain was bound to result in its transference elsewhere. When textiles arose as an industry in Britain, this most certainly was experienced initially as an affliction, but by the time the industry of Lancashire was dissolved, this was felt less as a freedom than as an arbitrary removal of a sense of purpose. Certainly, the abolition of the very reasons for the existence of the cotton towns did not come to their inhabitants as a cause for rejoicing, but dealt a blow to their sense of self and their function in the production of necessary articles of daily use. So much was cotton part of people's lives that Manchester had been called 'Cottonopolis', as though cotton itself had originated there, sprung up between the cobbles, or flourished in the humid tenements where it was transformed into garments. Cotton certainly became part of their bodies, since the dust and lint entered their lungs, creating then unnamed illnesses like 'mill fever', and respiratory diseases. In the 1861 census 'cotton weaver' was by far the most common occupation in Lancashire, ahead of 'servant', 'housekeeper' and 'labourer'.

And so the wheel came full circle: the textile baton was passed back to East Bengal/Bangladesh with the establishment of a large-scale garment industry in the country. The garment industry of Bangladesh (and elsewhere) could only emerge as the textile industry in the West declined. This occurred as the result of an increasingly globalized economy, where cheap labour could be recruited in parts of the 'developing' world, without the menace of serious organization and resistance on the part of the workers. For this to be established, it was necessary that alternatives to industrial capitalism should be cancelled; and this is what happened with the collapse of the Soviet Union and Eastern Europe in 1990. The nominal communism of China prudently forbore to interfere with global markets from which the country was to derive its great advantage.

This perspective—looking at how garments came to Bangladesh—gives a different view of the present. The events which lead over time, without design, to the rise and fall of trade and industry are often random and unpredictable. The spread and use of commodities, the combination of need, fashion and addiction in the creation of markets, remain constant. The experience of the twentieth century does not show any significant departure from this pattern. Although workers in the garment industry of Bangladesh mimic and echo the lives of earlier generations, the making up of items of clothing actually emerged in contemporary Bangladesh as the result of chance and historical accident. In the early 1980s, civil war in Sri Lanka disrupted garment manufacture there; while South Korea, which had earlier been a major contributor to the global textile industry, had become more developed and came to see clothing as a 'sunset industry'. Some of its entrepreneurs invested capital and trained people in South Korea to start up the industry in Bangladesh.

It began simply as assembling ready-made cloth; and although Bangladesh now is extending 'backward linkages'— spinning, weaving and printing—this is still on a relatively small scale, given that several million people are dependent upon the garment industry. More than 80 per cent of the five thousand factories are in Greater Dhaka, and altogether about ten million people are engaged in one way or another in garment production, finishing and distribution. It remains a fragile industry, inhibited by poor infrastructure, bureaucratic corruption, and a shortage of power—gas and energy. Port facilities, law and order, congestion and the black market limit its capacity for even greater expansion.

It has, however, transformed the lives of women, who no longer have to be agricultural labourers, maidservants or sex workers if they want to enter the labour force. Young women now have a voice in their family and society. They cannot go back to their former lives of submission and domestic drudgery. In the beginning, religious leaders in villages issued fatwas against women going into factories; but so many people now depend upon their remittances that the religious authorities no longer have the same power over those working women whose income plays an important role in the survival of whole communities. In the early 1980s, religious leaders said no one should marry a woman who had gone to work in a factory, and that she should be expelled from the family. But now in the villages they are proud of her; she has dignity and independence. This is a positive transformation that cannot easily be reversed. Although on marriage many women do revert to a more traditional role, there has been an awakening in the rural areas as well as in the cities.

It is a strange historic irony that the descendants of those who fled Dacca two hundred years ago should now have been summoned back to what has become a vast metropolis by a global apparel industry. The throng of people making for the capital city is on a scale unimaginable for those who once deserted it in the wake of the ruin of a livelihood of making fabrics. What has ousted them once more from a precarious rural belonging, always threatened by natural and human-made disaster, and sent them to seek another kind of fortune in the cities they evacuated in the early imperial era? From where does the 'demand' come for the products of their labour on the scale we have seen in the past three decades? It is exactly two hundred years after the ruin of Dhaka that its renewal—albeit in a chaos of traffic, overcrowding, violence and degrading living conditions—has taken place.

By 1860, there were 2,650 cotton mills in Lancashire, employing about 440,000 people. By this time, only 10 per cent were children and 56 per cent women. It was one of the few industries in Britain in which female labour dominated throughout its history. The production of cotton goods reached its peak just before the outbreak of the First World War in 1912; and then began the long decline of the Lancashire cotton industry, followed in the late twentieth century by the second great transformation of a city that then lost the reason for its turbulent, and for the workers, brutal, existence.

From my first visits to the garment factories of Dhaka, I was struck by images and memories which had an elusive familiarity: tales from the early industrial history of Britain, and indeed from its later stages, when the cotton factories of Lancashire, which in their heyday had displaced the weavers of Bengal, were also on the verge of extinction. These melancholy places in Britain that had given meaning to people's lives were also being made superfluous by a new global division of labour, in which there was no longer any place for them. Did the people of Lancashire have any inkling of the long story of displacement and destruction, which, beginning with the decline of the cotton industry in the early twentieth century, had culminated in the 1950s and 1960s in their own redundancy? Could they identify the twisted metal and glass, the shattered soot-encrusted bricks of their silent mills with the rusted looms and abandoned homesteads of a Bengal that had been ruined for the sake of their own now-defunct livelihood? Did they appreciate that the destructive power of a global market which had robbed them of purpose had similarly, in its earlier guise, extinguished the function of distant artisans of another time and place?

While labour draws more and more people into Dhaka, Lancashire is only the shell of what it was, albeit an ornamental shell, an altered décor having replaced the mills with their windows gilded by the sunset, their chimneys, their looms and machinery that shook and deafened those who tended them. Because Manchester and its dependencies lost their reason for existence at a time of rising affluence, it was, perhaps, not noticeable that something irreplaceable was being taken away. First of all, many of the looms were transported to India in the later nineteenth and early twentieth centuries, to be placed in structures that replicated there an architecture once familiar in Bolton and Blackburn. The coming of consumer society appeared to the once-more changed sensibility of former millworkers as a compensation, perhaps a belated reward for their proscribed function in the national division of labour. As malls and shopping centres gained prominence, the mills and warehouses, worn and blackened commercial structures, either fell into ruin or were transformed into places where people could dance, shop, eat or drink: a conspicuous liberation from the industrial rigours of their past.

In Lancashire, the sites of industry were to endure for a span of five or six generations; and although thrown up in haste to house an army of workers, many of the physical structures, particularly dilapidated tenements and palaces of industry, the workhouses and magistrates' courts, and especially the churches were to outlive their usefulness; so that these remained— monuments to an age that had violently reshaped the psyche of the people who had no choice but to make them their home. As late as the 1940s and early 1950s, many of the streets remained virtually unaltered, apart from the occasional motorized vehicle parked in the narrow road. Although the workers had been provided with paving, some houses were still lighted by gas, and remained unconnected to the main sewage system. In a frenzy of 'slum clearance', these were demolished in the 1950s, and replaced by geometrical shapes, cubes and rectangles, without ornament, unadorned spaces that would accommodate all the furniture, goods and amenities that had been wafted into the lives of workers with the coming of a society of consumption after the Second World War.

Enough of the original fabric of industrial cities remained in the deserted streets and forsaken houses to evoke the lives of the people; and indeed, a whole social history lay abandoned in the splintered glass, rickety furniture, the old artefacts and belongings which people had left behind when they migrated once more, sometimes journeys even shorter than those which had brought them into the towns and cities in the first place, since they were voyaging only to new suburbs, estates within the same urban settlement. In the 1960s and 1970s, whole streets were abandoned, and with them, the evocative paraphernalia of daily living: the greasy sofas where young women had wasted away with TB, the stopped clocks and deal tables, the worn-out chenille cloths, ornaments that had contained aspidistras or dusty geraniums, photographs of the dead stored in ancient chocolate boxes, brass fenders and coal scuttles, cracked teapots, china and clothing.

The effacement of the industrial past went hand in hand with the obliteration of memory of exploitation and loss. Not only were the slums demolished, the slag heaps grassed over, the sites of desolation covered with saplings, but the air was suddenly full of music: anthems to commodities, fruits of the publicity industry, seductive invitations to people to spoil, indulge and let themselves go—a soft caressing concern where previously all had been harshness and discipline. The purpose of human life had been redefined in the image of a world that wanted to shower its blessings upon those from whom they had been so long withheld. So it was that free offers, rewards, prizes, gifts became available to people who had only the day before gone hungry in cold tenements, walked unshod, suffered the sicknesses of malnutrition and want, and led lives of thankless labour, with only brief moments of snatched pleasure and enjoyment purloined from unwilling employers and punitive government. All of this occurred, of course, only from within the security of the welfare state, an arrangement that cared not only for the social ills that might befall anyone—unemployment, accident or misfortune—but also the existential certainties of ageing, enfeeblement and dependency.

This outpouring of grace was bewildering, for it appeared with the force of a revelation; and it required the most fundamental reappraisal of human purposes. People who believed they had been born to want and woe, and had made their dispositions accordingly, now discovered that self-realization was the purpose of life and that their highest duty was to themselves. This was confusing: so abrupt a change— far more rapid than that which had refashioned an agricultural labour force into an industrial working class—had important consequences. In the new environment, the shouts of joy and hosannas to consumption drowned out the greatest sense of loss that came with the new dispensation. The towns and cities of Lancashire had been constructed on a powerful material certainty: the making of necessary durable things, in the event, clothing, an undisputed necessity. The people employed in the mills had performed essential labour. All the ugliness and cruelty of industrial life had at its base an unanswerable purpose, and the people who worked were never called to question their function, even though they certainly did question the conditions and remuneration they received for it.

The decay of the cotton towns was repeated in all the other manufacturing centres of Britain. What had complacently, triumphantly, called itself 'the workshop of the world' saw its tools rusted, its machinery exported or sent for scrap, its buildings plundered, its chimneys collapsing in a cloud of red dust, its forges cold and silent. Industrial ruins littered the country; while roads cut deep wounds through the centres of towns, which became simply a topographical anomaly: and the 'bypass' avoided the heart. It would be unreasonable to expect that so sudden a shift in sensibility would not involve a certain 'friction', in the jargon of economics. Just as the making of the working class had yielded its casualties of the maladaptive and unadjusted, with its mental disorientation and growth of institutions—asylums, workhouses and orphanages—so the unmaking of the class was not a painless transition. The sweeping away of the streets broke webs of relationships and networks of kinship and propinquity, contracted families and led to a reduced sense of a common predicament. That this manifested itself in growing crime, mental and emotional disorder, isolation and above all, addiction, was simply attributed to natural human frailty, if not human nature itself. After all, if all that the heart could desire, all that the impoverished of industrialism had fought—and often died for—was now conceded to them, any dissatisfaction must be a consequence of individual inadequacy: any remaining evil was no longer socially determined, but the result of defective personalities.

Indeed, with the passing of the generation which had lived to see its dream of plenty realized—or was it perhaps a caricature of its longing for sufficiency and security?—the modified sensibility became the accepted norm. Society receded; politics became an importunate intrusion into the business of living, and labour was increasingly instrumental in the securing of the good things of life. Individual ambition and financial success were the criteria by which human beings were to be measured by the new assessors of achievement. There is no such thing as society, intoned Margaret Thatcher; and although she was ridiculed for it at the time, this is now an unacknowledged, but axiomatic, truth.

The culture of wanting, of affluence, of contentment, of consumption—and it has been categorized as all of these at one time or another—is now established in the former mill towns of Britain. But the vanished function haunts the towns and cities: the scribble of roads across their face suggests attempts both at the effacement of the lineaments of the industrial town and the urgency of escape from them. Some of the warehouses, factories and mills have been demolished. Others have been converted into 'luxury' flats, while some have become resorts of pleasure, where the old buildings mock the ghosts of those who laboured for the barest subsistence.

Manufacturing is here a buried civilization, obliterated by the palaces of merchandise—including garments from Bangladesh and elsewhere, the stitching of which is now invisible to the eyes of people who have raised their gaze from loom and machine and fixed it on the goods which it is now their privilege to consume. An epic forgetting has taken place, assisted by the landscaping of the old sites of labour, and their transformation into pleasure grounds, open spaces, caverns no longer of exploitation and grief, but of escape, leisure and enjoyment; and in the process, the poor are no longer those who work in the great mills and halls of production, but those excluded from the paradise of plenty which the majority now take for granted as the 'natural' setting for a human life. Indeed, with the removal of the places where people laboured, the purpose of life itself is changed. No longer called to labour for subsistence, the function of the people has been dispersed; and work is the key, not simply to livelihood, but to all that money can buy (and much that it cannot, but that is not always evident at the point of purchase). An epic shift has taken place in our sense of identity: nothing is apparently forgotten so swiftly as want and insufficiency, and if the young women of Dhaka replicate scenes of toil which the occupants of Lancashire knew only the day before yesterday, there is little enough to remind them: the garments they wear are so unlike the plain stuff they produced that any associational memory has been effaced; or, if it is thought about at all, it is that those people are at a lower stage of development than we, that we have known their afflictions, and eventually they will one day be released into the satisfactions we now enjoy.

But the current fragile privilege of yesterday's cotton operatives is not quite all it appears. The vanished sense of purpose takes its revenge. In the vacuum where human purposes fastened themselves to the creation of useful and necessary goods, the spaces must be filled; and indeed they are, by an even greater range of escapes than the dreary pubs, the doors of which were always reckoned the quickest way out of Bolton or Blackburn or Bury, when people were inadequately rewarded for a surfeit of labour. Addictions of other kinds beckon the disemployed of manufacturing: drugs, gambling, crime, but also shopping, and the deployment of the most addictive substance known to humanity, money, and the ways it is come by. Generations born to functionlessness where there was lately only exploitation suggest passage—not from misery into a peaceable sufficiency, but an inexorable movement from one extreme to another.

Yet, this is the vision that sustains the young women and men of Bangladesh. De-industrialization has its own miseries, as the people of Dhaka once learned, and as the people of Lancashire, who certainly have no option to return to any rural past, even if they wanted it, are now being shown.

In the former mill town, the main streets are closed to traffic on Friday and Saturday nights. Barriers are placed at each end of the street, like the frontiers of another country. But if this is the border of another state, it is of a state of consciousness, the threshold of the land of pleasure. This is the place where people seek 'fun', that flexible monosyllable that covers a wide range of experience. These streets, from which the echo of clogs, the hum of looms, the rattle of buckets washing away the soot and grime, the last sighs of the worn-out mill girl and the wasted labourer have only just faded, are now the portal to escape—an escapism from which there is no other exit.

When the pleasure seekers express their objective, the words evoke violence: they want to get smashed, rat-arsed, legless, out of their skull. They will use any means, permitted or prohibited, to get out of the place where they live, the circumstances of their lives, even the selves they have become.

If the search for pleasure is punitively relentless, is this because work disciplines, the old Protestant ethic, have deserted the lost significance of labour and migrated to the more compelling pursuits of leisure? The rhythms of enjoyment distinctly echo an older tempo of production—an irony accentuated by the fact that many clubs, bars, restaurants in the city centres are the sites of former mills, warehouses, pubs, even chapels, converted to urgencies no longer prompted by overseer, foreman or factory owner, but marching to the beat of international entertainment conglomerates, breweries, distilleries, tobacco, fashion and apparel industries. The inheritors of the toilers in mill and factory now serve as 'outlets' for the profusion of merchandise which their grandparents were compelled to produce.

Just as some of the physical structures of industrial servitude survive, despite their transformation into places of enjoyment, so the compulsions of labour haunt the obsessive pleasures of a new generation. The social and spiritual environment of the Protestant work ethic may have vanished, but the values remain, if vagrant and houseless; what is more natural than that they should find a lodging in the world that was to come, not, of course, in a fanciful paradise, but in this, the shining afterlife of industrialism, these post-industrial locations which are capitalism's realm of freedom.

It isn't only the garments worn by the crowds avid for enjoyment that have called into existence new cohorts of labour in South Asia: their 'demand' for drugs is also satisfied, brought by the cunning laws of economics by tortuous pathways from the rocky landscapes of Afghanistan, the high Andes or the fields of Myanmar. If the youth and energy of young women in Bangladesh are confiscated by familiar masters of factory owner and apparel exporter, those of the young of the West serve other lords than the caricature of capitalist in monocle and top hat, riding in his phaeton and scattering halfpennies to urchins on the roadway.

It was so much more straightforward when the streets of the mill towns were filled with smoke, the phalanx of bicycles and the regimented tread of boots on the pavement; when women pounded clothes in the vat of boiling water, whitened the doorstep, put a match to sooty fires and stood over gas stoves in a cloud of steam, their consolations were meagre: beer and pub singing, pigeon lofts and allotments, family gatherings for weddings, funerals and Christmases. What is most striking about these social and economic transformations is how effortlessly societies oscillate between extremes: the shift from iron discipline to intemperance, from a grinding culture of labour to a frenzied cult of pleasure; and how all this occurred without the people ever being consulted. No one ever asked if this was what they wanted. No one was ever invited to vote on the establishment of industry or its abolition. Epic changes take place behind the backs of people, unreached by the democratic freedoms that are supposed to be the distinguishing feature of our civilization.

When dawn breaks over the scenes of riotous desolation, the paramedic van is waiting, the police are still in attendance, the security guards in their black suits have the sombre vigilance of undertakers. Some young women totter towards a taxi, shoes in one hand, a bottle in the other. Debris—chip wrappings, polystyrene trays, broken glass, cigarette ends stained with scarlet, a gauzy stole from some unvisited factory in Bangladesh—is stirred by the wind, remnants of a city from which the people have now fled.

The global imperium, of which Britain was once an incarnation, has shown itself ready to shift its sites of exploitation in the world in its nomadic jhum cultivation of profit. In its newest phase, capital has become more adroit and protean than ever, assisted by the untraceable electronic mobility of its instantaneous transactions. What appeared as epochal, irreversible changes, when the people of Bengal were dispossessed of ancient skills, and the workers of Lancashire forced into labour settlements barely dignified by the name of cities, can now be seen as mere temporary expedients in a longer cycle: the psyche of the people has been made, unmade and remade in pursuit of an epic extractive project.

The weavers of Bengal, whatever ruin and disturbance they experienced, could nevertheless retreat into an older cultural tradition. The cotton workers of Lancashire, once their function had been discharged, had no return to their broken rural past; and in any case, it seemed to them that industrial society had become their 'natural' element, and that it would persist for the foreseeable future. When their factories were shuttered and abandoned, there was nowhere for them to go, and they were compelled to make their home within the global market—a flimsy arrangement, since this demands that they should not take root there: this form of globalism aims to keep them virgin of any cultural attachment, except that which emanates from the market itself. Variable, unpredictable, volatile, it requires that they remain forever available, to adapt to whatever it may next require of them. This migration into an established impermanence is, perhaps, the most disruptive and least reversible of all.

As for the workers in the factories of South Asia, they know that their abode is only temporary; if cheaper labour appears anywhere else in the world, the work they do will fly away, leaving empty the husks of the fragile, flammable buildings that briefly held them captive. In this sense, they have one advantage over their sisters in the former British cotton industry: they are under no illusion. The women of Lancashire had thought their way of life permanent. Whether or not the workers of Bangladesh would be able to return to the countryside, should their industry desert them in the years to come, is another matter; for that homecoming would be to landless exile, a situation of a different order from their ready assimilation into the rural economy of two centuries ago.

When the workers of Bengal have served their purpose in the fabrication of disposable apparel, will they inherit the rewards enjoyed by the descendants of yesterday's cotton workers in the Lancashire mill towns, and the ambiguous pleasures of an escapism from which there is no exit? And if so, by that time, what kind of social beings will the people of Lancashire, and all the others who have passed through the shadow of industrialism, have become? Will the world witness even more epic circularities than the cycle of industrialization, de-industrialization and re-industrialization that we have seen? Shall we face new forms of feudalism—not, of course, that of the cowed and diminished serfs in the fields of lords set above them by God, but a 'modernized' techno-peasantry, in thrall to global landlords of knowledge, dependent upon the technologies and expertise of new hierarchies of knowing and ignorance? Is it also conceivable that, with declining incomes in Europe, it might even become worthwhile for capital to recolonize the shells of Bolton, Blackburn or Manchester with the ghosts of the industry that once made them the centre of the world?

We have seen the mutability of lives responding to changing livelihoods and occupations, even within the unchanging purposes of profit—the only constant in a world of continuous flux and change. Will the industrial paradigm and its global market which gouge the treasures of the earth, the harvests of its land and waters, with such ferocity continue to intensify their pressure in the name of development, and if so, will large tracts of the world become scarcely habitable? Will the market become cosmos, leaving no alternative, no culture, no civilization, no other way of living outside of its constantly expanding frontier? What new demands will be made of us, we who were the spinners and weavers of Bengal, the cotton operatives of Lancashire, the garment workers of Dhaka, the ragpickers of the world? What shape will that culture take, and who will benefit from the apparently infinite pliability of cultivators-turned-workers, workers who have become cultivators once more, cultivators transformed again into workers or workers who have become the servicers of globalism? Or will the resourcefulness of humanity demand a new and more ample relationship with material resources, one that does not continuously deplete the reservoirs of human energy nor exhaust the limited treasures of a wasting planet?

Select Bibliography

Alvares, Claude. 1991. *Decolonizing History: Technology and Culture in India, China and the West: 1492 to the Present Day.* Goa: The Other India Press.

Bamford, Samuel. 1843. *Passages in the Life of a Radical* (1840–42). London: Published by Author.

Bannerjee, Sumanta. 1989. *The Parlour and the Streets: Elite and Popular Culture in Nineteenth Century Calcutta.* Calcutta: Seagull Books.

Bernier, François. 2011. *Travels in the Mogul Empire.* Trans. Irving Brock. Cambridge: Cambridge University Press. (Orig. Publ. 1670.)

Bolts, William. 1772. *Considerations on India Affairs; Particularly Respecting the Present State of Bengal and its Dependencies.* 2nd. London: J Almon, P. Elmsly, and Brotherton and Sewell.

Chakrabarty, Dipesh. 2000. *Re-Thinking Working Class History: Bengal 1890–1940.* Princeton: Princeton University Press.

Chattopadhyay, Bankim Chandra. 1882. *Anandamath.* Trans. (2006) Julius J. Lipner. Oxford: Oxford University Press.

Chaudhuri, Amit. 2013. *Calcutta: Two Years in the City.* London: Union Books.

Chaudhury, Pradip and Abhijit Mukhopadhyay. 1975. *Calcutta, People and Empire: Gleanings from Old Journals.* Calcutta: India Book Exchange.

Cobden, John. 1853. *The White Slaves of England.* Cincinnati: Henry W. Derby.

Dutta, Krishna. 2003. *Calcutta: A Cultural and Literary History.* Oxford: Signal Books Ltd.

Eden, Emily. 1866. *Up the Country: Letters Written to Her Sister from the Upper Provinces of India.* London: R. Bentley.

Embree, A.T. 1958. *Sources of Indian Tradition: From the Beginning to 1800.* Second revised edition, New York: Columbia University Press, 1988.

Engels, Friedrich. 2009. *The Condition of the Working Class in England in 1844.* Edited by David McLellan. Oxford: Oxford University Press. (Orig. Publ. 1887.)

Fay, Eliza, and W. F. Firminger. 1908. *The Original Letters From India (1779–1815).* Calcutta: Thacker, Spink and Co.

Fenton, Bessie Knox. 1901. *The Journal of Mrs Fenton: A Narrative of Her Life in India, the Isle of France (Mauritius), and Tasmania during the Years 1826–1880.* London: E. Arnold.

Gadgil, D.R. 1938. *The Industrial Evolution of India in Recent Times.* 3rd. London: Oxford University Press.

Ghose, H.P. 1944. *The Famine of 1770.* Calcutta: Book Company.

Graham, Maria. 1813. *Journal of Residence in India.* 2nd. Edinburgh: George Ramsay and Company.

Hamilton, Alexander. 1744. *A New Account of the East Indies.* London: C. Hitch, A. Millar.

Hammond, J. L., and Barbara Hammond. 1925. *The Rise of Modern Industry.* London: Methuen.

Habib, Irfan. 2006. *Indian Economy 1858–1914.* New Delhi: Tulika Books.

Heber, Reginald. 1829. *Narrative of a Journey through the Upper Provinces of India, from Calcutta to Bombay, 1824–1825 (With Notes upon Ceylon).* 4th. London: John Murray, Albemarle Street.

Hobsbawm, Eric. May 1958. "History and 'The Dark Satanic Mills'". *Marxism Today*: 132–39.

Hoggart, Richard. 1957. *The Uses of Literacy.* London: Chatto and Windus.

Hossain, Hameeda. 1988. *The Company Weavers of Bengal: The East India Company and the Organization of Textile Production in Bengal, 1750–1813.* Dhaka: The University Press Limited.

Huggins, William. 1824. *Sketches in India.* London: John Letts.

Hughes, Robert. 1986. *The Fatal Shore: The Epic of Australia's Founding.* New York: Vintage Books.

Hunter, William Wilson. 1899. *A History of British India.* Vol. 1. London: Longmans, Green, and Co.

Kay-Shuttleworth, James Phillips. 1832. *The Moral and Physical Condition of the Working Classes Employed in the Cotton Manufacture in Manchester.* London: J. Ridgway.

Kelman, Janet. 1923. *Labour in India: A Study of the Conditions of Indian Women in Modern Industry.* London: George Allen & Unwin.

Macaulay, T.B. 1907. *Macaulay's Essay on Clive.* With introduction, notes, etc. by H.M. Buller. London: Macmillan.

Mamoon, Muntassir. 2010. *Nineteenth Century East Bengal.* Dhaka: The University Press Limited.

Marshall, P.J. 2006. *Bengal: The British Bridgehead: Eastern India, 1740–1828.* Cambridge: Cambridge University Press.

Mitra, D.B. 1978. *The Cotton Weavers of Bengal: 1757–1833.* Calcutta: Firma KLM.

Mohsin, K.M. 1973. *A Bengal District in Transition: Murshidabad, 1765–1793.* Dacca: Asiatic Society of Bangladesh.

Mukerjee, Radhakamal. 1938. *Changing Face of Bengal: A Study in Riverine Economy.* Calcutta: University of Calcutta.

Nair, P. Thankappan. 1989. *Calcutta in the 19th Century.* Calcutta: Firma KLM.

Parks, Fanny. 1850. *Wanderings of a Pilgrim in Search of the Picturesque: During Four-and-twenty Years in the East.* London: Pehlam Richardson.

Prebble, John. 1962. *Culloden.* New York: Atheneum.

Roberts, Emma. 1835. *Scenes and Characteristics of Hindostan, with Sketches of Anglo-Indian Society*, vol. 1. London: W.H. Allen and Co.

Sen, Samita. 1999. *Women and Labour in Late Colonial Bengal: The Bengal Jute Industry.* Cambridge: Cambridge University Press.

Sharma, V. Suguna. 1998. *Studies in Indian Textiles.* New Delhi: Bharatiya Kala Prakashan.

Sinha, N.K. 1956. *The Economic History of Bengal*, vol. 1. Calcutta: University of Calcutta.

———. 1962. *The Economic History of Bengal—From Plassey to the*

Permanent Settlement, vol. 2. Calcutta: University of Calcutta.

————. 1970. *The Economic History of Bengal,* vol. 3. Calcutta: Mukhopadhyay.

Sinha, Pradip. 1965. *Nineteenth Century Bengal: Aspects of Social History.* Calcutta: Firma KLM.

————. 1978. *Calcutta in Urban History.* Calcutta: Firma KLM.

Smith, Vincent A. 1920. *Oxford History of India: From the Earliest Times to the End of 1911.* Oxford: Clarendon Press.

Taylor, James. 1840. *A Sketch of the Topography and Statistics of Dacca.* Calcutta: G.H. Huttman, Military Orphan Press.

Thomas, Frederic C. 1997. *Calcutta Poor: Elegies on a City Above Pretense.* New York: M.E. Sharpe.

Thompson, E.P. 1963. *The Making of the English Working Class.* London: Victor Gollancz Ltd.

Tocqueville, Alexis de. 1958. *Journeys to England and Ireland.* Tr. George Lawrence and K.P. Mayer. Yale: Yale University Press. (Orig. Publ. 1835.)

Ure, Andrew. *The Philosophy of Manufactures.* London: Charles Knight, 1835.

Viscount George, 2nd Earl of Valentia. 1811. *Voyages and Travels to India, Ceylon, The Red Sea, Abyssinia and Egypt in the Years 1803, 1804, 1805 and 1806.* Vol. 2 of 4 volumes. London: F.C. and J. Rivington.

Walsh, J.H. Tull. 1902. *A History of Murshidabad District (Bengal); With Biographies of Some of Its Noted Families.* London: Jarrold Publication.